FILM FUN:
A SCRAPBOOK

FILM FUN:
A SCRAPBOOK

JOHN HOYLES

L'Age d'Or, Hull.

L'Age d'Or
Hull, UK in 2013.

Email: drhoyles@drhoyles.karoo.co.uk
Copyright © John Hoyles 2013

All rights reserved. No part of this publication may be reproduced, stored in or introduced into a retrieval system, or transmitted, in any form, or by any means, electronic, photocopying, recording or otherwise, without the prior written permission of the author.

L'Age d'Or, Hull.

CONTENTS

1. **JOHN HOYLES CINEPHILE**   7
   *An Introduction

2. **THREE SPECIAL FILMS**   11
   L'Age d'Or **1930**
   Persona **1966**
   Ai No Corrida **1976**

3. **EIGHT SPECIAL DIRECTORS**   32
   *Chantal Akerman
   *Catherine Breillat
   *Michael Cacoyannis
   *Charlie Chaplin
   *Nelly Kaplan
   *Ken Loach
   *Roman Polanski
   *Ken Russell

4. **SHORT SUBVERSIVE FILMS**   57
   *An Adult Education Syllabus

5. **CINE-FEM**   62
   *A University Syllabus

6. **COMMUNIST CINEMA**   80
   Kuhle Wampe **1932**
   Cecilia **1982**

7. **ART AND PORN**   88
   *Unpublished Letter to *The Guardian*
   *Pornography Conference Handout
   *Joe Sarno's Erotic Aesthetic

8. CAPSULE REVIEWS   107
    *From Garbo 1926 to *Antichrist* 2009

9. SCRAPS   171
    *A to Z – Agora to Zetterling

10. TOP TENS   192
    *Top Ten Films
    *Next Top Ten Films
    *Top Ten British Films
    *Top Ten Shakespeare Films
    *Top Ten Erotic Films

THANK YOU / POST SCRIPT   197

APPENDIX   198
    *Malcolm Watson on Zulawski

CHAPTER ONE: JOHN HOYLES CINEPHILE

John Hoyles's encounters with the Seventh Art include:

*being frightened by *Snow White and the Seven Dwarfs* in Swansea during the Second World War

*hearing the Headmaster say 'Make it go blurred' whenever there was a kissing scene in the Ealing Comedies shown at Kingswood School, Bath (early 50s)

*sexual gropings in the cinemas of Stoke-on-Trent

*the discovery of Bergman and Antonioni in the Cambridge University Film Society 1957-60

*savouring the delights of French film culture (Eisenstein, Renoir, Clair) in Paris (early 60s)

*a nocturnal visit to a clandestine cineclub in a Trotskyist-occupied deserted village in the French Alps (1968)

*attendance at the week-long Godard Forum (Hull 1973), the famous Buñuel Day-School (Bridlington 1981), and the International Festival of Hungarian Cinema (Eger 1984)

*the 1995 centenary foundation in Hull University of a course on Cinema and Totalitarianism (22% Firsts, average mark 68, best essay winning the Larkin Prize on Makavejev's *WR Mysteries of the Organism*)

*active participation in the 1996 Aberdeen University International Film Culture History Conference, with fantastic memories of the great English director Peter Watkins and the great American critic Sandy Flitterman-Lewis *the 1999 establishment in Hull University of the Cine-Fem module, allowing students to examine great films by women directors under the sign of the Female Gaze

*active participation in the BBFC/Aberystwyth University Focus Group on Cinema/Video Censorship (2006) with special reference to the BBFC cuts to Catherine Breillat's *A Ma Soeur*

*speaker at Manchester Arts Cinema Conference on Pornography and Censorship, together with Anna Span and the BBFC

TOUCHSTONES

Cinema is the opium of the people, the heart of a heartless world. (Karl Marx, adapted by John Hoyles)

Film is the greatest teacher, because it teaches not only through the brain, but through the whole body. (Pudovkin)

There is no such thing as art for art's sake. ... Works of art which lack artistic quality have no force however progressive they are politically. (Mao-tse-Tung 1941-2)

The highest and the lowest are always closest to each other in the sphere of sexuality. (Freud)

I like my movies made in Hollywood. (Richard Nixon)

To make a film all you need is a girl and a gun. (Godard)

The test of a work of art is in the end our affection for it, not our ability to explain why it is good. (Kubrick)

The unconscious holds no negatives. (Freud)

Great art is always flanked by its dark sisters, blasphemy and pornography. (Geoffrey Hartmann)

Each art breeds its fanatics. The love that cinema inspires however is special. It is born of the sense that cinema is an art unlike any other: quintessentially modern; distinctively accessible; poetic and mysterious and erotic and moral - all at the same time. (Susan Sontag 1996)

We are all 15 and a half in our hopes. We always want to believe it's the first time - it's that feeling of life that can't be reasoned by the adult mind, to think that we may change the world. (Catherine Breillat)

Only the perverse fantasy can save us. (Goethe to Eckermann)

CHAPTER TWO: THREE SPECIAL FILMS

1. *L'AGE D'OR* 1930
Annotated extracts from Paul Hammond, *L'Age d'Or*, BFI 1997.

Section One: SCORPIO RISING

The Entomology Student
The intertitles are not Buñuel's work; they came with *Le Scorpion languedocien* (1912). Furthermore they're verbatim quotation from Jean-Henri Fabre's ten-volume *Souvenirs entomologiques* (1898-1907). Buñuel was a Fabre enthusiast, having read him as an entomology student in Madrid. Fabre: 'The scorpion of Languedoc on the termination of the hymeneal rites allows the female to devour him without attempting to employ his weapon, the venomous dagger.' (11)
Scorpions Also Suffer From Coitus Interruptus
Although Fabre is nowhere mentioned by name his ideas form the latent content of the film which images the hymeneal rites of a bungling heterosexual couple. The theme of libidinal frustration is even fleetingly announced in the *objet trouvé*. We see a shot of two scorpions, tails entwined in erotic embrace. Suddenly a third arachnid charges through them, sundering the blissful dancers. (12)

Section Two: PRIMITIVE BANDITS

Hand of the Great Wanker
Rope tugged through pitchfork; this anguishing onanistic ritual was improvised on the day. I see the hand of a great wanker here; Dali. (15) [cf. Dali *The Great Masturbator* 1929]

11

Two Ranks of Cinema
Following Rank - Otto, not J. Arthur, although he too is ever-present in the movie - Dali and Buñuel considered that reality's adjustment to the unconscious, and not the other way round, is what marks the true development of humankind. (16) [cf. Otto Rank *The Incest Theme in Literature and Legend* 1912]

Mallorca and the Axis of Evil
For Dali and Buñuel, fervent hispanophobes in 1930, Mallorca connoted all that was feudal, God-fearing, reactionary. In 1926 Rivera and Mussolini signed a pact to further their geopolitical ambitions in the Mediterranean. Spain's claims to Tangiers were recognised in return for an Italian base on Mallorca. Mallorquins, then, are metonyms for fascist realpolitik. In July 1936 the Italians would land and the islanders side with Franco. (18)

Section Three: THE MALLORCANS

Sex Death
"Considered objectively, copulation seems both risible and tragic to me. It's so very like death." Buñuel. (22)

Shit Orgasm
Modot the crapule goes into a brown study, and in his voluptuous vision sees Lys sitting on the john. She has a constipated expression. To the sound of flushing we cut to archive footage of molten lava, bubbling mud. Modot licks his lips. As Dali said at the time, 'One loves entirely when one is prepared to eat the shit of the beloved.' (22)

Animal Rights
Hearing a puppy bark, Modot the enragé breaks away from the cops and gives it a mighty boot. (When Eric Mottram showed *L'Age d'or* in Cambridge in 1950 the only complaint came from the RSPCA! Ah, the English.) Modot's indifference tells us that morally he's marching to a different drum. (22)

Ruling Class Garbled Speech
The bantam Governor begins his peroration. A discourse on collectivising the land was dubbed in a strangled French. Phrases like 'raw material' and 'common clay' echo the cloacal mud we've already seen a-bubbling. Did Chaplin crib the idea of garbled speechifying for the statue-unveiling in City Lights (1931)? (23)

Civilisation as Shit
Mendelssohn takes over from Wagner as the deluded debauchee is escorted away. The trowel of cement the Governor places a-top the granite block is one more turd. (23)

Freudian Libido Theory with Added Bakhtin
Hollywood silent comedy luxuriated in Bakhtin's 'material bodily lower stratum': shit, piss and spunk to you and me. There are endless examples of victims covered in mud, paint, tar, eggs, feathers. Conversant with Freudian libido theory, Buñuel and Dali consciously used the oral, anal and phallic as the armature of their movie. (24)

Dali Rewrites Freud
Dali's theory, developed during 1929-30, and essentially a rum rewrite of Freud, argued that reality must be understood phenomenologically as the sublimated and endlessly displaced expression of unspeakable soma. He classified the returning repressed signifiers as our old friend putrefaction, plus blood and excrement: an unholy trinity shot through with Thanatos. (24)

Section Four: ROME

Pope's Concordat with Mussolini
The Pope gives a blessing from the balcony of St Peter's. Taped to his cracked window is a scribbled note to a cousin: the Vicar of Christ has renewed the mortgage. As with the Primera-Mussolini 'Mallorca' pact, there's a precise historical allusion here: to the Lateran Treaties of 1929 wherein the Papacy agreed to restrict its temporal sovereignty to the

Vatican City in return for lire from the Italian state. The next shot shows a limo in a Roman street. Are Pius XI and cousin aboard, en route to visit the landlord, Mussolini? (25)

Dali Versus Buñuel

Buried for 50 years, by 1981 *L'Age d'or* could be seen again and it seemed obvious that Dalinian imagery suffused the film. (Ask yourself: were hysteria, scatology and onanism the pet subjects of Buñuel, or of Dali?). (30)

Modot's Onanistic Fantasy

Modot has time-travelled to Rome. Here he is, in shit-stained suit, all basic instinct, still cuffed to, and by, his minders. Passing a hoarding, he fixates on a poster of a woman's be-ringed hand reaching for a 'Leda' powder puff. Modot fantasises his lover's ring-finger twitching onanistically; a quivering swatch of hair has replaced the beauty aid and adds to the genital illusion. The arched digit is poised like a scorpion's tail to bring *la petite mort*. Modot's delusions persist as a sandwich-man passes with an ad for 'Anitta' nylons. Stopping before a bookshop window - the Librairie Espagnole, where Buñuel's fiancee Jeanne Rucar worked - the scoptophile bites his lip at a Man Ray-esque photo of a swooning beauty. (30)

Lya Lys's Horny Bandage

Cued by a shift from Mendelssohn to Wagner, a match cut reveals Lys on her couch, duplicating the swooner's Bernini-like posture. (And echoing the moribund Peman.) In Anitta hose, Leda has been a swan to herself. As the camera dollies back unsteadily we see that her bodice is undone and her ring-finger suspiciously bandaged: another play on words, because 'bander' means both 'to bandage' and 'to feel horny'. (31)

Masturbation Gags

We go from Wagner to direct sound. Lys encounters her mother. Seeing her offspring's bandaged finger curled over the page of a book, the Marquess makes enquiry. Contemporary audiences hooted when she asks, '*Tu as la main bandé?*'. Yes, the lass's finger's been afflicted for a week. (31-2) The masturbation gags keep coming. Is this a highfalutin porno movie? When Lys enquires after her papa we cut to him in his laboratory, vigorously shaking a bottle of liquid plugged by his ring-finger. Like father, like daughter! (32-3)

Fighting the Fascists
Lord Muck takes time from hailing a taxi to kick a blind war veteran to the ground. A fulsome provocation, this, given that the Anciens Combattants were the most powerful political lobby in the land. In 1927 the right-wing of this anti-democratic movement took the name 'Les Croix de feu'. With the ascension after 1929 of the retired colonel Francois de la Roque, the 'Crosses of Fire' became a para-military force organised along Mussolinian lines. They would play a major part in the fascist riots of February 1934 which ushered in the *Front Populaire*. (36)

Section Five: LIEBESTOD OR AMOUR FOU

High Class Putrefaction
To strains of Schubert, an intertitle announces that the Marquises of X will be receiving guests in their magnificent property outside Rome. We recognise the Marquis as Lys's self-abusing father. The flies stuck to his face signify he's a 'putrefact'. (36)

From Sacrament to Excrement via the Blasphemous Ostensory
A Rolls brakes, a footman lifts out an ostensory, a woman's stockinged leg steps on to the running board. It was when the ostensory - a piece of altar furniture used to display the consecrated host at Catholic Mass - appeared that the fascists started laying about. In Surrealist parlance the Holy Sacrament was the 'Holy Excrement'. Buñuel and Dali invented many a poem about the host: with moustache and prick; coming out of a nightingale's arse, saluting; combating ants. (40)

Class Consciousness

Faced with the disruptive presence of the plebs the Mallorquins don't bat an eyelid. Like the scorpion, they have an immense instinct for self-preservation. The tumbrils of the Terror are history, so the ghastly horse and cart that trundles across the room with its carousing Cloggies is politely ignored. A similar fate awaits the maid, torched by an exploding kitchen range. (41)

Wankers United

When the edgy Lys strokes her unbandaged ring-finger a dissolve superimposes a butler feverishly fingering a smeared decanter. 'You're all wankers!' seems to be the message. (42)

Proles and Aristos

The gamekeeper's over-reaction to his son's mischief is cross-cut with the under-reaction of the aristos to prole violence. Sadism is ubiquitous, part of everyday life. (43)

Modot as Basil Fawlty

All hell breaks loose. A slapped Marquess has more worth than a slaughtered child. The snarling Marquis has to be held back; no flies on him now! Modot defends his outrageous action with the same insouciance as Ortiz (the gamekeeper). Lys, the object of his unwavering gaze, is exalted. He bows to the serried fists and leaves, sad sack dress in tow. She dutifully consoles her snivelling mum. Seconds later the churl is back, gesticulating to Lys to go outside. It's as if Modot has no memory of the slap. The amnesiac Basil Fawlty crosses the salon, ignoring the glaring toffs, who are, anyway, too polite to eject him a second time. The show must go on; the orchestra is tuning up. (44)

Passion and Society from Courtly Love to Wagnerian Liebestod

For Denis de Rougemont the 12thC romance of Tristan and Iseult established the very notion of love in the Occident. In short, what the lovers love is less each other than the fact of loving. Each loves the other not as they really are but as a mirroring of their personal desire for oneness. Driven by nostalgic narcissism, the lovers' passion can subsist only by placing obstacles in its path. The absolute obstacle, and thus passion's true object, is death itself. Rougemont takes Wagner to be the first to have uncovered the latent meaning of the archetype. (46)

Love Sublime and Ridiculous

We cross-cut from the aristos taking their seats on the terrace - one concert-goer's menses could stain her dress, suggested Dali - to the over-anxious lovers tumbling from their seats in the garden. A statue of Venus presides over their farcical and prolonged coitus interruptus. Modot, his eyes glazed, takes Lys's fingers into his mouth - her ring is visible - she his. The oral sadism is belied by the ecstatic smile on the faces of Modot and Lys, and the joyous reciprocity of their cannibalistic gesture. (47)

Cinema Dreams Cunt

Dali had big ideas for the love scene. He's found, he said, a way of realising Buñuel's 'longstanding dream of showing a cunt in cinema'. The amorous woman should incline her head so her lips were 'north-south', so to speak, and in big close-up. Then a dissolve, to superpose the labia of a depilated vagina. Or alternatively the superimposition of a decollete framed by a feather boa - 'pubic hair' - with the lips gradually seceding to a heaving bosom. Dali was practising 'critical paranoia' here, a methodology inspired by the dissolves of film language. His idea revamped the images in *Un Chien* when breasts metamorphosed into buttocks, a hairy armpit into a sea urchin. (47)

Penis Power

The conductor onanistically taps his baton – *une baguette*, which also means 'prick' - on his rostrum. Wagner varooms and the startled lovers bang heads. (47)

The Great Suck

In frustration Lys turns to Venus's big toe and gives it the full Mae West treatment, sucking lustily. 'Ah! the young girls who lift their dress / And wank off in the bushes / Or in the museums / Behind the plaster Apollos' (Peret). Lya's an oral sublimator. (48)

Mad Love and the Cosmic Fuck

The vibrato Wagner steers them to orgasm. Lys is wide-awake, rapt. 'I've been waiting for you so long', she ejaculates. 'What joy to have murdered our children!'. The matron's a Messalina at heart. The gamekeeper's infanticide was predictive, the Minister's accusation justified. Paul Eluard's voice speaks for Modot, whose face is lacerated, left eye sanguine, lips horribly rouged. 'Mon amour, mon amour, mon amour', enunciated the way poets do: 'Mon ameuur,' (I'd conjecture that Lys's lines are spoken by Eluard's lover, Nusch.) We're reminded of Fabre on insect courtship, on the sadism of the female and masochism of the male during copulation. Love can make you lose your head. (49)

Section Six: THE MARQUIS DE SADE AND JESUS CHRIST

Blasphemy Rules OK
We're told to expect the arch-sodomite the Duke of Blangis. The castle door opens and out steps Jesus. Twenty years ago this blasphemy seemed archaic. Now that religious fundamentalism has returned to plague the world it resonates again. (52-3)

Misogyny, Christianity and Desire
The six female scalps hanging from the leaning cross sashay obscenely in the swirling wind; one more symbolically functioning object, another holy relic, a last gag linking hair and symptom. The Christian symptom, the image says, is genocidal hatred of women. The same could be said of the vaginophobic pornology of Sade: did Buñuel twig this when he equalled Christ and Blangis? Eight seconds later *L'Age d'or* is done, spent, its final burst of Nietzschean laughter doing little to resolve the ambivalence of Buñuel (and Dali) towards femellitude. The problematic of desire can be exercised, not exorcised. Desire is impossible, desire is. (57)

Conclusion

L'Age d'or is no longer a *film maudit*. Neither is it wholly domesticated. A holy relic can always move the faithful fetishist. Caught like an arachnid in amber, in the amber glow of its own golden age, Buñuel's second film remains an object of fascination, of perturbation, of productive nostalgia. The dagger of the projector beam may yet bear some poison. (69)

2. *PERSONA* 1966

Bergman's most famous films include: *Summer with Monika* 1953, *Smiles of a Summer Night* 1955, *The Seventh Seal* 1956, *Wild Strawberries* 1957, *The Virgin Spring* 1960, *The Silence* 1963, *Persona* 1966, *Scenes from a Marriage* 1973, *Autumn Sonata* 1978, *Fanny and Alexander* 1983.

The Silence 1963

The final part of Bergman's trilogy (after *Through a Glass Darkly* and *Winter Light*) is a bleak and disturbing study of loneliness, love and obsessive desire. Sisters Ester (Thulin) and Anna (Lindblom), together with the latter's young son, book into a vast but virtually empty hotel - the only other guests are a troupe of dwarf entertainers - in a country seemingly occupied or threatened by war. Once again exploring the conflicts between physicality and spirituality, Bergman candidly portrays Ester's latent Lesbian desire for her sister, as well as Anna's own compulsive sexuality (she picks up a waiter and brings him back to the hotel). Despite the overt eroticism, the sisters' craving for emotional warmth is filmed in a cold objective style; in this way, Bergman's severe symbolism emphasises both the seeming impossibility of, and absolute necessity for, human tenderness in a Godless world. (Nigel Floyd, *Time Out Film Guide* 2000)

Persona 1966

Bergman at his most brilliant as he explores the symbiotic relationship that evolves between an actress (Liv Ullmann as Elizabet Vogler) suffering a breakdown in which she refuses to speak, and the nurse (Bibi Andersson as Alma) in charge as she recuperates in a country cottage. To comment is to betray the film's extraordinary complexity, but basically it returns to two favourite Bergman themes: the difficulty of true communication between human beings, and the essentially egocentric nature of art. Here the actress (named Vogler after the charlatan/artist in *The Face*) dries up in the middle of a performance [of *Electra*], thereafter refusing to exercise her art. We aren't told why, but from the context it's a fair guess that she withdraws from a feeling of inadequacy in face of the horrors of the modern world; and in her withdrawal, she watches with detached tolerance as humanity (the nurse chattering on about her troubled sex life) reveals its petty woes. Then comes the weird moment of communion in which the two women merge as one; charlatan or not, the artist can still be understood, and can therefore still understand. Not an easy film, but an infinitely rewarding one. (Tom Milne, ibid.)

Hour of the Wolf 1967
In its exploration of the nature of creativity, haunted by the problem of whether the artist possesses or is possessed by his demons, *Hour of the Wolf* serves as a remarkable companion piece to *Persona*. (Tom Milne, ibid.)

Cries and Whispers 1972
Thulin in period costume is undressed by her maid, which says all there is to say about clothes, disguise, repression. *Cries* is about bodies, female bodies, in extremity of pain, isolation or neglect (the cards are heavily stacked). Karin (Thulin) mutilates her cunt with a piece of broken glass and, stretched out on her marital bed, smiles through the blood she's smeared across her mouth at her husband in celebration of a marriage that's a 'tissue of lies', Maria (Ullmann) finds herself lacking a thread that would tie her irreversibly to life. Bergman's hour remains resolutely that of the wolf. (Verina Glaessner, ibid.)

Susan Sontag on Cinema of Cruelty
It is not that Bergman is pessimistic about life and the human condition - as if it were a question of certain opinions - but rather that the quality of his sensibility, when he is faithful to it, has only a single subject: the depths in which consciousness drowns. If the maintenance of personality requires

safeguarding the integrity of masks, and the truth about a person always means his unmasking, cracking the mask, then the truth about life as a whole is the shattering of the whole facade - behind which lies an absolute cruelty.

It is here, I think, that one must locate the ostensibly political allusions in *Persona*. Bergman's references to Vietnam and the Six Million are quite different from the references to the Algerian War, Vietnam, China in the films of Godard. Unlike Godard, Bergman is not a topical or historically oriented filmmaker. Elizabeth watching a newsreel on TV of a bonze in Saigon immolating himself, or staring at the famous photograph of a little boy from the Warsaw Ghetto being led off to be slaughtered, are, for Bergman, above all, images of total violence, of unredeemed cruelty. They occur in *Persona* as images of what cannot be imaginatively encompassed or digested, rather than as occasions for right political and moral thoughts. In their function, these images don't differ from the earlier flashbacks of a palm into which a nail is being hammered or of the anonymous bodies in a morgue. History or politics enters *Persona* only in the form of pure violence. Bergman makes an "aesthetic" use of violence - far from ordinary left-liberal propaganda.

The subject of *Persona* is the violence of the spirit. If the two women violate each other, each can be said to have at least as profoundly violated herself. In the final parallel to this theme, the film itself seems to be violated - to emerge out of and descend back into the chaos of "cinema" and film-as-object.

(Susan Sontag, 'Bergman's *Persona*', in *Styles of Radical Will* 1969. Also in Lloyd Michaels ed. *Ingmar Bergman's Persona* 2000.)

Pauline Kael Against Interpretation
Though it's possible to offer interpretations, I don't think that treating *Persona* as the pieces of a puzzle and trying to put them together will do much more than demonstrate ingenuity at guesswork. It's easy to say that the little boy reaching up to

the screen is probably Bergman as child; and he may also represent the nurse's aborted baby and/or the actress's rejected son. But for this kind of speculation (and one would have to go through almost every image in the movie this way) to have any purpose, there must be a structure of meanings in the work; I don't think there is one in *Persona*. We respond to the image of the little boy - not because he's Bergman or an abortion but simply in terms of the quality and intensity of the image - but we don't know why it's in this film. (Pauline Kael *New Republic* 1967, in Michaels 2000).

John Simon on Art and Life
I can only guess at the ultimate meaning. The artist and the ordinary human being need each other, but this is a love-hate, a fight for absolute power over the other. Their complete communion is illusory and painful - only a dream, a nightmare - yet also real enough, perhaps to mark them both. Life and art batten on each other, art sucking life's blood, life trying to cajole or bully art into submission, into becoming its mirror. The result of the strife is madness, whether feigned or real hardly matters. Relatives, lovers, friends, all who are sucked into this conflict, suffer along with the principal combatants. The rest is, at best, a draw. And, with luck, a magnificent film. (John Simon, *The New Leader* 1967, in Michaels 2000).

Roger Ebert Manfully Rises to the Occasion!
Shakespeare used six words to pose the essential human choice: "To be, or not to be?" Elizabeth, a character in Ingmar Bergman's *Persona*, uses two to answer it: "No, don't!" She is an actress, who one night stopped speaking in the middle of the performance, and has been silent ever since. Now her nurse, Alma, has in a fit of rage started to throw a pot of boiling water at her. "No, don't!" translates as: I do not want to feel pain, I do not want to be scarred, I do not want to die. She wants ... to be. She admits ... she exists.

Persona (1966) is a film we return to over the years, for

the beauty of its images, and because we hope to understand its mysteries. It is apparently not a difficult film. Everything that happens is perfectly clear. and even the dream sequences are clear - as dreams. But it suggests buried truths, and we despair of finding them. *Persona* was one of the first movies I reviewed, in 1967. I did not think I understood it. A third of a century later I know most of what I am ever likely to know about films, and I think I understand that the best approach to *Persona* is a literal one. It is exactly about what it seems to be about. "How this pretentious movie manages to not be pretentious at all is one of the great accomplishments of *Persona*", says a moviegoer named John Hardy, posting his comments on the IMDB. Bergman shows us everyday actions and the words of ordinary conversation. And Sven Nykvist's cinematography shows them in haunting images. One, of two faces, one frontal, one in profile, has become one of the most famous images of the cinema.

Elizabeth (Liv Ullmann) stops speaking in the middle of *Electra*, and will not speak again. A psychiatrist thinks it might help if Elizabeth and Nurse Alma (Bibi Andersson) spend the summer at her isolated house. Held in the same box of space and time, the two women somehow merge. Elizabeth says nothing, and Alma talks and talks, confessing her plans and her fears, and eventually, in a great and daring monologue, confessing an erotic episode during which she was, for a time, completely happy.

The two actresses look somewhat similar. Bergman emphasizes this similarity in a disturbing shot where he combines half of one face and half of the other. Later he superimposes the two faces, like a morph. Andersson told me she and Ullmann had no idea Bergman was going to do this, and when she first saw the film she found it disturbing and frightening. Bergman told me, "The human face is the great subject of the cinema. Everything is there."

Their visual merging suggests a deeper psychic attraction. Elizabeth, the patient, mute and apparently ill, is stronger than Alma, and eventually the nurse feels her soul

THREE SPECIAL FILMS

being overcome by the other woman's strength. There is a moment when her resentment flares and she lashes back. In the sunny courtyard of the cottage, she picks up the pieces of a broken glass, and then deliberately leaves a shard where Elizabeth might walk. Elizabeth cuts her foot, but this is essentially a victory for the actress, who has forced the nurse to abandon the discipline of her profession and reveal weakness.

Elizabeth looks at Alma, seeming to know the glass shard was not an accident, and at that moment Bergman allows his film to tear and burn. The screen goes blank. Then the film reconstitutes itself. This sequence mirrors the way the film has opened. In both cases, a projector lamp flares to life, and there is a montage from the earliest days of cinema: jerky silent skeletons, images of coffins, a hand with a nail being driven into it. The middle break ends with the camera moving toward an eye, and even into the veins in the eyeball, as if to penetrate the mind.

The opening sequence suggests that *Persona* is starting at the beginning, with the birth of cinema. The break in the middle shows it turning back and beginning again. At the end, the film runs out of the camera and the lights dies from the lamp and the film is over. Bergman is showing us that he has returned to first principles. "In the beginning, there was light." Toward the end there is a shot of the camera crew itself, with the camera mounted on a crane and Nykvist and Bergman tending it; this shot implicates the makers in the work. They are there, it is theirs, they cannot separate themselves from it.

Early in the film, Elizabeth watches images from Vietnam on the TV news, including a Buddhist monk burning himself. Later, there are photographs from the Warsaw Ghetto, of Jews being rounded up; the film lingers on the face of a small boy. Have the horrors of the world caused Elizabeth to stop speaking? The film does not say, but obviously they are implicated. For Alma, horrors are closer to home: She doubts the valiidity of her relationship with the man she plans

25

to marry, she doubts her abilities as a nurse, she doubts she has the strength to stand up to Elizabeth.

But Elizabeth has private torments too, and Bergman expresses them in a sequence so simple and yet so bold we are astonished by its audacity. First there is a dream sequence (if it is a dream; opinions differ), in which Elizabeth enters the room of Alma in the middle of the night. In a Swedish summer, night is a finger drawn by twilight between one day and the next, and soft pale light floods the room. The two women look at one another like images in a mirror. They turn and face us, one brushing back the other's hair. A man's voice calls, "Elizabeth". It is her husband, Mr Vogler (Gunnar Bjornstrand). They are outside. He caresses Alma's face and calls her "Elizabeth". No, she says, she is not Elizabeth, Elizabeth takes Alma's hand and uses it to caress her husband's face.

Inside, later, Alma delivers a long monologue about Elizabeth's child. The child is born deformed, and Elizabeth left it with relatives so she can return to the theatre. The story is unbearably painful. It is told with the camera on Elizabeth. Then it is told again, word for word, with the camera on Alma. I believe this is not simply Bergman trying it both ways, as has been suggested, but literally both women telling the same story - through Alma when it is Elizabeth's turn, since Elizabeth does not speak. It shows their beings are in union.

The other monologue in the movie is more famous: Alma's story of sex on the beach involving herself, her girlfriend and two boys. The imagery of this monologue is so powerful that I have heard people describe the scene as if they actually saw it in the film. In all three monologues, Bergman is showing how ideas create images and reality.

The most real objective experiences in the film are the cut foot and the threat of boiling water, which by "breaking" the film show how everything else is made of thought (or art). The most real experience Alma has ever had is her orgasm on the beach. Elizabeth's pain and Alma's ecstasy were able to break through the reveries of their lives. Most of what we

think of as "ourselves" is not direct experience of the world, but a mental broadcast made of ideas, memories, media input, other people, jobs, roles, duties, lusts, hopes, fears. Elizabeth chooses to be who she is. Alma is not strong enough to choose not to be Elizabeth. The title is the key. "Persona". Singular.
(Roger Ebert on *Persona* in the *Chicago Sun-Times*, 7 January 2001)

A Personal Addendum
It has been suggested that there is a more intimately personal aspect to the content of *Persona*. While shooting the film Bergman was half-way between his personal past and his personal future, between his ex-girlfriend Bibi Andersson (Alma) and his new and long-term girlfriend Liv Ullmann (Elizabeth). The dialectical and symbiotic relationship between the two women and their genial director perhaps constitutes more than tittle-tattle, adding as much meaning as spice to the film's significance, thus fulfilling perhaps Susan Sontag's call for less hermeneutics (interpretation) and more erotics (pleasure/*jouissance*) in critical theory and practice.
(FJH March 2010)

3. *Ai No Corrida* 1976

Yes, it's out on video, even in Pudding Island, the most ferociously tender film ever made about sexual obsession.

Watch it in the light of the following touchstones: "Pornography is an appropriate means to cure our society from its genital panic" (Otto Muehl); "To imagine is no crime" (The judge in Buñuel's *The Criminal Life of Archibaldo de la Cruz*).

See if you agree that *Ai No Corrida* measures up to the highest standards of great cinema as laid down by Jean Vigo, when he said of Buñuel's *Un Chien Andalou*: "Although primarily a subjective drama fashioned into a poem, it is nonetheless, in my opinion, a film of social consciousness, and too arid an analysis, image by image, is impossible in a good film whose savage poetry exacts respect."

I believe *Ai No Corrida* measures up to these touchstones. It is not just *saké* and saliva: it is a work of genius comparable to the "naked and angry" mad lovers in *The First Lady Chatterley*; to the mad love in *Wuthering Heights*; and to the *amour fou* to be found above all in *L'Age d'Or*, but also in Genet's *Chant d'Amour*. But, as is often the case, especially in Britain, all this comes wrapped in the nasty brown paper of censorship.

The BBFC, Pornography and Censorship

In 1930 Eisenstein visited London, failed to get *Potemkin* unbanned and lampooned Britain's censors: "One of them is blind and probably deals with the silent films, another one is deaf and so gets the sound films; the third one chose to die while I was in London".

In 1976 *Ai No Corrida*, with its erections, non-simulated fucking, fellatio, egg in vagina, heroine yanking little boy's penis, children throwing snowballs at old man's genitals, was banned in England. It was shown in a London cinema club in 1978 with penis yank cut, and briefly unbanned, with 8 seconds of penis-yank zoomed out of frame in 1991. In Japan, where pictures of pubic hair are banned, every explicit scene was air-brushed into a white haze by the censors. Oshima was prosecuted and only found innocent after 4 years in court. Briefly in 1982 a video of the film was available for rental from corner shops in Britain.

In 1985, in a fit of Orwellian newspeak, the British Board of Film Censors (BBFC) transmogrified itself into the British Board of Film Classification (BBFC). Euphemism and hypocrisy are after all eminently British virtues.

In 1989 Genet's gay classic *Un Chant d'Amour* (1950) was banned by Hull City Council, preventing my students from seeing a film relevant to their Literature and Totalitarianism course.

In 1992 the BBFC rule on male erections was refined/defined as the Mull of Kintyre test (i.e. the male performer's penis must never appear more tumescent than the aforesaid Mull of Kintyre (see a map of Scotland).

In 1994 The Guardian reported on the BBFC's so-called ILOOLI rule ("inner labia is out but outer labia can be in, but clear distension of labia would still be cut").

In i998 Lars von Trier's *The Idiots* passed the British censor with a very brief shot of penetration not cut.

In 1999 Catherine Breillat's *Romance*, with scenes of non-simulated penetration and fellatio, passed the British censor with only very small cuts (including one real ejaculation which, believe me, does have artistic/symbolic significance).

And in 2000 *Ai No Corrida* is at last released on video in Britain (albeit with the 1991 penis yank still zoomed out of frame).

These are the facts. They are worth knowing. But the personal is also political. Personally I don't understand why the BBFC cut the penis yank (presumably on the grounds that it verged on paedophilia) and not the snowballing of the old tramp's genitals. This discrimination could be construed as ageism.

I saw the film once in Paris, once in London, once on video. In Paris the film had a special dispensation from the Minister of the Interior to be shown in public. The queue outside the cinema was harangued by some passing Maoists who objected to bourgeois consumers paying to see "illusions in colour!". In London we were not allowed in past the entrance curtain till the previous showing had finished. I still remember the haunting theme music audible from behind the curtain. It was shown in a cinema club. You had to wait 24 hours after joining. One woman, so a friend told me, could not wait that long and in radical protest against Pudding Island protocol proceeded to pee all over the foyer carpet. As for the video, that was quickly regulated out of existence under the Video Nasties Act.

The dirtiest great film ever
Oshima's film is dirty, like all dirty films, a product of the sexual fix. It is also a dirty film, unlike most dirty films, a product of the poetic imagination. Yes, as Susan Sontag has shown us in her work on Georges Bataille's *Story of the Eye*, there is such a thing as the pornographic imagination. And Oshima's film tackles what is normally brushed under the carpet: sex and death, sado-masochism, totem and taboo, jouissance and transgression, perversion and fetishism. And incorporating all these all too human characteristics, there is the overriding rhythm of Tenderness (which you may recall was Lawrence's original title for *Lady Chatterley's Lover*). Not that Oshima is a Lawrentian, given that in his film the life-

force moves inexorably to the death-wish.

This is not the place to rehearse these themes image by image, but viewers may wish to anticipate some of them: Sada's slow dribble of semen and saliva over Kichi's penis; Kichi licking Sada's menstrual blood; the mock wedding ceremony when a virgin is deflowered with a bird-shaped dildo; Sada sniffing Kichi's kimono in a train toilet; Sada forcing her bespectacled old teacher to slap her face and pinch her nipples harder; Sada laying a previously inserted hard-boiled egg; Sada munching a tuft of Kichi's pubic hair; the penis and knife in Sada's hands in extreme close-up; the prick that springs to attention and 'speaks'; Kichi finding the taste of Sada's tears very salty; the intercourse between Kichi and a 68 year-old woman who looks happy, then serious, then very serious, then dead; soldiers on the march (make love not war subverting Japanese militarism); the long, carefully crafted sex and strangulation scenes (a reprise of the jouissance in *L'Age d'Or* when we hear 'Mon amour, mon amour, mon amour' as blood streams down Modot's face in extreme close-up); the porcelain stoppered *saké* jar, spinning like a top in close-up (recalling the sexually symbolic water-tap earlier); Sada yanking Kichi's overworked flaccid penis (recalling the earlier scene with the little boy); the mysterious stadium sequence (what does it mean?); and of course the ultimate castration and death ('when arrested holding the wrapped packet of Kichi's penis, Sada was radiant with joy').

The whole film is saturated with colour and sound. You never forget those kimonos, or the haunting melody of the theme music (3 rising notes, then one falling, on a wind instrument).

CHAPTER THREE: EIGHT SPECIAL DIRECTORS

1. Chantal Akerman

Interim report on Chantal Akerman, b. Bruxelles 1950.

Films from 1968 to 1975.

Saute Ma Ville 1968. Chantal's grenade for 1968, aged 18. *L'Imagination au Pouvoir* as they used to shout. A startlingly surrealist short film in which Chantal, rebel without a cause, brave and narcissistic, nihilistic and suicidal, trashes her flat for the revolution (symbolically of course!). B+

La Chambre 1972. Short but slow exercise in minimalism. Nothing much to write home about. C

Hotel Monterey 1972. Oh dear! Homage to New York. But dire to watch. Gives minimalism and Belgium a bad name. D

Je Tu Il Elle 1975. A tour de force. Chantal as actress and generic woman traverses three phases of existence. 1. Imperious solipsism, alone in her flat, narcissistically spooning caster sugar out of a bag into her mouth. That is JE and TU. 2. Encounter with the male of the species, a proletarian married truck-driver who gives her a lift while she gives him a hand-job. That's it. That is IL. 3. Chantal and her erstwhile girlfriend make love with naked *brio* in a scene which surpasses any other similar thing in world cinema. The movement of the bodies is abrupt, spasmodic, and the soundtrack like that of birds flapping their wings in a cage. Never have I seen the shudder of the loins (Yeats, 'Leda and the Swan') so well reproduced. You understand, after ten minutes of that on the screen, that lesbian love leaves you utterly shagged beyond any prick stuff. That is ELLE. Note that in each sequence there is food being munched. A

Jeanne Dielman 1975. This is by reputation her chef d'oeuvre. Delphine Seyrig aged 41 plays the lead some years after doing *Last Year in Marienbad* and *The Milky Way*. After two hours performing her household tasks with immaculate precision, she starts dropping a couple of things on the floor. This film is the *ne plus ultra* of minimalism *a l'etat pur* (as they say in Latin and French). All I will say is that it never flags (though the viewer might), that there is a hilarious scene with a baby which you cannot not laugh out aloud at, and that the end is as wonderful as the end of Catherine Breillat's *Perfect Love*! A

So folks, a great experience, rather better than I had feared. I heard that Varda was born in Bruxelles. So, with two of the greatest women directors on his doorstep, Jacques Brel can't have been that lonely.

Final report on Chantal Akerman. Films in my collection 1976-2000.

News from Home 1976. Homage to New York and to Letters from her Mother. Streets, subways and waterfront, reduced to minimalist tedium. Famous dissolve into Whistlerian image of water and sky-line. Later I found out she was under the influence (*nefaste* in my opinion) of Babette, a Belgian dabbler in all the extreme avant-garde arts (mainly photography). C

Les Rendez-vous d'Anna 1978. Return to Europe. A kind of trans-europ-express. Moscow to Paris (wow what a journey), with stops in various places for encounters which are either meaningful or meaningless. Occasional oomph seeps out of the minimalism, and at least the excesses of New York are left behind. One of the best bits for me were the two vast railway stations. Bruxelles Nord and Bruxelles Sud, as if Brussels were the largest metropolis in the world. B+

Extras - *Babette*. A sincerely disingenuous woman, not to be trusted. She led our Chantal into arid formalism and mistakenly believed that Delphine Seyrig had got on really well with Akerman, whereas it was obvious, and Chantal had to point it out to her, that Seyrig at first refused to follow Akerman's instructions and found great difficulty in submitting to Akerman's radical aesthetic. D-

Extras - *Natalia*. Nice cinema-verite conversation between Akerman and her mother. The family came from Ternow, Poland. Natalia was a concentration camp survivor, a very ordinary petit-bourgeois Belgian housewife, a proud mother with no graces and airs whatsoever. Touching stuff, especially when Chantal tried to approach the experience of those Polish Jews who were very nearly all exterminated. B+

Extras - *Aurore*. Memories shared with her leading actress in *Rendez-vous d'Anne*. Akerman came across Aurore's naked body on the front of a magazine, claimed she was too beautiful to figure in an Akerman film, and when she asked Aurore if she had seen *Je Tu Il Elle* and if she didn't think that the lesbian love-making with those two naked bodies was crude, we got the wonderful reply that No, No, it was poetry, pure poetry and something that had helped her find her way in the world. BA

J'ai Faim J'ai Froid 1984. A fantastically brilliant short film about two very young teenage girls who go on a spree, mostly of eating - but then of sexual experiment - in the spirit of Chytilova's *Daisies* and Breillat's inimitable pubescent girls in search of adventure and reality. Done with sheer anarchist abandon and dadaist glee. BA

Night and Day 1991. Two taxi drivers (who resemble Ant and

Dec) share the same girlfriend. For most of the film one knows and the other doesn't. One works nights and the other works days. The woman takes all this in her stride, without scruple, a latterday Anais Nin with touches of *Jules et Jim*. The style and dialogue is almost childish (child-like). It is almost Varda's *Le Bonheur* in reverse. The woman eventually (either 'cos she's shagged out or dismissive of male jealousies) walks out of both relationships, boldly, along a brightly lit Parisian boulvard. B+/A-

The Captive 2000. Adaptation of the Prisoner episode in Proust. Accomplished work, with the aplomb of Breillat's *Last Mistress* but not its spectacular eroticism or satiric wit. Still, it does make you think about Proust, gender politics and the male obsession with lesbians. As the American guy in IMDB put it with characteristic yankee honesty - 'I never realised there was so much girl-on-girl action in Proust.' A-

That's it folks. Am putting Akerman to bed for the next few months and moving on to some light relief with Sirk and Leigh. (14 April 2009)

2. Catherine Breillat

Known now for her latest releases (*Romance* 1999 and *A Ma Soeur* 2001), Breillat's previous films include *Une Vraie Jeune Fille* 1976, *Tapage Nocturne* 1979, *36 Fillette* 1987, *Sale Comme Un Ange* 1991, and *Parfait Amour!* 1996. But her scandalous debut goes back to 1967 when her first novel *L'Homme Facile* (*A Man for the Asking*) was published. Breillat was only 17 and the novel was banned for under-eighteens. The protagonist L. (= Elle) prefers rape to consensual sex and the text established Breillat as a would-be latterday Rimbaud, disordering language and the senses in all directions in a pornographic phantasmagoria of female fantasy. Breillat never abandoned her adolescent obsession. Her crazy quest culminates in her latest two films.

Three Cheers for Breillat: Bravo!

In her lively and literate review of 'the works of filmmaker Catherine Breillat', entitled *A Matter of Skin* (1999), the American critic Kathleen Murphy calls Breillat 'a wild child who matured early, a provincial loner steeped in the likes of Sade and Lautreamont'. Breillat's 'pagan eye rejects the Christian rupture of body and soul to remarry skin with spirit in a potent metaphysic of sex', and 'in today's cinematic climate of carnal benightedness this is a consummation devoutly to be wished'. According to Murphy, Breillat 'reverses the infantilisation and masculinisation of American sexual imagination', and she concludes, 'taking sex seriously is what Breillat's art is all about.'

Interviewed in 2001 about *Romance*, Breillat says: 'The film is not about Paul and Marie. It's about the dichotomy of womanhood. The woman cut in two. Every society has created laws to exercise power over women and to exclude certain parts of women, and they use the excuse that it is to preserve the dignity of women.' On the question of censorship, art and porn, Breillat says: 'One cannot forbid an image. If the image is masturbatory, then the film is an X-rated film because sex becomes an object rather than the subject. But in *Romance* sex was the subject so it could not be an X-rated film. In the porno film there is no director whose gaze we follow. The director is just a utility. An image without intention or without meaning does not exist. It is funny that the censors managed to obliterate this fact for 25 years. It is very political to forget this fact. It makes it possible to present images and to tell people that the image is proof of something. But an image is always a manipulation.' Breillat was obviously influenced by Oshima (director of *In the Realm of the Senses / Ai No Corrida* 1976), who had argued that: 'Obscenity does not exist because to show a thing renders it "not obscene". Only hidden things and things that are not shown can be obscene.' Which is of course irrefutable etymologically since 'obscene' means 'off-stage'.

Breillat's remarks on *A Ma Soeur* are equally enlightening. On the significance of the exquisitely formed 15 year-old Elena and her podgy 12 year-old sister Anais, she notes: 'To be as beautiful as Elena is not a real gift in life. She becomes a fantasy for men, an object of desire, and she's so young she cannot understand why. You are made by the way people look at you. What makes Anais so beautiful is that nobody's looking at her and making her ugly. She actually likes herself.' On the implication that the film's ending makes Anais subvert her violation by embracing her attacker and denying to the police that rape took place, Breillat argues that female masochism is culturally imposed and questions whether it is possible for women to be 'sexually liberated' when all sexual narratives remain dominated by men. And, in a reference back to her own adolescent novel, Breillat sums up the thesis of *A Ma Soeur* in the following trenchant manifesto of 1968 utopian desire: 'We are all 15 and a half in our hopes. We always want to believe it's the first time - it's that feeling of life that can't be

reasoned by the adult mind, to think that we may change the world. You resign yourself to becoming an adult, but actually we have idealistic dreams. That's what I'd call being 15 and a half, but without the teenage misery.' And that's what I'd call the life-enhancing provocation we will find (if we want to) in all Breillat's work I have so far seen.
(For more on Breillat's *A Ma Soeur* 2001, see Capsule Reviews)

3. Cacoyannis

Funny thing. In the Cambridge University Film Society 1957-1960, we caught a first glimpse of the New Wave, those films now regarded as the greatest generation in the history of cinema. But the one director whose first three films we saw without knowing who he was or what they were, was Cacoyannis. So we saw *Windfall in Athens* 1953, *Stella* 1955 and *The Girl in Black* 1956. As most of us had studied Greek at public school and were bound for long vacation tours of Greece in 1959 and 1960, these films made a big impression on us. The actresses were stunning, Elli Lambeti, Melina Mercouri, Irene Papas.

Since then of course Cacoyannis hit the big time with *Zorba the Greek* 1964. *Time Out* slams this film as a stupid vehicle for Quinn's over-the-top histrionics. It is a very good film, capturing the spirit of Kazantzakis's novel and bringing out the very best in Lila Kedrova and Irene Papas. Cacoyannis was offered big jobs in Hollywood and thankfully refused them all. A Greek Cypriot who spent some time in London, Cacoyannis went on to make some fine films in Greek, especially the Euripides trilogy of *Electra* 1962, *The Trojan Women* 1971, *Iphigenea* 1977. He was blacklisted and in self-imposed exile during the rule of the fascist colonels 1967-74. He worked closely with the anti-fascist militants Theodorakis (music) and Mercouri (actress, married to Jules Dassin, later minister of culture in a socialist government and famous for trying to get the Elgin Marbles back to Athens).

The dvd of Zorba has an audio by Cacoyannis. The film is full of action, atmosphere and extras (local Cretan peasants). Its feel-good humanitarian ending hangs on the friendship/love between the Dionysian Quinn and the Apollonian Alan Bates. And that is Kazantzakis's philosophy, the conflict between the flesh and the spirit, the physical and the intellectual. My only complaint is that this reconciliation takes place after the death of the two women in the film. And it is those two women who carry the main weight of the film, ideologically and aesthetically. The death of these women does demonstrate the backwardness of peasant society in southern Crete around WW1. Irene Papas is an 'available' and sexually attractive young widow. All the villagers want to sleep with her. One young lad is so smitten he commits suicide. Irene Papas fancies Alan Bates and after much encouraging from Zorba they get it together in her tiny hut of a house. Then the young lad's father organises a lynch mob and in spite of Zorba's attempt to save her, Irene Papas is stabbed to death in the square in front of all the sex-starved peasants. Lovely Greek Tragedy. Irene Papas's dying body is covered by the only local she trusted, a finely portrayed village idiot straight out of Buñuel's *Viridiana*.

And, as if that were not enough for us poor spectators, catharsis is added to catharsis as the splendid Lila Kedrova has her house (*The Hotel Ritz*) trashed by local ancient hags acting like vultures to loot her of all her property and trinkets as she gasps in Zorba's arms on her deathbed.

These two deaths have a specific cultural-historical context and so make total sense. BUT (and this is no doubt as much due to Kazantzakis and the Greek culture of EROS and THANATOS as to Cacoyannis), I personally cannot take seriously the 'happy ending' of homoerotic matiness between the two men, which seems almost to depend on the sacrifice of the two women. And for me it is the two women who carry the film as actresses - Zorba is almost a caricature of Greek excess and Alan Bates a mere cipher of Anglo-Greek repression (his brief affair with Papas has no effect on his willy-wet-legs nature). But Papas and Kedrova - they are in another league, along with Helen of Troy, Elektra, Iphigenia, Clytemnestra, Cassandra and all those other Greek women who have forged the consciousness of our European race.

To be yet discovered are: *A Matter of Dignity* 1957, *Eroica* 1960, *The Day the Fish came out* 1967, *Sweet Country* 1986 (on Chile 1973), *Up Down and Sideways* 1993, *The Cherry Orchard* 1999. Oh, and one odd one I've already seen *Attila*

Rape of Cyprus 1975 - a passionate pro-Greek polemic on the Cypriot war between Greeks and Turks - so partisan that the philosophically eirenic Kazantzakis who wrote even-handedly about the Turkish occupation of Greece in *Christ Recrucified* would probably not have approved - but then he was dead by then, so who knows.

Dr Hoyles, O level Greek (early for responsions) c.1954. (August 2011)

4. Charlie Chaplin 1889-1997

Select Filmography:
The Kid 1921, *The Gold Rush* 1925, *City Lights* 1931, *Modern Times* 1936, *The Great Dictator* 1940, *Monsieur Verdoux* 1947

The London Years
Charlie Chaplin was born in London on 16th April 1889. Both his parents were music hall entertainers and Charlie started appearing on the stage while still a child. His father, Charles Chaplin, deserted the family and eventually died of alcoholism. His mother, Hannah Chaplin, found it increasingly difficult to find work on the stage and in 1895 the family entered the Lambeth Workhouse. Later, Charlie's mother had a mental breakdown and was sent to the Cane Hill Lunatic Asylum.

The Kid 1921
Stunningly sentimental but amazingly effective. This film reminds us that Chaplin was much closer in time to Dickens than to us. He tear-jerks us to and past the limits of modern cynicism and makes it work. The penultimate reel which distils the whole tale into a fantasy of love spoiled by jealousy, is a complete delight in and of itself. (IMDB user comment)

Freud on Chaplin
In the last few days Chaplin has been in Vienna but it was too cold for him here and he left again quickly. He is undoubtedly a great artist; certainly he always portrays one and the same figure; only the weakly poor, helpless, clumsy youngster for whom, however, things turn out well in the end. Now, do you think for this role he has to forget about his own ego? On the contrary, he always plays only himself as he was in his dismal youth. He cannot get away from those impressions and humiliations of that past period of his life. He is, so to speak, an exceptionally simple and transparent case. The idea that

the achievements of artists are intimately bound up with their childhood memories, impressions, repressions and disappointments, has already brought in much enlightenment and has, for that reason, become very precious to us. (early 30s)

Chaplin Psychoanalysed

Generations of filmgoers have laughed with tears in their eyes at Chaplin's scenes in *The Gold Rush* where his boyishly innocent Little Tramp naively attempts to woo Georgia, a wistfully soulful dance-hall prostitute, away from her hollow life as a good-time girl in a boomtown saloon. But few people realise that the creation of Georgia - like the creation of so many of his other film heroines - borrowed heavily from and reflected dramatically details of the life experience of his own mother Hannah. Chaplin lost his mother to mental illness when he was still a child. It was that loss and the scars it left that later shaped Chaplin's development of an alter-ego screen character whose core identity was the rescue and repair of damaged and fallen women. Read from a psychoanalytical perspective, *The Gold Rush* retraced (and symbolically corrected) the original real life circumstances which had ultimately led to his mother's mental illness, probably resulting from an incurable case of third stage syphilis. Like Georgia, Hannah Chaplin was in a gold rush (she was in South Africa when gold was first being discovered). And also like Georgia, she may have been a prostitute. (Weissman 1996)

"Look Up Hannah" Speech

Greed has poisoned men's souls - has barricaded the world with hate - has goose-stepped us into misery and bloodshed. ... Soldiers! Don't give yourselves to these brutes - who despise you - enslave you - who regiment your lives - tell you what to do - what to think, and what to feel. ... You are not machines ...Don't hate! Only the unloved hate. (*The Great Dictator* 1940)

Kafka on Chaplin

That's a very energetic, work-obsessed man. There burns in his eyes the flame of despair at the unchangeable condition of the oppressed, yet he does not capitulate to it. Like every genuine comedian he has the bite of a beast of prey, and he uses it to attack the world. He does it in his own unique way. Despite the white face and the black eyebrows, he's not a sentimental Pierrot, nor is he some snarling critic. Chaplin is a technician. He's the man of a machine world, in which most of his fellow men no longer command the requisite emotional and mental equipment to make the life allotted to them really their own. They do not have the imagination. As a dental technician makes false teeth, so he manufactures aids to the imagination. That's what his films are. That's what films in general are. (Janouch *Conversations with Kafka*). [NB Kafka died in 1924 and only saw some of Chaplin's very early stuff.]

Chaplin and Hitler

In the crazy apocalyptic year 1916, in Zurich, in the magic mountains above the trenches, Lenin, still a superfluous man, awaits his turn, and Dada (a nonsense word for a nonsense world) denies even that a terrible beauty has been born. From the holocaust of World War One (8 million killed, 25 million disabled), in the form of the not-so-Chaplinesque archetypal 'little man', Corporal Hitler, the seeds of a second holocaust are germinated. (Hoyles, *The Literary Underground* 1991, 27) [Chaplin and Hitler were both born in 1889.]

Taylorism Triumphant

In Zamyatin's *We* (1920) Taylorism is triumphant. This is the word of Fritz Lang's *Metropolis* (1926) and Charlie Chaplin's *Modern Times* (1936). What is more, in Zamyatin's world, what Gramsci describes as 'the attempts made by Ford, with the aid of a body of inspectors, to intervene in the private life of his employees, and to control how they lived', especially with regard to 'the sexual question' and 'alcohol', have almost totally succeeded. (Hoyles 101)

Zany Slapstick
Kafka's comic genius, like Chaplin's and Keaton's, taps this vein of random zany slapstick. But it can also give the reader a headache (or make us weep), because the comic version of ludic absurdity is part and parcel of that same totalitarian world of mass-society where the organic and the human is perpetually tripping up on the banana skin that has become the mechanised escalator of daily life. (Hoyles 164)

Torture Machines
One of the secrets of this amazing narrative (Kafka's *In the Penal Colony* 1914) is the way in which it combines a harrowing description of torture to death by machine, and a comic subtext not far removed from the mechanical mishaps of Charlie Chaplin in *Modern Times*. (Hoyles 196)

Human Rights
Charlie Chaplin's campaign for the rights of the little man (and its accompanying modes of sentimentality, pathos and melodrama) are contained within the magic machinery of comedy. Kafka's material, like Chaplin's, may include the heat of righteous indignation, but his medium is cool, controlled and ultimately comic. The countless fortuitous beauties of both artists are a product of their understanding and mastery of the absurd. (Hoyles 220)

The Marvellous and the Absurd
As so often in Kafka, this knife-edge ability to fuse fantasy and satire gives full play to both the marvellous and the absurd. And it is that double view of the machinery of the modern world which links Kafka with Chaplin and Mayakovsky. They are all amazed by the intricate beauty and power of Taylorised efficiency, and they are all appalled when the machine devours its own workers. (Hoyles 222)

The American Dream and Western Civilisation's Discontents

In *Amerika* (1912/1927), Kafka's tramp, half way between Chaplin and Beckett, carries the spirit of the deracinated outsider into the very heart of our civilisation, as embodied in the Hotel Occidental. (Hoyles 224)

5. Nelly Kaplan

She has made two brilliant and one decent film.

1. *La Fiancee de Pirate* (1969), aka in USA, *A Very Curious Girl*, or, *Dirty Mary* – (trust the Yanks to lower the tone). Demythologises the persecution of witches, in militant feminist as opposed to liberal-humanist fashion. The witch burns the inquisitors.

2. *Nea: A New Woman* (1976), sometimes has the New Emmanuelle soubriquet to capture the soft-porn market. Demythologises the Pygmalion myth. Teenage writer of erotica overwhelms patronising bookseller and publisher who seeks to appropriate her for his own nefarious purposes. As I remember, she blows him up with explosives, after a torrid affair in which she loses her virginity in order to improve her writing.

3. *Plaisir d'Amour* (1980). Somewhat creaky allegorical plot. Demythologises the Don Juan myth. Thus, a 40 year-old playboy gets his come-uppance from a trinity of sexy women, grandma, mother and daughter, but really all the same person. Half way between the three witches in *Macbeth* and Angela Carter territory.

Nelly Kaplan's partner Claude Mayovski seems to have had a hand in all her films. The couple remind me of Agnes Varda and Jacques Demy. Mayovski and Demy are the lightweight entertainers, Kaplan and Varda the serious investigators and feminist ideologues.

Kaplan is an ultra-feminist and anarchist and surrealist. She demythologises like Angela Carter and Marina Warner. She has a continental (Argentinian?) ferocity, but never loses her comic feel-good dimension. Apart from these three films her other stuff seems trivial and Makovski-dominated. But what they lost in their artistic collaboration they must have gained plentifully (like Varda and Demy) in their life together. It is not easy to be ferocious and gentle. D.H.Lawrence was quite good at it.

Incidentally there is a nice reversal of the cliche in *Plaisir d'Amour*. As the song goes, the pleasure is brief and the sorrow (chagrin) is long. Kaplan seems to see this as a male view-point and turns it upside down. For women, the pleasure is long and the sorrow short. Women last longer as men's erections slump. As she gleefully reminds us, the literal meaning of dithyramb is 'a song to erect the penis'.

In Kaplan's *Charles et Lucie* (1980), a road movie very popular in the States (Nelly tells us) there is a wonderful shot of the Green Ray, even more splendiferous than the one caught at the end of Rohmer's *Rayon Vert* (1986). Nelly got there first!

You may know some of this already, but until a few weeks ago I'd never heard of Nelly Kaplan. It appears that only *Nea* exists with English subtitles, probably because it is included in a truly atrocious collection of 'French Erotica' put out by the Australians (sic). Such is the white anglo-saxon mentality, on the look out for the dress malfunction, the escaped tit and moony bum. Mind you, Kaplan had difficulty with the Pompidou Ministry of Information in 1969. A ministry man told her she could only have her film released if the heroine was killed off. Kaplan made sure this insult got into the papers, and she triumphed over the censorship. But, until Giscard came along and liberalised cinema censorship, she had to cover up her topless drawing of Nea on the posters. I feel I have justified my pension for doing nothing. So, sock it to them, cinephiles of the world, you have nothing to lose but your subtitles. (12 October 2008)

6. Ken Loach

Riff Raff is OK as a 'Play for Today', clear, didactic to a T, preaching to the converted, what our Ken does best. *Raining Stones* is more ambitious, existential, with a touch of *Godot* throughout. But the metaphysical comedy (unlike in Chaplin) never really escapes the old political nostrums of the long-term unemployed, the fecklessness of the workers, the chirpy Orwellian humour of proletarian speech-rhythms, blarney from the lower depths, the working man's only defence against the hand he has been dealt by the nasty bosses who (like the poor) will always be with us, since Lenin, Stalin and Trotsky failed to get rid of them.

But, as for *Ladybird Ladybird*, that is another thing entirely. Certainly one of Loach's most powerful dramas since *Cathy Come Home*. The figure of Maggie, Magna Mater, Life-force and thorn in the side of the social services, is truly epic, Homeric, Brechtian. Her acting is so powerful that she carries us beyond the finely tuned dialectic (feckless detritus of dysfunctional motherhood versus the benign welfare state set up by the Labour Movement to look after us from cradle to grave). We see both sides in this dialectic. Which side are we on. We are conflicted (as the Americans like to say). Maggie is a hypermanic nasty piece of work who should be looked after by being put away in a secure unit. She is also a metaphysical fertility symbol of how the life-force cannot be denied by any social engineering, rehabilitation, or Malthusian eugenics. And so our Ken gets his Cathy to come home again into our living rooms.

Like Zola, like Pialat, Loach's *Ladybird* transcends the easy appellation of naturalism. It is nearer to Rimbaud, whose '*je est un autre*' has just been mentioned on the French radio I have on in the background. Zola's Nana was raped, sexually abused as a child, like Loach's Maggie. But even if this provides sufficient cause for what then ensues, it is never presented as an excuse, or even explanation, by Zola or Loach.

What Maggie and Nana have in common is the life-force which may rush into negative and unproductive avenues, but which cannot be put down.

When Maggie gives a rapid account of her abused childhood, it is almost an interpolated insert (a gesture of rationality and causality to conform with the politically correct nostrums of the left-liberal ruling elite). It reminds me of old Arnold Kettle (lovely Marxist in the CPGB) telling us that Heathcliff is as he is 'cos he was found in the slums of Liverpool. Yes, I believe Terry Eagleton came from those parts as well. Heathcliff and Maggie (and Nana) have a rage that cannot be put down to a sufficient cause in socio-economic, or even psycho-sexual, terms. But they are perhaps all characters for whom *'je est un autre'* may be a motto. They are out of place, displaced, strangers to themselves, let alone to others and the powers that be. 'Rage' in French is 'rabies', it is that biological.

And then, oh dear, there is poor old Ray Winstone (actually a lovely family man), roped in to do some more psychopathic domestic violence. There's a thick prole in *Nana* who is almost as awful – but she still loves him of course, even when nearly beaten to death. Brecht's 'Ballad of Sexual Dependency' will now be sung to ram home the point.

And it says that Loach's film is based on actual facts. How many well-paid social workers are needed to keep Ray Winstone under control? The poor wretched social workers, set up presumably by the social-democracy to replace the nuns and Mother Teresas of feudal Catholicism - no wonder they've got a bad name. Where in what art-form on earth are they heroines? No - they are nasty, taking babies away from their carers. Isn't the strongest image of this benevolent cruelty the removal of Chaplin's little boy by do-gooders in *The Kid*? And this image was predominant in *Cathy Come Home*, and it was the persistent causal theme of the plot to the 2001 remake in modern dress of Zola's *Nana*. Lou Doillon (Charlotte Gainsbourg's half-sister) undresses in front of, and sleeps with, half of the French ruling class, in an attempt to get her little boy back from the social workers!

Maggie is of course magnificently infuriating. Her swearing is industrial. She is her own worst enemy. Surely she has to be taken into care to stop her sleeping with psychopathic retards and producing babies on a factory conveyor belt.

At this point my notes become illegible. But it would appear that Loach falls for the Third World solution. Hence the hero from Paraguay who has somehow escaped the machismo of the latinos, and who, as an illegal asylum seeker has all the credentials to tame and rescue our deviant scouse lumpen-prole. Well, maybe it is true, maybe it happened, but it comes across as a utopian Trotskyist device to satisfy our Ken's progressive conscience.

Sorry to be so long-winded. Of course what is wrong with *Raining Stones* is its meretricious Roman Catholic plot. Our noble prole is a wretched papist, obsessed with his daughter's first communion dress. He is such a bigot that he doesn't even listen to the only sensible bloke in the film, his Roman Catholic priest! This (in spite of the little girl's Mouchette-like inability to understand the catechism) gives the whole film a sickly hue, which is the mark of George Galloway and his ilk, the working class Catholics of Scotland among whom Loach's principal screen writer is pre-eminent, and (when he with religiose modesty speaks with Loach on dvd commentaries), Glaswegianly incomprehensible.

7. Polanski

You come to films either through personal acquaintance in specialised corners, or through Hollywood hype. Polanski's public reputation rests on his American middle period 'shockers', *Rosemary's Baby* (1968), *Macbeth* (1971) and *Chinatown* (1974). Yet arguably these 'famous' films (together with the wooden *Tess* of 1979) are hollow works of sound and fury compared to the earlier work when he was still making a name for himself. His 1959 short *Two Men and a Wardrobe*, which I first saw in a student Film Society, is a masterpiece of the absurd (surrealism with cosmic pretensions), and this world-view is fleshed out in his three greatest films, *Knife in the Water* (1962), *Repulsion* (1965) and *Cul-de-Sac* (1966). The way in which relationship and isolation breed absurd violence is under wraps in these films, economically controlled in a well-timed pressure-cooker of cinematic devices.

Cul-de-Sac is Holy Island in Northumberland, cut off by the tide twice a day. Grown men there still remember the mess left by Polanski's crew, one even remembers as a boy spying in the dunes to catch a glimpse of the naked Françoise Dorléac. The film is heavily pregnant with threatening meaning that is never made explicit. This is the only Polanski film that one might compare with Antonioni's *L'Avventura* (1959). Somehow, in America, with *Rosemary's Baby* and the 1969 vicious murder of his eight month pregnant wife Sharon Tate by the Manson gang, Polanski lost the plot, went berserk, let the cat out of the bag. Hollywood production values took over. Nothing strange about this. It had happened to Fritz Lang from Germany, Renoir from France, Milos Forman from Czechoslovakia. And so, the gratuitously vulgar violence in *Macbeth* was laughed to scorn by schoolchildren taken to study their exam text. Every spurt of blood was cheered like a goal in football. And so the dumbing down goes on.

It is still true that Polanski's genius has a long way to fall into mediocrity. Certainly his *Dance of the Vampires* (1967) which is comparable to Mel Brooks' *Young Frankenstein* (1974), is in a class above the more publicly vented Hammer school of horror. And, by way of postscript to this somewhat mean and meagre tribute to a Polish genius, I should add that I now believe that *The Tenant* (1975) is one of Polanski's greatest films, and the film indeed in which (as opposed to his 1975 *Tess* with its dedication to Sharon Tate) he resurrects his genius out of the ashes of the Manson murders. And while his Oscar-winning *Piano* (2002) is more worthy than wonderful, a hidden gem has just surfaced here in Hull - it is the dvd of *A Day at the Beach* (1970) with the director credited as the unknown Heresa in which Polanski pulls off an amazing *tour de force* of the banal-absurd genre in the immediate aftermath of the murder of his wife.

Finally, given the ongoing predicament in which Polanski has found himself under a kind of house arrest in Switzerland for unsorted sexual offences dating back to the 70s in America, and the threat of extradition hanging over his head as his wife and young children languish in Paris, Polanski fans will want to check out an excellent documentary on all this - Marina Zenovich's *Roman Polanski: Wanted and Desired* (2008).

More Polanski. Poor old Polanski. Thank God he's banned in America. *Rosemary's Baby* was his first American film. It was a huge success, probably his most famous film for the Hollywood infected globalised masses. *The Tenant* was apparently a total flop, commercially and critically. It is clear to me that *Rosemary's Baby* is a well-made pot-boiler with the wretched whining Mia Farrow an absolute minus and with nothing for us to grasp other than Exorcist-type occult mumbo-jumbo. *The Tenant*, on the other hand, is bright and intelligent throughout, cast in the spirit of Kafka, and with Polanski himself and Isabelle Adjani playing out of themselves with exquisite black humour and sublime mad love. Polanski is building out of that body of work comprising *Repulsion*, *Cul-de-Sac* and *Le Bal des Vampires*, and taking us beyond them into a new place. Adjani is gorgeous, her excessive sex-appeal muted by an enormous pair of glasses. This mixed persona doesn't prevent her grabbing Polanski by the balls in a cinema at the beginning of the film. Polanski is Joseph K in *The Trial*, and the left-over traces from *Rosemary's Baby* are nicely contained within the hilarity of paranoia. *Rosemary's Baby* is so ponderous, literal and Sirk-like. So, let Polanski remain in Paris, and keep Hollywood away from him (once he gets out of that Zurich house arrest of course). (4 November 2009)

8. Ken Russell

Ken Russell, don't you love to hate him, the thinking man's Michael Winner, the man who is for ever over the top. Well ... For my money, Ken is one of the few major talents in English cinema (that contradiction in terms according to Truffaut). His early television films on *Elgar* (1962), *Delius* (1968) and *Debussy* (1965, at last available after 40 years under an embargo by the Debussy family heirs) were gems of cinematic invention as well as fascinating documentaries. And although his full-length film on Tchaikovsky, *The Music Lovers* (1971), described by the director as a 'love story between a homosexual and a nymphomaniac', can be consumed as tasteless kitsch, it does make you think about Tchaikovsky's music. Even the early *French Dressing* (1963), though obviously hopelessly dated at one level has a certain panache; its controlled high spirits bear some comparison with Tony Richardson's marvellously poetic *A Taste of Honey* (1961).

D.H. Lawrence who lambasted cinema in *The Lost Girl* and whose painting of an early cinematic kiss is intended to convey horror, perhaps inevitably became Ken Russell's favourite novelist for adaptation purposes. Both men were expressionists, prepared to kick against the pricks and go over the top. *Women in Love* (1969) is a masterpiece of translation. A great novel becomes a pretty bright film, a classical interpretation which never betrays the book and never annoys the Lawrentians among us. The falling off in the embarrassingly trite and meretricious versions of *The Rainbow* (1988) and *Lady Chatterley* (1993) is appalling to behold. [PS I have since revised my views here - and I now think that his *Lady Chatterley* is a tour de force that bears comparison with Pascale Ferran's outstanding French version of 2006.]

But it is *The Devils* (1971) where Ken's virtues and vices confront each other most dramatically, 50% Jarmanesque kitsch, 50% expressionist experiment - sometimes you lap it up, sometimes you throw it up, the proverbial dog's dinner.

Unfortunately we are not able to measure *The Devils* against a more sober and Marxist version of the same 17thC events, since Kawalerowicz's *Mother Joan of the Angels* (Poland 1961), which I saw in Leipzig (DDR) when it first came out, is as far as I know not available. [Now, 2011, it is of course out on dvd and is certainly less strikingly sensationalist than Ken's masterpiece.]

Personally, in spite of his baroque affectations and tendency towards Catholic kitsch and blasphemy, I regard Ken Russell as English cinema's Savage Messiah, saving us of course from the dominant culture's Ivory Merchants and long Georgian summers. And *Savage Messiah* (1972), like his early films on composers, was a pretty good study of the artist as a young man - in this case Gaudier-Brzeska, who was a bit like Russell himself, a Vorticist.

CHAPTER FOUR: SHORT SUBVERSIVE FILMS

World Cinema and Political Radicalism: Art Cinema Shorts in an Age of Extremes 1919-1990

20thC history takes on a visionary hue when viewed through the fantasies and documentaries of the seventh art. Short films (programmes normally less than an hour long) allow students to spend the second half of each session discussing and arguing about what they have just seen. These films are classics, carefully chosen to reflect the highest and brightest achievements of 20thC cinema. And they reveal the extreme conditioning, visions, utopias and anti-utopias which mark the violent history of our epoch.

1. Luis Buñuel *UN CHIEN ANDALOU* France 1928 (15)
    Arguably the most notorious and shocking film of all time.
    Luis Buñuel *LAS HURDES* Spain 1932 (28)
    A cool callous documentary with a sting in its tail, upsetting and hilarious.

The juxtaposition of these two films by the master of surrealist cinema raises far-reaching questions about fantasy as reality, reality as fantasy, the conflict between reason and imagination, dream and documentary, as well as the relationship between Freud and Marx, liberation and subjection. The films are anti-fascist, but not in obvious ways. Melies (magic) and Lumiere (ultra-realism) preside over these terrorist bombs.

2. Robert Wiene *THE CABINET OF DOCTOR CALIGARI* Germany 1919 (45)
    The seminal film of German expressionism, prophetic of Hitler's rise to power.

This studio-bound fantasy with its crazy design and plot gives us a gothic horror story where the post-WW1 world is turned upside down. The benevolent director of the lunatic asylum turns out to be a psychopathic killer - or does he? - isn't that just our disordered imagination? What do you think?!

3. Charlie Chaplin *THE KID* USA 1921 (50)

Revolutionary sentiment and social realism galore from the scintillating tramp. Life in the slums with society's rejects, outsiders up against the pompous hypocrisies and violent cruelties of a ruling class in need of overthrow. Compare the kitchen-sink naturalism here with Caligari's extreme artificiality.

4. Luis Buñuel *L'AGE D'OR* France 1930 (60)

Revolutionary surrealism in all its blasphemous obscenity. Buñuel's greatest film tackles Civilisation and its Discontents in the same year as Freud's text of that title. Right-wing rioters invaded the cinema in an attempt to stop this frontal onslaught on all bourgeois values (church, state, family etc). Celebrating the surrealist theory of mad love, and simultaneously sublime and absurd, blissful and hilarious, this film was banned for a generation.

5. Jean Vigo *ZERO DE CONDUITE* France 1933 (45)

An anarchist bomb combining bleak naturalism and magic surrealism. Vigo's masterpiece (influential on Lindsay Anderson's 1968 *If*) is a vicious blast against educational sadism, a call for a Popular Front progressive education (to come in 1936). Compare A.S.Neill's Summerhill experiment in practical anarchism. Banned for a generation, Vigo's film celebrates with mordant wit and blissful dream sequences the rebellion that lies at the heart of us all when we say to our elders and betters: 'Monsieur, je vous dis merde!'

SHORT SUBVERSIVE FILMS

6. Sidney Bernstein *A PAINFUL REMINDER* GB 1945 (1985) (70)

The holocaust documentary they dared not show. Commissioned by the British authorities as a contribution to the denazification programme following the collapse of the Third Reich, this documentary was immediately withdrawn on the grounds that it would demoralise the cadres needed to reconstruct West Germany. It was only released forty years later and then very rarely shown. Please note: images of concentration camps are not for the faint-hearted. Compare Claude Lanzmann's *Shoah* where Auschwitz is approached via the memories of witnesses with not a single shot of the victims.

7. Kenneth Anger *FIREWORKS* USA 1947 (15)

Real sailors produce gay sado-masochistic reverie. The oneiric homosexual imagery and exploding phallus clearly had a big influence on Genet's film three years later.

Jean Genet *UN CHANT D'AMOUR* France 1950 (25)

Homosexual prisoners break down the walls with flower power. This gay love story (with no soundtrack) is a revolutionary poem from the scandalous outsider of outsiders, Jean Genet, author of *The Thief's Journal, The Maids, The Balcony* etc. Banned in many places (including for a time in Hull).

Kenneth Anger *SCORPIO RISING* USA 1963 (27)

Homoerotic transgression with legendary rock'n'roll soundtrack. An underground tribute to bikers' rituals from the author of the scandalous *Hollywood Babylon*. Intercut with Sunday School film of Jesus, to create gorgeous blasphemy.

8. Santiago Alvarez *HANOI TUESDAY 13TH* Cuba 1966 (35)

Vietnam War documentary not likely to be seen in Hollywood. Excellent example of communist agit-prop. Arguably makes *Apocalypse Now* (the best American film on the subject) seem pathetically self-indulgent (given the casualties on the Vietnamese side).

Marisol Trujillo *PRAYER FOR MARILYN MONROE* Cuba 1985 (8)
An astounding indictment of American Imperialism. This Cuban woman director provides a coruscating sequence of images to a celebrated poem by Ernesto Cardenal (Nicaraguan priest, poet and minister in the Sandinista government, famous for being on the receiving end of a papal finger-wagging rebuke). This film is propaganda and poetry, ending in the crescendo of Blake's Jerusalem.

9. Ken Russell *ELGAR* GB 1962 (55)
England's dreaming. The outrageous (Catholic) film director's take on the sober (Catholic) composer of Land of Hope and Glory. Combines ecstatic celebration with timely deconstruction of the jingoist myth.

Yuri Norstein *TALE OF TALES* USSR 1980 (30)
Russia's dreaming. Voted number one animated film of all time, this gentle but rigorous poetic film encapsulates the spirit of Russia. Its brilliance dazzled the censors who suspected it contained some dissident allegory which they could not find.

10. Tony Harrison *V* GB 1988 (37)
England's nightmare. The best of Harrison's film poems, *V* raises complex questions of class, culture, language and poetry, through a meditation on the activities of football hooligans in a Yorkshire cemetery. Conservatives tried to get the BBC to ban it. Why?

Jan Svankmajer *DIMENSIONS OF A DIALOGUE* Czechoslovakia 1982 (10)
Jan Svankmajer *THE DEATH OF STALINISM IN BOHEMIA* Czechoslovakia 1990 (10)

Czechoslovakia's nightmare. These are brilliant surrealist animations which are both visually stunning and thought-provoking. They go beyond treating Czech politics under a Stalinist regime and make us think about subjection and liberation within the human condition under whatever regime.

CHAPTER FIVE: CINE-FEM

Women Filmmakers and the Female Gaze
"One isn't born a woman, one becomes one." Simone de Beauvoir *The Second Sex* 1949.

"DS/ID: Deesse/Idee: Goddess/Idea: Two kinds of Citroen car. Two kinds of women." Agnes Varda, *Cleo de 5 a 7* 1961.

Manifesto 1999
Let us study some strong films made by women (including one by a token man), which raise questions about the power of the moving image, the power of propaganda, the power of dream and desire.

Traditionally women were in front of the camera, not behind it; as in literature and all the arts, they were high and low objects rather than subjects, But, although marginalised and often neglected, these films constitute an alternative cinema, with aesthetic and ideological qualities which at least match, and in some ways surpass, the achievements of films directed by men. It remains to be seen how far these films are gender-specific, what contribution they make to the feminist agenda, how far they contest, subvert or reverse the so-called male gaze, how far they build up an alternative female gaze, and how far they open up radical strategies, in form and content, with which to confront a world and an art so often gone dead or mechanical in heart and head.

Let us address the aesthetics and politics of women's cinema - not cinema exclusively about women, or even exclusively for women, but cinema made by women for the world, without which neither the cinema nor the world can be truly emancipated.

Sandy Flitterman-Lewis once said that she preferred teaching film within an English Department, rather than in a Cultural Studies or Media Studies or Communications context. And I agree. While not ruling out work on cinema which stresses the sociological dimension, I find it more rewarding to treat cinema as a fine art which has more in common with literary studies than with television and commerce. The same values operate in film as in literature, values which I call aesthetic and ideological. Hollywood is not thereby excluded, but it is marginalised (which, given its global hegemony is what it deserves).

In the last thirty years, hypostasised theory has clogged film criticism (e.g. the journal called *Screen*), as it has literary criticism (e.g. totemic French theory from Derrida, Lacan, Foucault to Kristeva, Irigaray, Cixous). I do not rule out sophisticated psychoanalytical or post-structuralist approaches, but I prefer the more straightforward combination of Marxism and Formalism which accompanied the production of modernism in all the arts. Trotsky accepted that Shklovsky's Formalism was 'necessary but not sufficient'. And my old school friend Peter Wollen, with 'signs and meaning' in the title of his first book, also sanctions this approach.

Cine-Fem Films on Video. The Selected Works. A Brief Descriptive Catalogue.

Leni Riefenstahl, *Triumph of the Will* Germany 1935.
    Hitler in all his glory. Fascinating Fascism (Susan Sontag). Every woman adores a fascist (Sylvia Plath).

Larissa Shepitko, *The Ascent* USSR 1977.
    Soviet partisans under the Nazi yoke in WW2. Communist humanism.

Leontine Sagan, *Maidens in Uniform* Germany 1931.
Banned by Goebbels. Lesbian cult film. A Prussian girls boarding school. No men.

Marie Epstein, *La Maternelle* France 1933.
Nursery school kids act in Popular Front film. More poetry than propaganda. Neglected classic of world cinema. Bears comparison with Vigo's *Zero de Conduite* 1933.

Agnes Varda, *Cleo de 5 a 7* France 1961.
A pop singer waits two hours (the length of the film) to find out if she has cancer. The 'mother' of the (exclusively masculine) French New Wave (Godard, Truffaut etc) tells us how a woman 'looks' (in both senses, as object and as subject of the 'gaze').

Vera Chytilova, *Daisies* Czechoslovakia 1966.
Dada lives in the Prague Spring. The most formally revolutionary and modernist film produced by the otherwise male dominated Czech New Wave. *Jouissance* (pussy) galore.

Marta Meszaros, *The Two of Them* Hungary 1977/1979.
Hungarian sisterhood burns bright in the unlikely setting of a communist hostel for factory workers from the countryside. The personal is political (and vice-versa).

Karoly Makk, *Another Way* Hungary 1979/1982.
Lesbian dissident journalist struggles against the dead hand of Stalinism and marriage. A poised, sparkling and trenchant study in nonconformity.

Mai Zetterling, *Scrubbers* GB 1982.
Violence and passion in a girls' borstal.

Lizzie Borden, *Working Girls* USA 1986.
Workers in the sex industry spill the beans.

Agnes Varda, *Vagabond* (*Sans Toit Ni Loi*) France 1985.
A female drop-out discovers there is no place for her in France.

Jane Campion, *Sweetie* New Zealand 1989.
A female misfit descends into catatonia and mayhem. A life-affirming film which negotiates a vertiginous path between tragedy and comedy.

Margarethe Von Trotta, *The German Sisters* West Germany 1981.
An enlightened left-wing analysis of the Baader-Meinhof Red Army Fraction with special reference to the human cost of Marxist armed struggle on bourgeois intellectual young women (such as Ulrike Meinhof).

Margarethe Von Trotta, *Rosa Luxemburg* West Germany 1983.
A sympathetic tribute to the Polish Jew who (ignoring nation, race and gender) embraced Marxist internationalism and founded the German Communist Party out of the ruins of the Second International. She was battered to death following the failed Spartacist uprising of 1918-1919 by Hitler-type free-corps militia under the eyes of the emerging Weimar Social-Democratic Republic.

Beeban Kidron, / Amanda Richardson *Carry Greenham Home* GB 1983.
Classic documentary of the Greenham Common women's protest against American cruise missiles.

Mary Harron, *I Shot Andy Warhol* USA 1995.
Valerie Solanas of SCUM (Society for Cutting Up Men) Manifesto fame weighs into the shadowy unreal Warhol set with bright crazy feminist brio.

Critical Quotes and Questions
General

As for women, they are dominated by four authorities - political, clan, religious and masculine. The authority of the husband is getting shakier every day (1927).
In the world today all culture, all literature and art belong to definite classes and are geared to definite political lines. There is no such thing as art for art's sake. (1941)
Works of art which lack artistic quality have no force, however progressive they are politically. (1942)
An army without culture is a dull-witted army, and a dull-witted army cannot defeat the enemy. (1944)
Letting a hundred flowers bloom and a hundred schools of thought contend is the policy for promoting the progress of the arts and the sciences and a flourishing socialist culture in our land. (1957)
(Mao Tse Tung *Little Red Book* 1966)

Film is the greatest teacher, because it teaches not only through the brain, but through the whole body. (Pudovkin)

Each art breeds its fanatics. The love that cinema inspired, however, was special. It was born of the sense that cinema was an art unlike any other: quintessentially modern; distinctively accessible; poetic and mysterious and erotic and moral - all at the same time. (Susan Sontag *Guardian* 2 March 1996)

The image of women in the cinema has been an image created by men. The emergent women's cinema has begun the transformation of that image. (Claire Johnston, Notes on Women's Cinema 1973, Kuhn 150)

The cinematic apparatus, as a social technology that transcends the work of individual directors, was and is fully compromised in the ideology of vision and sexual difference founded on woman as image, spectacle, object and locus of sexuality. (Teresa DeLaurentis 1984, SFL 1)

The American cinema is entirely dependent, as is psychoanalysis, on a system of representation in which the woman occupies a central place only to the extent that it's a place assigned to her by the logic of masculine desire. (Raymond Bellour 1979, SFL 1)

Cleo's transformation hinges on the turn of phrase "How do I look?" This question, traditionally connoted as feminine, is displaced from its passive, objectified meaning ("How am I seen, how do I appear in the eyes of the world?") to its active complement ("How do I see, how is the world viewed by me?"). (Sandy Flitterman-Lewis 1996, 269)

1. Epic Cinema in the Totalitarian Epoch

Triumph of the Will is a masterpiece of style and editing, which in turn are the very techniques used to manipulate reality and create emotionally effective propaganda.

Leni Riefenstahl's poetic style of disorientation and her disturbing depiction of people as architecture contribute to both the art and the ideology of the film. (Marie Saeli IDFF 486)

Leni Riefenstahl behind the camera is a more dangerous phallic woman than any vamp or femme fatale. (FJH)

Leni Riefenstahl, the maker of Fascist documentaries in the 1930s, is ironically the only woman director whose name is a household word. (Laura Mulvey VAOP 113)

It was not only the American women's movement, with its commitment to forgotten women artists, which made it possible for LR's films to be shown at women's film festivals under the 'pure' aspect of 'fascinating' aesthetics: this was encouraged also by a view of art which fails to see politics in aesthetics. (Annette Brauerhoch, in Kuhn 1990)

The Ascent reflects the Russian obsession with the horrors of The Great Patriotic War, but unusually is both steeped in religious symbolism and ready to acknowledge the existence of the less than great Russian collaborator. The true battle is not with the Nazis, who hover in the background as mere extras, but between the Russian Nazi investigator and Sotnikov, the captured partisan who finds the spiritual strength to go to his death unbeaten. (Sheila Johnston *Time Out* 1998)

Fascism seeks to aestheticise the political, Communism to politicise the aesthetic. (Walter Benjamin)

Riefenstahl and Shepitko have this in common: nationalism in their hands becomes mythic and religious. (FJH)

Shepitko's art humanises and inspires where Riefenstahl's dehumanises and infects. (FJH)

In the epic cinema of the totalitarian epoch we can identify a specific (albeit contradictory) female gaze: heroically phallic in the case of Riefenstahl, heroically Christian in the case of Shepitko. (FJH)

2. Education, Education, Education

Its subversive anti-Fascist, anti-patriarchal themes seem astonishing when one realises that *Madchen in Uniform* was shot in Germany just two years before Hitler's rise to power. In the early 1970s interest in the film was revived by women's film festivals and it has come to be seen as the first truly radical lesbian film. The audience is reminded that although the school is a feminine space (indeed there are no male characters in the film) it is surrounded and even permeated by ubiquitous male authority. Sagan's cinematography is an excellent example of what Lotte Eisner calls "*stimmung*" (emotion), which suggests the vibrations of the soul through the use of light. Sagan uses superimposition to convey moments of deep attraction between the teacher Fraulein von Bernburg and her student Manuela. The fusion of their images suggests the strength of their bond. It was a technique used 30 years later by Bergman in *Persona*. (Gretchen Elsner-Sommer IDFF 1990, 274)

Marie Epstein's work is about a particular relation to childhood which has to do, powerfully and fundamentally with feminine desire. (153)
In posing an authorial voice from another site of desire, Epstein's film engages new modes of organising meaning, new articulations of the gaze, not only in its poetic texture but in its fictional structure as well. (166)
La Maternelle contextualises its focus on the affective relationship between a maternal figure and the female child within a detailed highly realistic description of life in the Parisian slums. It thus combines crucial elements in a dramatic psychic scenario of familial relations with the populist French films' concern for contemporary social problems and the accuracy of quotidian detail. The double entendre of the film's title reinforces the thematic duality of the film. Literally the "nursery school" where most of the film's action takes place, *La Maternelle* symbolically refers to the emotive relationship that constitutes the film's core. (188)
(Sandy Flitterman-Lewis 1996)

In Prussian boarding school and Parisian nursery school alike, the female gaze subverts social relations. (FJH)

Poetic realism is too feeble a phrase to do justice to the vision and critique contained in these two films. (FJH)

There is more to education (reactionary or progressive) than what goes on in the classroom. (FJH)

3. Sixties New Wave

Through its central problematic of woman-as-image, *Cleo de 5 a 7* (1961) offers a critical examination of reified categories and definitions of woman while proposing the necessary inscription of sociality in constructions of femininity. The film traces the process by which Cleo, the woman-as-spectacle, becomes transformed into an active social participant, rupturing the oppressive unity of identity and vision and appropriating the gaze for herself in a new appreciation of others in the world around her. This transformation is intimately bound up with processes of self-reflection. But, whereas self-reflection means narcissistic self-absorption in the first part of the film, it means self-recognition - mediated by an awareness of others - in the latter half, (Flitterman-Lewis 268-9)

Daisies is Chytilova at her most formalist. The 'moral messages' of her films are simply libations that enable her, and her friends among the critics, to defend the unashamedly formalist films and the healthily satirical presentation of social reality they contain. This is corroborated by Chytilova's many clashes with the Czech political authorities, from an interpellation in Parliament calling for a ban on *Daisies* because so much food - 'the fruit of the work of our toiling farmers' - is destroyed in the film, to her being fired from the Barrandov studios after the Soviet invasion of 1968, to her 1975 open letter to President Husak printed in *Index on Censorship* 1976. In each instance she won her case by a combination of publicly stated kosher ideological arguments, stressing the alleged 'messages' of her works (e.g. for *Daisies*: 'irresponsibility and recklessness lead to a bad end'), and of backstage manipulation, not excluding the use of her considerable feminine charms. In her integrity, artistic boldness and originality, in her ability to survive the most destructive social and political catastrophes, Chytilova is a unique phenomenon in Czech cinema. (Joseph Skvorecky IDFF 94)

The only important women directors of the French and Czech New Waves, Varda and Chytilova make revolutionary films in revolutionary ways. (FJH)

The New Wave carries a New Look, making us see the world differently. (FJH)

The sobriety of French cinéma-vérité and the dazzle of Czech Dada each contribute in their own way to the sixties' counter-culture, to the sexual revolution and to a new sexual politics. (FJH)

4. Seventies Feminism in Hungary

Marta Meszaros's films deal with realities usually ignored in East European cinema: the subordination of women, conflicts of urban and rural cultures, antagonism between the bureaucracy and its employees, alcoholism, the generation gap, dissolution of traditional family structures and the plight of state-reared children. In the mid-sixties Meszaros joined Mafilm Group 4 where she met Miklos Jancso, whom she later married. In *The Two of Them* Juli has a daughter (Zsuzsi) and alcoholic husband (Feri), and Marie directs a hostel for working women and tolerates a lack-lustre husband (Janos). Juli and Marie enjoy more rapport with each other than with the men in their lives. Situations depicting humiliation and discrimination against women recur. (Louise Heck-Rabi IDFF368)

I am a feminist, if you like, in that I believe the fundamental question of any relationship to be the need for people - men and women alike - to understand themselves. As I see it, the problem of today is the quest for companionship by men and women alike. It is not primarily a quest for sexual partners, rather it is a search for companions, for friends. I tell banal, commonplace stories - I portray things from a woman's angle. I am being sensitive in a different way from men. My shots work out differently too, and it's a different world that emanated from my films. The principal problem of feminism is the male view of us women; the way they look upon us. As long as men view us only as objects of sexual gratification, love machines, beings of a lower order, we women shall only be a kind of "third world". Artists are a crazy lot, they are taking a good many liberties. But what does a factory girl do? (Marta Meszaros Mafilm Interview 1979)

Opening and closing - in a circular flashback movement on the classic cold war cliché of the corpse by the mist-enshrouded watchtower, *Another Way* cunningly undercuts expectations aroused by its 1958 Hungarian setting. For the body belongs to a female reporter punished for loving Truth, Freedom and Beauty - in the form of other women. Probing the interface of professional and sexual integrity, Makk troublingly links 'deviant' lesbianism with a commitment to impeccably democratic ideals. Not just a film of Big Themes though: the love scenes sail close to the wind, steering an unsteady course between voyeurism and candour, (Sheila Johnston *Time Out* 1998)

The journalist girl (Eva) lives under the stress of a double "perversion"; on the one hand she is lesbian; on the other hand she is unable to tell lies or even to make compromises. And these are two "perversions" which rarely lead to a happy end anywhere in the world. I wanted to make it so that the spectator, having seen the film, would not remember primarily that he has seen a story about homosexual love. I may as well tell you that for Jankowska and Szapolowska [Jadviga Jankowska, who won the Cannes Film Festival Best Actress prize as Eva, and Grazina Szapolowska as Livia, were Polish actresses brought over in the absence of any Hungarian actresses willing to play the part of a lesbian], it was an extraordinary alien task even to touch each other's body: the first few rehearsals degenerated into bouts of silly tittering. However the inner command of histrionic talent bound them to go through the sequences, even if gnashing their teeth - perhaps that was what has given the story fresh nuances and flavours we had not expected. The theme of homosexual love never aroused my interest before, and it was only in connection with making this film that I found that homosexuality was a penal offence in this country and that it was only struck from the Penal Code around 1954-5. However I was not interested in the social aspect of this subject, it was the psychological aspect of the theme that held my interest. I am intrigued by vulnerable heroes or heroines who are finding themselves in situations of distress; it was this possibility of a film that appealed to me in Galgoczi's novel. (Karoly Makk, 1982 Interview)

The Two of Them gives us a warmly humane female gaze; *Another Way* gives us a trenchantly provocative male gaze. Meszaros has modestly opened up a space for Makk to sparkle in. (FJH)

Where Meszaros deals with the banal and the commonplace, Makk highlights the extraordinary. Meszaros is interested in the everyday reconciliation of opposites, Makk in the fiery tragedy of a double "perversion". (FJH)

Western audiences tended to read these films for their sexual politics; but in the context of the advanced thaw in Stalinism taking place in Hungary in the 1970s (a thaw which would lead inexorably to the fall of the Berlin Wall), these films have primarily to be read as critical reflections on that progress towards socialism with a human face. Female companionship, sisterhood and lesbianism are as much tropes and metaphors, as subjects in their own right. (FJH)

5. Prison and Prostitution

Scrubbers follows the career of two Borstal girls: a lesbian orphan who busts herself back inside to rejoin her faithless lover, and a single mother who, separated from her child, puts an ever-increasing gap between them by her escalating violence. But blatant audience manipulation backfires: the more the mother bashed her way through the film, the less your sympathies are engaged. A script which bridles with a grim wit more akin to *Porridge* than *Scum* (1979)-in-a-skirt, and a filtered use of colour so dense it appears to be shot in black-and-white, are both points in favour. But no amount of effing and blinding, unconvincing slow-motion violence, scatological inventiveness, and buckets of flying excreta, can hide the fact that *Scrubbers* is a very noisy film that manages to say nothing novel. An entertaining washout. (Frances Lass *Time Out*)

Born in Sweden, Mai Zetterling made her debut as a film actress in 1941 aged 16. She appeared in films by Sjoberg and Bergman before turning to filmmaking in the 1960s. In *Alskande par / Loving Couples* (1964), *Night Games* (1966), *Girls* 1968, and *Amarosa* (1986), Mai Zetterling concentrates on lesbianism, women's sexuality, problems in reaching maturity, and madness. (Astrid Soederbergh Widding, in Kuhn 1990)

In *Working Girls* Lizzie Borden takes an axe to the Hollywood image of the prostitute. Focusing on Molly, a college girl who's trying to make some cash, prostitution is viewed as an economic alternative, another business in the world's financial capital. The overriding unsung leitmotif is that of a procession (of clients, rituals, preparations). The cold reality of Borden's vision is reminiscent of Frederick Wiseman's examination of

American institutions. But whereas Wiseman's seemingly neutral recording of a nightmare works, Borden's calculated dramatic reconstruction falters as one set of stereotypes is substituted for another. Wooden lines stand in lieu of dialogue, caricatures in place of characters. (Steven Goldman *Time Out*)

Borden's first feature, *Born in Flames* (1983), set in a post-revolutionary New York City, is a radical futuristic feminist fable about sexual politics, race, class and the role of the media. *Working Girls* has a more conventional narrative structure and deals in a non-moralistic way with prostitution as 'a viable economic alternative' for middle-class women. The sex scenes - shot from the women's point of view - are non-voyeuristic and unerotically demystifying. Many women who had supported the radical feminist implications of *Born in Flames* considered it contradictory that Borden could make this apparently uncritical film on prostitution. However, it is precisely Borden's undogmatic feminism which has allowed her to tackle important - and controversial - issues for women. (Ulrike Sieglohr, in Kuhn 1990)

The problem with semi-documentary dramatic reconstructions is how to avoid sensationalism (voyeurism) on the one hand and didacticism (propaganda) on the other. (FJH)

Can the female gaze de-glamorise the sex and violence associated with prisons and brothels? (FJH)

6. Deviants and Outsiders

Sans Toit Ni Loi / Vagabond, Varda's lyrical requiem to Mona, a teenage tramp discovered dead from exposure, shows (in flashback) her last few months and her effect on people she met: a smart middle-class professor [tree agronomist] mesmerised and repelled by the fierce young woman, peasant drudges to whom she inspires romantic dreams of freedom, a dour *soixante-huitard* [philosophy student turned goatherd], now the most conventional [drop-out] of all. Varda boldly explains nothing about Mona, who simply holds up an unflattering mirror to others' follies, prejudices and fears. Spare, poetic images of the mid-winter Midi are offset by the warmth and vigour of the well-chosen, largely unprofessional cast, with a formidable central performance from Sandrine Bonnaire. (Sheila Johnston *Time Out* 1998)

Vagabond is a film about looking, but a kind of looking which is quite precise: in its massive project of reformulating both the cinematic gaze and its object - the body of a woman - it restructures relations of desire, both in the text (desire of its characters) and for the text (desire of its viewers). The film engages with issues of sexuality and representation, narration and address, in a textual meshwork that is at once a systematic reflection on cinematic meaning and on socially constructed conceptions of femininity as well. In a film that is part social investigation and part feminist inquiry, Varda redefines cinematic visual pleasure just as certainly as she interrogates "femininity" and its cultural representations. She devises new textual strategies that rework the function of narration; she disrupts the patriarchal logic of vision by reconceiving the voyeuristic gaze, and she provides a discursive space for questions of sexuality, reflecting what it means to be a woman and to represent one's own desire. (Flitterman-Lewis 285-6)

In *Sweetie*, Kay fears darkness and the secret, stifling power of plants, her teenage sister Dawn is crazy, throwing tantrums at all and sundry, and dreaming unrealistically of stardom. When Dawn and her bombed-out boyfriend arrive unannounced at the suburban home Kay shares with her equally loopy lover Lou, all hell breaks loose. Tragedy looms. And all is played, partly as comedy. Campion's first feature is a remarkable, risky exploration of the weird and wonderfully surreal undercurrents that can lie just beneath the surface of everyday suburban life; ordinary folk harbour dark unfathomable obsessions, phobias and desires, and a familiar world is unsettlingly distorted by grotesque close-ups, harsh overhead angles and narrative ellipses. Amazingly, as she veers without warning from black comedy to bleak melodrama, she manages to make us laugh at and like her confused, barely articulate characters, so that her denouement is simultaneously ludicrous and deeply affecting. *Sweetie* confirms Campion as a highly original movie talent. (Geoff Andrew *Time Out* 1998)

The female deviant may be a victim, but she tells us more about our society than the well-adjusted do. (FJH)

7. Red Revolution in Germany

The German Sisters. Inspired by the cases of Gudrun Ensslin - the Baader-Meinhof terrorist and Stammheim 'suicide' - and her journalist sister, Trotta once again takes up questions of the roots and potential paths of women's resistance and revolt, creating a disturbing mosaic of personal and state histories around a sisterly relationship of intriguingly contradictory complexity. As in *The Lost Honour of Katharina Blum*, terrorism itself is an offscreen phenomenon, its ramifications at the personal level, and its unlabelled reactionary equivalents, marking the film's painful subject across at least a generation: from two schoolgirls watching film of the concentration camps to a young son almost burned alive in the 80s because of his now notorious parentage. A bold assertion of the continuity of history, from the culture most willing to deny it, and fine, accessible political film-making. (Paul Taylor *Time Out* 1998)

Rosa Luxemburg. Red Rosa has a lot going for her when it comes to the myth factory: female, lame, Polish Jew, internationalist, pacifist, revolutionary, imprisoned on nine separate occasions, a leader of the Spartacists in their brief revolutionary success in post-war Germany, and cruelly murdered in 1919. The film won awards at Cannes and Berlin, two for Sukowa in the title role, and utterly splendid she is too, conveying a delicate mixture of strength and vulnerability. The film, however, falls badly between the two stools of personal chronicle and politico-historical analysis, despite the intriguing use of archive newsreel footage and the sterling contributions of Sander (as Karl Liebknecht) and Olbrychski (Leo Jogiches). (Steve Grant *Time Out* 1998)

Trotta's films combine lucid political analysis with fine feminist sensibility. (FJH)

Trotta's heroines carry the weight of German bad conscience in their souls. (FJH)

8. Feminist Agit-Prop

Carry Greenham Home. You don't have to be a woman to watch this documentary by National Film School students, but it certainly helps. Seven months spent sharing the experiences of the peace protesters at Greenham Common has produced a faithful picture, but rarely a compelling one. It is moving to witness the bleak conditions in which the women continue their fight, and solidarity has a way of making you want to participate in its victories. But protests get nowhere by being innocuous, and the film's virtue - its unflinching honesty - brings about its defects: a bland directorial eye, an assumption that they have your sympathies, and if they don't, they're not worth having. To maintain its momentum, the peace movement needs to make constant inroads on the flagging public consciousness. (Suzie Mackenzie *Time Out* 1998)

I Shot Andy Warhol. Engrossing, informative and beautifully performed account of the psychological turmoil and various other pressures that led Valerie Solanas, founder and sole member of SCUM (Society for Cutting Up Men), to gun down Andy Warhol. Despite a long, rather too self-conscious party scene, complete with Velvets, various superstars and conversation on couches, the re-creation of the Factory and its population is mostly spot on. Taylor's paranoid but spikily intelligent Solanas is a triumph, as is Dorff's Candy Darling. And if Harris is perhaps a little too enervated as Andy, the film's sharp take on sexual politics, the allure of fame and the artistic pretensions of a vanished era lend it substance a-plenty. There's a score by John Cale, too. (Geoff Andrew *Time Out* 1998)

One suspects that the Greenham Common Women and Valerie Solanas would make strange bedfellows, and yet they represent two kinds of fundamental feminist theory and practice, contributing to the struggle against sexist militarism and the struggle against the cult of male celebrity. What kinds of feminist consciousness do these two films raise, and with what conviction? (FJH)

Postscript
This university course was established in 1999 with the films I had to hand. The following masterpieces of women's cinema would certainly have been included had they been available:

Mai Zetterling, *Loving Couples* Sweden 1964
Mai Zetterling, *Girls* Sweden 1968
Agnes Varda, *Le Bonheur* France 1965
Agnes Varda, *L'Une Chante, L'Autre Pas* France 1977
Catherine Breillat, *Romance* France 1999
Catherine Breillat, *A Ma Soeur* France 2001

CHAPTER SIX: COMMUNIST CINEMA

1. Slatan Dudow and Bertolt Brecht *KUHLE WAMPE* Germany 1932

Some Background Material on "the only Communist film to come out of Weimar Germany".

NB This film was banned by the SPD before being banned by the Nazis. The film makes no reference to either Nazis or Jews.

German Politics
1912 The SPD (German Social-Democratic Party, 'Marxist', Second International) became the largest party in the Reichstag.
1914 First World War. Collapse of Second International.
1918-19 Formation of the Weimar Republic. Failed Spartacist (Bolshevik) Uprising led by Karl Liebknecht and Rosa Luxemburg. Foundation of KPD (German Communist Party, Third International).
1920 Foundation of Nazi Party, NSDAP (National Socialist German Workers Party).
1923 Hitler Beerhall Putsch, Munich.
1924 Hitler writes *Mein Kampf* in Landsberg Prison.

REICHSTAG ELECTIONS	SPD	KPD	NSDAP
May 1924	21%	13%	7%
December 1924	26%	9%	3%
May 1928	30%	11%	3%
September 1930	25%	13%	18%
July 1932	22%	15%	37%
November 1932	20%	17%	33%
March 1933	18%	12%	44%

Presidential Election March 1932:
>Hindenburg
>(Conservative militarist supported by SPD)   50%
>Hitler   30%
>Thalmann (KPD)   13%

KPD Slogan 1932: "AFTER HITLER OUR TURN". KPD called SPD "social fascists".
Remmele (KPD Reichstag Leader) 14 October 1931: "Once the Fascists are in power, the united front of the proletariat will be established and it will make a clean sweep of everything [violent applause from the Communists]. We are not afraid of the Fascist gentlemen. They will shoot their bolt quicker than any other government ['Right you are!' from the Communists].
30 January 1933 - Hitler appointed Chancellor.

Wilhelm Reich
The Mass Psychology of Fascism 1933. The Three-Layer Theory:
1. The surface layer: the average man is reserved, polite, compassionate, responsible, conscientious. There would be no tragedy of the human animal if this surface layer of the personality were in direct contact with the [third layer] deep natural core. This is unfortunately not the case. The surface layer of social cooperation is not in contact with the deep biologic core of one's selfhood. It is borne by a second layer.
2. The second layer: this intermediate character layer consists exclusively of cruel, sadistic, lascivious, rapacious and envious impulses. It represents the Freudian unconscious, or what is repressed.
3. The third layer: this is the deep biologic core of one's selfhood. The natural sociability of the deepest third layer, the core layer, is foreign to the liberal.

The Politics of this Psychology
Let us now transpose our human structure into the social and political sphere. In the ethical and social ideals of liberalism we recognise the advocacy of the characteristics of the surface

layer of the personality, which is intent on self-control and tolerance. This liberalism lays stress upon its ethics for the purpose of holding in suppression the 'monster in man'. our layer of secondary drives, the Freudian unconscious. The liberal deplores the perversion of the human character and seeks to overcome it by means of ethical norms, but the social catastrophes of the 20thC show that he did not get very far with this approach [cf. George Dangerfield *The Strange Death of Liberal England*, ed.]. Everything that is genuinely revolutionary, every genuine art and science, stems from man's natural biologic core. Thus far, neither the genuine revolutionary, nor the artist or scientist has won favour with masses of people and acted as their leader, or if he has he has not been able to hold them in the sphere of vital interest for any length of time. The case of fascism, in contrast to liberalism and genuine revolution, is quite different. Its essence embodies neither the surface nor the depth, but the intermediate layer of secondary drives.

John Hoyles interprets: Reich was a communist and psychoanalyst belonging to both Internationals. If Layer 1 = SPD, Layer 2 = NSDAP, Layer 3 = KPD, then to get from 1 to 3 you have to pass through 2. This did not work. The Nazis put the Communists in concentration camps and Wilhelm Reich, expelled from both Internationals, ended up bonkers in Eisenhower's America with his orgone box.

2. Humberto Solas *CECILIA* Cuba 1982

Part One

Have you come across the Cuban film *Cecilia* by Solas? After watching the first hour I was overwhelmed by intellectual delight and had to take a siesta. The film is in the Cuban Masterworks Collection, was made in 1982 and is a historical costume drama set in the Cuba of 1830.

I may have been over-impressed, but this film (just the first half remember) seemed to be a powerful piece of Marxist-Humanist analysis such as we are not used to seeing.

For example. A sexist man somewhat exasperated by the coyness of a potential conquest says "Are you a woman or a book?". To which the somewhat liberated woman replies: "A book, but with particularly piquant parts banned by the Pope".

For example: A nice bourgeois man says "I thought the English were outlawing the slave trade out of benevolence." To which a proto-marxist woman says: "It's not benevolence that makes the world go round. The English want Spain to outlaw the slave trade so they can sell their machines to us. Machines will take the place of slaves."

The weakness of man is symbolised in the comment "one whiff of a woman and you're lost".

The film is saturated in gender/race/class consciousness. All in costume drama which has a whiff of Visconti's *The Leopard* about it, and thankfully none of the bland complacency of BBC2 Jane Austen.

The theme and cause of the film is independence. Uprising and general Cuban rebellion against Spanish Colonialism. And there is a strong presence of African Congo Voodoo practices, seen as a site of resistance to mainstream colonial Christianity.

Cecilia is a fantastically beautiful mulatto woman,

wooed by a ruling class white man, who eschews (with difficulty) the wiles of falling in love with him. She manages to use the power of her beauty to advance the political cause of the rebels.

Haiti is seen as a source of anti-colonial rebellion and black power (a generation after theBlack Jacobin revolution of Toussaint l'Ouverture).

There is also some subtle play on the idea of bourgeois society as a theatrical game in which love and courtship are shown as part of the society of the spectacle. And where authentic reality is associated with rebellion, class struggle and uprising. Here then is more than a whiff of Situationism. And one is reminded of Genet's *The Balcony*.

All in all, we are reminded of the class struggle dramatised in *The Leopard* by the dialectical slogans Solas gives us: THE WORLD HAS TO CHANGE versus THE WORLD WON'T CHANGE.

This weekend I shall gird up my loins to watch the second half of this film. Let's hope I'm not disappointed!

Part Two

Ultimately *Cecilia* was not quite what I was expecting. A flawed masterpiece I think. The 19thC novel of the same name was the definitive Cuban text. Solas has tried to turn it into a post-Castro marxist piece, not quite successfully. The accretion is not organically integrated into the original.

So much so indeed that I expect many left-wing critics might regard it as a monumental love-epic akin to *Gone with the Wind*.

Cecilia is not prepared to infiltrate the hacienda ruling class in the interests of revolution. She is really in love with Leonardo. There's lots on love as salvation (and not always signalled as a bourgeois illusion).

The mix of love and politics is heady enough. A whiff of Flaubert's *Sentimental Education* pervades the piece (though with leftist humanist tendency rather than Flaubert's cynical nihilism).

There is a plenitude of love imagery between Cecilia and Leonardo. This is happy love-making, once she abandons her strategic frigidity and cock-teasing coyness. The fruits of love (as in Keats's 'The Eve of St Agnes') include watermelons, bananas and lots of other succulent greengrocer produce. The eroticism is endorsed by the director (close-ups of the couple sharing slices of water-melon and covered with white rose-petals). They drink white wine. The scene is sensual, fleshly, even gross. Throughout the film, close-ups (especially of Cecilia) reveal an unusual amount of liquefaction (tears, sweat - like the pores of Marvell's coy mistress).

Cecilia says "Lies!" to Leonardo's proposal of marriage 'cos she is of different class and race. "I'm not even white", she says. The love is real but impossible.

When Leonardo confronts his 'intended' Isabella (posh white ruling class) he calls his kiss an advance payment on a transaction (the marriage hearse).

There follows the most graphic and leftist presentation of slavery, as Leonardo shows Isabella how the slaves live on her hacienda. Negroes of both sexes are stripped, flogged, tied to posts as in crucifixion. This is the world of *Whity* (Fassbinder) and *Black Snake* (Russ Meyer).

The scene is lingered over with scores of extras. Solas had made the most costly and lavish film in Cuban history. The white racist owners and their running dogs strip and torture a black woman and maul her naked breasts, all in close-up; her face covered in spittle, sweat and tears. Then they strip and castrate a male slave. We see the knife and genitals in close-up.

All this Isabella is forced to witness. And then the slave revolt begins. The masses rise. They storm the hacienda with battering rams. It's the Bastille all over again. OR IS IT?

It turns out that all this is just Isabella's bad dream. In her nightmare she sees Leonardo being lynched to death by the mob. She wakes in a cold sweat and screams (just a soupcon of Buñuel's *Discreet Charm* here).

Cut to Jose Dolores, our implacable cool rebel leader, a curly haired mulatto who argues with Cecilia that there are more important issues than love - i.e. the armed struggle. Close-up of pistol and sword in box. Jose tells Cecilia that only when the slaves are freed will women (all women) escape their suffering and gain their human rights.

There's a fantastically powerful scene where Leonardo and Isabella are pictured as lovers in a large mirror. They are exactly that: a picture of love. They kiss and canoodle in the authorised fashion (as Emma Bovary imagined her own love-life out of books). Isabella, as proud and gorgeous as a Velasquez portrait, pulls down her blouse to reveal her slip-veiled cleavage. Leonardo's hands grope and grasp her breasts as she declares to her fiancé: "I am no book Leonardo - I am a woman". Wow! And this reverses literally Cecilia's retort to Leonardo at the beginning of the film ("I am a book").

The posh groping of the tits, in high romantic splurge, is real enough. But it is in a mirror. Passionate kisses ensue, so much so that Isabella has to point out that it's not long till December (wedding) and that Leonardo should be patient. The shot is gorgeous, her head thrown back in studied abandon and anticipated ecstasy, their lips pressed courteously together and her breasts held firmly in his manly grasp. The scene contrasts strongly with the mauling of breasts and rape of slaves in the previous scene.

Then, when Leonardo is next with Cecilia, he says "That thing with Isabella is pure farce". Cecilia answers (a cliché perhaps, but true nonetheless): "Isabel in the house. She keeps her honour. And I'm the mistress hidden away."

So - is Leonardo the noble bourgeois torn between two worlds, one dead (or moribund at least), the other powerless (as yet) to be born? Or, is he, as Cecilia thinks in her anger, the little male baby in need of a mother in his two women?

Cecilia thinks he is "a detestable white man, one who lives from the sweat of whipped slaves". But of course she also loves him. Tragic tears. Tragic music with heavy drumbeats.

In close-up she screams an unholy wail, with a carefully constructed mesh hair strategically arranged to cross her right eye, left nostril, left edge of mouth, down across her chin. This is hot stuff. On her own, with Leonardo gone, she sinks to her knees on the stone floor and utters "My Love" (reminded me of *L'Age d'or*).

Well, the rebellion has been organised, but betrayed by somebody. Leonardo, who has given mild support to the rebels by not revealing the whereabouts of a runaway slave, is denounced to the authorities. According to his mother (brilliantly acted, cruel bastard), her son has become the victim of the wiles of a whore (Cecilia).

The plot unravels like a Puccini opera, and Leonardo is too late to stop Cecilia throwing herself to death from a high tower. Well that smacks of King Kong or The Hunchback of Notre Dame.

So perhaps it is all an old 19thC tear-jerking epic romance onto which have been grafted some of the Cuban Communist Party's creative trimmings.

That's all folks. Are you a book or a man? Are you a book or a woman? Solas *Cecilia* 1982 on Cuba in 1830.
[typed for blog on International Women's Day 8 March 2011]

CHAPTER SEVEN: ART AND PORN

Nomenclature. What do we call it? Art-Porn? Porno-Art? Arthouse Porn? Hard Core Eroticism? Hard Core Film Art? The Pornographic Imagination?

1. Unpublished Letter to *The Guardian*

A Reply to John Patterson's Article PORNO-ART (*Guardian* July 2007).

At last a piece with some intellectual content in The Guide. It is in my opinion unduly dismissive of what has happened since *Last Tango*. John Patterson might like to consider the following.

1.The apartheid (separate development) situation in which art and porn are prevented from coming together, or even cross-dressing, has cultural/historical reasons behind it. This is to do with the censors' classification system (eg. in France, UK and USA) whereby porn is assigned to a ghetto (R18, sex shops, sex cinemas etc.). Attempts to cross this apartheid are severely controlled. Anna Span, for example, wants to make 18 certificate movies with a pornographic dimension, but the BBFC forces her back into the R18 ghetto.

2. Pauline Kael's wowing of *Last Tango* ("Brando and Bertolucci have changed the face of an art-form") ignores what later was often remarked upon, namely the absence of Brando's penis. And it is worth remembering that a generation later Bertolucci somewhat made up for this self-censorship in *The Dreamers*.

3. The issue is also clouded by class. Trash can dabble in porn. Art is above trash. Crossing that apartheid were films often considered failures because of their obscene mix of art and porn. Exemplary in this kind of mongrelised miscegenation of genres are *Salon Kitty*, *Caligula*, *The Night Porter*. However one judges these films (and personally I find *Night Porter* to be a masterpiece comparable to Visconti's *The Damned*) they fall into the self-fulfilling trap of mixing high and low (therefore bad).

4. There is a snobbery that can ruin careers here. Elizabeth Berkley, we are told, suffered severe setbacks in her career for performing as a trash nude dancer in Vorhoeven's *Showgirls*. She only redeemed herself by doing an English Literature degree and showing she was in fact a jolly decent actress in the stupidly named film *Student Seduction*. Likewise Maria Schneider had trouble wiping away the scandalous nature of her nakedness in *Last Tango*, running away from playing Caligula's sister, becoming a cipher of herself in Antonioni's *The Passenger* and then disappearing from the face of the screen. Since then things have somewhat changed so that Eva Green could morph from her extreme exposure in the art-porn of *The Dreamers* into a James Bond girl (in her case a commercial rather than artistic promotion).

5. Which brings me to my main point. It is simply not true that since *Last Tango*, art-house directors with no feeling for eroticism, and very little to teach us about it, have prevailed. Go and see Bruno Dumont's films (*Vie de Jésus*, *L'Humanité*, *29 Palms*, *Flandres*). These films are brave, experimental and, even if you don't like them very much, brilliant attempts to advance the art-porn synthesis. Dumont comes from Bailleul between Dunkirk and Lille, as god-forsaken a place as can be found on the French map. In his films the spirit of place acts as an objective correlative to the taboo-breaking exploration of the human condition, kinky and perverse, banal and quotidian. Winterbottom has pushed the barriers in *Nine Songs* and

succeeded in breaking the false dualism operated by the BBFC (no to erect penises, real sex, yes to soft-core clichés). Above all there is the divine Catherine Breillat who needs a paragraph of her own.

6. Breillat and her sister (ironically or prophetically) had tiny parts in *Last Tango*, that iconic film which marked both a turning point and a matrix for future development in cinema history. Breillat's first book *L'Homme facile*, written when she was 17 was banned for under-18s. Her first film *Une vraie jeune fille* was banned for 30 years. It still stands as the template of her later work, combining the normalisation of the sexually perverse with satire, comedy and generally intelligent critique of morals and manners. The generation of genre apartheid only breaks down with the bursting forth of *Romance* (1999). Culture, even the law, is ready to be transformed with this film. Together with the ground-breaking *A ma soeur* and *Anatomy of Hell* (the latter accompanied on dvd by a scintillatingly profound hour-long talk by Breillat), provide a trilogy which John Patterson sadly ignores. This whole vein is now open, even in America (e.g. *Short Bus*). It is a struggle worth supporting. *Madame Bovary* and *Les Fleurs du Mal* were banned in 1857, *Lady Chatterley* banned till 1960. The Republic of Letters will flourish against every prurience and hypocrisy that can be thrown at it.

Forgive me if I have taken Patterson's piece in the *Guardian* too seriously. But it did engage me, made me think, and that can't be a bad thing. Still, I rest my case. Patterson is wrong.

2. Pornography Conference Handout

Handout of Quotes for Manchester Art Cinema Conference on Pornography. Speakers: BBFC, Anna Span, John Hoyles.

1. To my chamber where I did read through *L'Escholle des filles*, a lewd book, but what to do no wrong once to read for information sake. And after I had done it I burned it, that it might not be among my books to my shame, and so at night to supper and to bed. (Pepys 1660s)

2. Yes, citizens, religion is incompatible with the libertarian system. Never will a free man stoop to Christianity's gods. One more effort; since you labour to destroy all the old foundations, do not permit one of them to survive, for let but one endure, tis enough, the rest will be restored. ... Ah triple bloody fucking God! ... my sperm flows ... tis lost, by bleeding little Jesus! ... Your daughter is old enough to do what she pleases, she likes to fuck, loves to fuck, was born to fuck, and if you do not want to be fucked yourself, the best thing for you to do is to let her do what she wants. (Sade 1795)

3. The male is obsessed with screwing; he'll swim a river of snot, wade nostril-deep through a mile of vomit, if he thinks there'll be a friendly pussy awaiting him. (Valerie Solanas 1967)

4. We cannot choose to have both eros and pornography; we must choose between beauty and silence. ... In 1977 (USA) pornographic films earned four billion dollars, as much as conventional films and the entire music industry combined. ... The pornographer calls himself rebellious when he is actually a loyal son. In the name of pleasure he gives us violence. (Susan Griffin 1981)

5. Porn is a body of material diverse in form and quality - some is tasteless, sexist, poorly made, some is educational, aesthetic, visionary. (Anarchist-Feminist position, *Freedom* 1986)

6. In a world grossly paralysed with introspection and constipated by delicate mental meals, this brutal exposure of the substantial body comes as a vitalising current of blood. The violence and obscenity are left unadulterated. (Anais Nin, Preface to Henry Miller, *Tropic of Cancer* 1935)

7. My work is psychic subversion, aiming at the destruction of the pseudo-morality and ethic of State and Order. I am for lewdness, for the demythologisation of sexuality. Pornography is an appropriate means to cure our society from its genital panic. (Otto Muehl in Vogel 1974)

8. The aim of surrealism is to destroy all censors and to liberate man's libidinal anarchist and marvellous impulses from all restraint. ... All bodily secretions are considered taboo because we remain chained to notions of the body's uncleanliness and animality. ... To those who abolish taboos, nothing human is alien. (Vogel 1974)

9. The sexual revolution has been neutralised by the sexual industry. ... The libido longs for another breakthrough against values which worship mechanical efficiency and bureaucratic order. But what happens if people with an armed character structure adopt a posture of complete sexual freedom? (Frankl 1974)

10. Pornography and totalitarianism both set up power relations which dehumanise the individual, violate privacy and create a concentration camp mentality. ... The actions of the mind when we masturbate are not a dance, they are a treadmill. ... The standardisation of sexual life, whether through controlled licence or compelled puritanism is an

essential component of totalitarian politics, because our dreams are marketed wholesale. (Steiner 1965)

11. Pornography is one of the branches of literature - science fiction is another - aiming at disorientation, at psychic dislocation. ... Its celebrated intention of sexually stimulating readers is really a species of proselytising. Pornography that is serious literature aims to "excite" in the same way that books which render an extreme form of religious experience aim to "convert". ... The emotional flatness of pornography is thus neither a failure of artistry nor an index of principled inhumanity. The arousal of a sexual response in the reader requires it. Everyone, at least in dreams, has inhabited the world of the pornographic imagination. ... Paul Goodman wrote: 'The question is not whether pornography, but the quality of the pornography'. (Susan Sontag 1967)

12. There is a capitalism of the sexual and we live under it; there is a multi-million pound industry which spreads sexuality like butter on all its products. The discourse and representation of orgasm is an alienation, a fix, blotting out subjectivity and politics. (Stephen Heath 1982)

13. Robin Morgan's "pornography is the theory, rape the practice" is a woefully inadequate explanation of the causes of sexual violence against women. ... When hard core begins to probe male pleasure with the same scrutiny it devotes to female pleasure, when erection, penetration and ejaculation are no longer primary self-evident measures of male pleasure, then a realm of female pornutopia may be at hand. ... Kate Millett is wrong. We do not need eroticism instead of pornography. ... The erotic and the pornographic interact in hard core. The one emphasises desire, the other satisfaction. Depending on who is looking, both can appear dirty, perverse or too explicit. ... Explicit pornography can teach us many things about power and pleasure that once seemed mystified and obscure. (Linda Williams 1990)

SELECT BIBLIOGRAPHY

Simone de Beauvoir "Must We Burn Sade?" (1951-2)
Susan Brownmiller, *Against Our Will* (1976)
George Frankl, *The Failure of the Sexual Revolution* (1974)
Susan Griffin, *Pornography and Silence* (1981)
Stephen Heath, *The Sexual Fix* (1982)
Marquis de Sade, *Philosophy in the Bedroom* (1795)
Lynne Segal ed., *Exposed: Sexuality and the Pornography Debate* (1992)
Valerie Solanas, *SCUM Manifesto* (1967)
Susan Sontag, "The Pornographic Imagination" (1967 in Georges Bataille, *Story of the Eye* 1928/1979)
George Steiner, "Night Words" (1965) in *Language and Silence* (1968)
Amos Vogel, *Film as a Subversive Art* (1974)
Linda Williams, *Hard Core: Power, Pleasure and the 'Frenzy of the Visible'* (1990)
Linda Williams ed., *Porn Studies* (2004)
Linda Williams, *Screening Sex* (2008)

3. Joe Sarno's Erotic Aesthetic

Joe Sarno (1921-2010) has been called the master and inventor of the proto-pornographic sexploitation film genre of the 1960s and 1970s. That's a mouthful designed to lift what the common spectator might regard as a nondescript porn merchant into a potential artistic genius. Was he a genius or a jerk, as one American communist once asked of Picasso?

Having mis-spent several days studying the films of Joe Sarno now readily available on dvd, I thought it worth while calling attention to this cinematic genre, sometimes categorised under the title Retro Seduction, and highlighting in a somewhat disordered fashion some of the issues arising which have a bearing on the relationship between Art and Porn.

What was clear to me, watching fourteen Sarno films as they appeared on dvd in 2010 (the year of his death aged 88) was that these films maintained a consistent middle way between hard-core porn and soft-core porn. I was curious to find out how, why and where Sarno was able to make hot erotic films, with art-house production values, without falling into the mechanical operation of matter and motion in graphic genital close-up or cheating the viewer with the tired nostrums of Hollywood-type simulated sex.

Since they fell between these two well-defined genres, Sarno's films were marginalised. I'd never heard of him let alone seen one of his films until last year. Indeed he himself stopped making these films once hard-core porn took over the market of hot erotica, and the attempts to mix art and porn were stymied by changes in the censorship laws from around 1976. What I find in Sarno is a rich vein of creative cinema which has been marginalised into a niche sub-cultural genre which cannot be fitted into either mainstream or hard-core porn as we now know it. It is a consequence of the revised censorship rules that after 1975 Sarno had no option but to make a whole series of hard-core in order to survive economically.

Sarno's peculiar erotic aesthetic in the period 1967-1975 can be summed up as a concentration on female pleasure as revealed on women's faces when in the throes of foreplay, intercourse and orgasm. This is his choice and it goes against the prevailing phallocentric tendency in western erotica. Of course there are circumstances as well as world-views involved here. Given that under the censorship laws of the period, it was not possible to show an erect or active penis or any signs of penetration, Sarno was obliged to centre his erotic gaze elsewhere. So we get lots of lesbianism, lots of heavy petting and lots of close-ups of the female face. Sarno is happy to exploit these circumstances to produce a female-friendly (if not feminist) type of porn.

And so we get a series of films which have a classy art-house style and yet cannot escape the label of sexploitation. And so he gets called the poor man's Bergman (some of his Swedish work was shot in Bergman-land including studio and personnel, so we are told). His films could be seen as soft-porn thrillers, but they nearly always have lots of psychological insights. He is too sweatily erotic to be accused of Lesbian chic. There is so often a sense of Lesbian utopianism as a critique of the limits of masculinity, a ploy exploited by the French intellectual feminist pornstar and director Ovidie in her hard-core *Lilith*. Elements of Lesbianism are of course often used to spice up heterosexual activities (and Ovidie herself is not immune to that ruse), but they also often offer a vision of ultimate sexual liberation beyond the anxieties, angst, and fear and trembling associated with phallocentrism.

Linda Williams in her extensive work on porn wonders whether porn will ever be able to show the female equivalent of the male money shot. Female ejaculation has appeared (as squirting) in recent hard-core American porn, and the phenomenon has been argued over in learned articles. It is a pity however that Linda Williams seems to have overlooked Sarno. For it is arguable that Sarno produces the goods which are lacking in male-oriented porn. The mechanics of the female money shot are of course problematic (squirting performers like Cytherea notwithstanding), uncertain, invisible, obscene in the sense of off-scene, off-stage. But Sarno is at least aware of all this. On the question of 'simulated' sex versus 'real sex', he is unusually lucid and prescriptive. Of course women can fake an orgasm and porn directors can fake a female money shot. What is important for Sarno is that if it is faked it be faked really well. So his sex scenes go well beyond polite simulation.

Sarno developed a skill with his Swedish actresses which is uncanny. Marie Forsa in particular didn't mind doing real sex in front of the camera but she ensured her contract did not allow visual evidence of penetration or close-ups of her genitals to be shown in the edited film. So Sarno's erotic aesthetic allowed real sex to take place, indeed he encouraged it, but not for it to be seen in graphic close-up of the genitals, only in graphic close-up of the face. Of course arms, mouth and legs could be opened, but it was the face that was shown doing the work. Christina Lindberg was quite good at this (though she required a double if real sex were to take place), Marie Liljedahl (from *Inga* onwards) was very good at this, and Marie Forsa was Sarno's ultimate expert at this. But, according to Sarno's wife and assistant director, Peggy (and with her I am in total agreement), the actress who gave the most sexually expressive performance in any of Sarno's films was the Swedish singer (she wasn't even a real actress!) Cathja Graff (in *Laura's Toys*).

A digression on the relative value of body parts in cinematic representation: If we grant Sarno's mastery of the female face as a displacement and condensation of genital excitement, we may extend the thought to Truffaut who fetishises women's legs: "The legs of women are compasses which circle the globe giving it its balance and harmony." And then there is Buñuel who in his chaste distaste of kissing and naked flesh condenses and displaces the genital embrace to the fetish of toe-sucking (and then to keep his distance from the flesh, a marble statue's toe). Of these three strategies, I feel that Truffaut's is the least artistic and most prurient, for by legs he means, but avoids saying, what is between those legs; that Sarno is expressively artistic with his facial signifiers; and that Buñuel is inventively the equal to Sarno in his fine surrealist fetishism.

Here then are some random notes on the Sarno films I have seen.

1. *Vibrations*, 1968 (1967). Ultra-kink... sex-happy Julia ... uptight young sister ... nightly orgies... an offbeat psychologically twisted skinflick.

2. *Inga* [*Jag - en oskuld*], 1968 (1967). The most acclaimed masterpiece of erotic cinema ever created. Starring Marie Liljedahl, Playboy's Sex Star of 1971 who does a sensational masturbation scene. Filmed entirely in Sweden. Inga finally decides to give in to the cravings of her aching heart and stirring body. Swedish version plus English dubbed version. Sarno & Peggy audio. Marie Liljedahl interview. Inga's character is nicely established as an obsessive Strindberg reader who hates mini-skirts. Her masturbation scene wowed the USA and was carefully shot with her lying on her back, her face and rolling head in the foreground, the real sexual activity discreetly obscure in the background. It was Marie's first film, aged 16-17. A striking prop is a series of mechanical toy soldiers which Inga plays with fetishistically in her bedroom. The toy marches across the floor, a displacement perhaps for her auto-eroticism and a symbol of her virginal desire for a real man. The plot echoes Laclos' *Dangerous Liaisons* with the mature sexually sophisticated characters manipulating the ingenue into adult experience via seduction and corruption. The Greta character, played by Monika Stromerstedt (who later became a Swedish Judge) was

originally (until Sarno discovered Marie) meant to play the central role. As she says helpfully rather than maliciously to Inga, 'it is natural for a girl to want sex'. There's a touch of Bergman's *Summer with Monika* in the film's atmosphere. Sarno used Bergman make-up artists to good effect, producing a natural look. The Swedish title was originally *I a Virgin*, 'about strong women'. *Inga* was one of the first x-rated films in the US, and Sarno remembers it was banned in Denver, Colorado at the request of one of his more self-righteous Roman Catholic friends. Marie Liljedahl made a few more sex films in Germany on the strength of her success in *Inga*, but as she says in her 2001 interview, the rest of her life has been spent looking after her daughters, helping them to become ballet-dancers, the very profession from which Sarno plucked her in the first place.

3. *All the Sins of Sodom*, 1968. Shocking sensual dramatic erotic tale of lust and obsession. Photographer's work ethic, works and career destroyed by pleasure principle and libido of interfering females. Shot in brilliantly lit b/w in New York. Lays foundations of Sarno's erotic aesthetic (orgasm in the face). Sarno interview. Peggy Sarno (who plays photographer's secretary) audio. She forgot she was in it! The story line oscillates between realistic narrative and soft-porn spectacle and is not without its grotesqueries (eg. a hugely comic industrial vibrator). But the prevailing mood is that of existential humanity operating in a confined space. Sarno filmed in the narrow confines of his brother-in-law's New York flat, almost entirely inside one small room, one minuscule corridor ending in the mysterious cul-de-sac of the communal lift, from which the said brother-in-law grins like someone out of Samuel Becket. The space is emblematic, symbolising the interior space of each character, a space of eroticism, a space of conspiracy, a space for suspense and surprise, a solipsistic space, a space of separated bodies, a space for sexual experiment where bodies come and go, talking of Michelangelo, or at least of photographic art. This is

a space in which any landscape recedes into meaninglessness. I am paraphrasing and plagiarising Michael J. Bowen's nice little booklet. As he, the Sarno expert par excellence puts it, *All the Sins of Sodom* strikes a perfect balance between the poverty of means available and the spatial and psychic realities of human erotic experience. And you never forget the miraculous lighting in this film which transforms a small ordinary room into phantasmagoric wonderland.

4. *The Indelicate Balance*, 1969. Shot in Sweden in three weeks. Centres on brother-sister, mother-son incest. Far from prurient Sarno shows Freudian understanding of psycho-sexual politics of the family. Awakening of sexual identity causes crisis in family loyalty. Soundtrack: Shostakovich 8th Symphony. Peggy Sarno audio.

5. *Daddy Darling*, 1970. Danish-produced soft-sex psychodrama featuring father-daughter incest. Joe and Peggy interviews.

6. *The Seduction of Inga* [*Nagon att alska / Inga and Greta*], 1971 (1969), Sequel to 1967 *Inga*, starring sensational Marie Liljedahl in her steamiest role ever. Inga is (again!) forced to reconcile an aching heart with a tireless young body that can't say no. Two versions of film. Lots of extras. Sarno discovered the 17year-old novice actress Marie Liljedahl in the Stockholm Ballet Company and transformed her from Inga 1967 (New York 1968) into an international sex symbol. Lesbianism, masturbation and incest galore. Soundtrack by Benny and Bjorn, later ABBA (1973).

7. *Swedish Wildcats*, 1972. Starring Diana Dors and Christina Lindberg. Set in Copenhagen brothel. Susanna & Karin tire of passionless encounters with perverse clients & long to experience true love.

8. *The Devil's Plaything* [*Vampire Ecstasy* / *Veil of Blood* / *Der Fluch der Schwarzen Schwestern* / *The Curse of the Black Sisters*], 1971 (1969). Campy creepy carnal smorgasbord of sensuous sensations, coffins and castles, blood drinking and satanic rituals, crawling with unclothed starlets. Mostly German cast speaking broken English but with one big new star, the 16 year-old unknown untried Swedish actress Marie Forsa. Shot in 22 days in a real German castle near Munich. Chris Nebe producer audio. Sarno & Neve interviews.

9. *Baby Love*. 1974. Starring 17 year-old Marie Forsa, guaranteed to get your pulse racing. Swedish Sex Collection. Uncut, restoring 47 minutes cut in England by BBFC. 15 certificate in Sweden.

10. *Confessions of a Young American Housewife*, 1974. With the seductive and luminous Rebecca Brooke, the legendary Jennifer Welles and the long-lasting Eric Edwards (all porn stars). The plot centres on mother-daughter lesbian incest. This is the first appearance in a Sarno film of his heroine of choice Rebecca Brooke who projects a persona that is fragile and intense. She is synonymous with Sarno's soul-searching mid-70s psychodramas. She was soon to appear in Radley Metzger's notorious 1975 *The Punishment of Anne* (aka *The Image*, from Catherine Robbe-Grillet's sado-masochistic novel). Rebecca's real name is Mary Mendum. She was great friends with the Sarnos. Peggy noted that she was from outside Chicago, dirt poor, with beautiful breasts, piercing eyes, a wonderful sense of humour and competent as a seamstress and cook. The film tells the story of the sentimental education of the returning mother Jennifer into free love and sexual therapy. A liberated swinging foursome beckons, but Jennifer is in love with the delivery boy and opts for a normal happy married life. The dvd comes with a booklet by Michael J Bowen, Sarno's biographer and intelligent enthusiast who did more than most to revive and resurrect Sarno's films for dvd viwers.

11. *Laura's Toys*, 1975. This, along with *All the Sins of Sodom*, is my favourite Sarno film. Let Blurb and Critic speak for me and themselves. The Blurb says: "Laura and her husband Walter - an archaeologist - are spending a working summer on a small Swedush island. An affair between Walter and Anna his demure young female assistant leads Laura back into the arms of a female ex-lover." *Laura's Toys* stars Rebecca Brooke, Eric Edwards and Cathja Graff - a mixed American and Swedish cast. As in *All the Sins of Sodom,* there is a strong theme (reminiscent of *The Bacchae* of Euripides) of the female pleasure principle subverting and destroying the dominant male work ethic. Sexual anarchy, sexual liberation confront and undermine the authority of the boss. The critic Troy Howarth writes: " Sarno's films can best be described as a study of the human face in its most intimate moments of arousal and satisfaction. Sarno again explores the sexuality of the female characters while pushing the traditionally male dominated pornographic spectacle to the background. The husband is less a driving force than a pawn in a game (hence the title *Laura's Toys*), while the female characters are for once allowed to speak their minds and function as something other than eye candy. This is an unusual approach in American erotic cinema, which traditionally objectifies and even minimizes females as little more than slabs of meat. Similarly, in his refusal to go in for gynecological close-ups, the director creates a palpably erotic climate. In forcing the viewer to use their imagination, Sarno skillfully avoids the repetition that mars so many films of this ilk, which tend to fall into a predictable pattern of foreplay, unlikely sexual acrobatics and inevitable popshot finales. The approach works: the close-up of Cathja Graff's face contorted with pleasure is far more sexually dynamic than the usual close-up of Eric Edwards groping at her genitals. With her petite build and olive complexion, Graf looks gorgeous without the aid of make-up. She plays her role in English very well and her sex scenes are all the more effective because she is so obviously aroused. When she says the porn staple, I'm coming, for once we really

believe it." The erotic passion is convincing not only because Sarno's orgasm-in-the-face technique is so palpable; it is also convincing in its graphic language, as for example when Laura, with a mixture of jealousy and lust gets the hots for her husband's archeological assistant to the tune of "I'd like to stick my fist up her runic passage." Finally we should note that it is perhaps significant that Cathja Graff's performance owes much to the fact that she was not an actress at all, but a musician. Pure documentary then?! The extras include audio by Eric Edwards.

12. *Butterflies* [*Broken Butterfly* / *Baby Tramp* / *Blafferen*], 1975. *Butterflies* is marketed as Sarno's most explicit film available in the Swedish Sex Collection. There are two versions on the dvd. The Soft at 112 minutes and the Hard at 93 minutes. This is where it gets interesting, both historically and aesthetically. Why you might ask is the soft version so much longer than the hard? Well, the answer is: INSERTS. Hardcore inserts have been added (with body doubles probably), and a lot of the soft foreplay has been cut to make room for them. The longer soft version is the Director's Cut. This marks a point in history (1975) when Sarno's specialist erotic aesthetic was being challenged, and indeed overtaken and defeated by the rise of hardcore. The body of the film reflects this bifurcation. It is probable that Sarno wanted the soft version to prevail. In any case it is harder than any soft porn ever was. The leads are Marie Forsa, now at the ripe old age of 17, and Harry Reems fresh from his moment of fame with Linda Lovelace in *Deep Throat*. The couple got on like a house on fire, on and off set. They followed the Sarno recipe to the letter, maximum real sex but no gynecological close-ups. So, at the end of Sarno's period of authentic experimental eroticism, his aesthetic is being 'improved' with hardcore inserts to satisfy the new post-*Deep Throat* publicly allowed porn consumers. The hard version is of course of both historical and aesthetic interest. It comes across as botched, an outward and visible sign if ever there was of the as yet unsolved problem of fusing (or even

just mixing) art and porn. As yet unsolved? Perhaps not. Catherine Breillat and others have recently struggled manfully to transcend what they regard as a false dualism. And that deliberately oxymoronical 'manfully' is of course central to the issue. Sexual politics and feminism, as well as censorship laws and aesthetic taste set us high mountains to climb. So, in 1975, the very year when Breillat's *Une Vraie Jeune Fille* was made (but not of course released or shown until the end of the century), Sarno signs out with his special starlet Marie Forsa giving her last important performance as a sexually precocious teenage rebel, in bed with the redoubtable superstud Harry Reems, who couldn't believe his luck. The dvd is obviously a collector's item and comes with a generous load of extras.

13. *Abigail Lesley is Back in Town* [*The Secret Garden*], 1975. Starring Rebecca Brooke, James Gillis, Jennifer Jordan, Eric Edwards, Jennifer Wells. These porn stars usually had some theatrical experience. To begin with the porn was very much a sidekick. As James Gillis tells us, his own introduction to porn came while he was nightly performing Shakespeare in a New York theatre and fucking girls for a porn loop in the afternoons. At $30 a time it was easier work than taxi driving. No doubt when picked up by Sarno he was able to find a middle way between the porn loop and Shakespeare. Blurb: "When Abigail Lesley returns to her old fishing village hometown, it sends a sexual tidal wave through the small community that has both men and women knocking on her door." Michael J. Bowen writes: "Abigail is a minor masterpiece, a stunning achievement in the field of non-explicit erotica. It beautifully illustrates Sarno's profound intuition for vibrant on-screen sexuality. Believing that eroticism and aesthetic aspiration need not serve two different masters, Sarno struggled visibly to maintain that delicate balance between sex and story (spectacle and narrative). Mary Mendum (Rebecca Brooke) in particular has earned a reputation as Sarno's quintessential siren, her sculpted

features simultaneously evoking a profound composure and a deep vulnerabiliy. But the film's secret weapon is Sarah Nicholson (Jennifer Jordan), Baypoint's unrelenting yet sympathetic provocateur. This actress's wit, insouciance, jaded persona, seductive Marlene Dietrich type voice, and vaguely maternal sensibility have never been better highlighted." Sarno shot the film in his home town, Amityville, on Long Island, NY. Since the film's video release in 2004, Abigail has been screened at numerous international venues, such as the Toronto Film Festival and the Cinematheque Francaise. It forms the centrepiece of the Sarno revival, organised by Bowen and company from Austin, Texas. It is combined with *Laura's Toys* on the key dvd of the Retro Seduction series, a double feature with copious extras, including a remarkable 2010 commentary by Joe Sarno himself, at the end of his long career, passing the torch of independent erotic cinema to a new generation.

14. *Suburban Secrets* [*Lust for Laura*], 2004 (2006). The dvd incorporates a Director's Cut (153), a Hot TV Cut (83), a Sarno interview (2009), and lots of extras. According to the blurb, the film bristles with sexual and psychological intensity and will appeal to women. It's a clever mix of realism, sexual fantasy and wit, reprising a generation after he'd stopped doing this kind of thing his old erotic aesthetic for a new generation of admirers. Of particular note is the actress A.J.Khan playing the office secretary Louise. She sits at her desk pretending to be a budding creative writer, but in fact spends her spare time composing porn and wanking. Throughout the film she has a wonderful way with words, she is witty, expressive and a provocatively sexual militant (a kind of amalgam of Henry Miller and Anais Nin). One of her memorable lines is spoken with a mix of wonder and world-weariness: 'I must admit I am somewhat hooked on masturbation.' As Sarno puts it, with Lawrentian emphasis: "The sex means a great deal because you care about the people. The story is never built around the sex - the sex is built into the story. This keeps my films away

from sexploitation." According to my notes from last year (can this be true?) the leading women in the film, Laura, the New York fashion model, and Judith, the local lawyer seek to extricate themselves from any male connexion by performing cunnilingus on each other, so keeping their cunts semen-free. They perform the longest lesbian love scene in all Sarno. The steamy eroticism does not prevent the film from being screamingly funny, grounded as it is in the locale of a provincial lawyers office. And the vision of a lyrical lesbian utopia is accompanied by a comic male character Johnson, the office clerk who has a Mary Whitehouse mission to clean up the sexual stables. Johnson spies on the lesbians but is of course converted to join in the sexual cavortings he seeks to abolish. And so Sarno in advanced old age becomes the leading American director to bridge that gap of a whole generation, just as in France Catherine Breillat picks up the sexual militancy she had tried to set in motion with *Une Vraie Jeune Fille* (1975). Sarno and Breillat - not obvious bed companions - but there is a link between *Lust for Laura* (I prefer that title) and Breillat's *Romance*. The art-porn syndrome has been well and truly resurrected.

CHAPTER EIGHT: CAPSULE REVIEWS

Niblo *THE TEMPTRESS* USA 1926
It was as *The Temptress* that Greta Garbo first made her mark on Hollywood. Barely out of her teens, a Swedish import, barely speaking English, she set herself up as the legendary star of American silent cinema. The film has an intriguing complex plot. But for me the most interesting aspect is the way in which Hollywood neutered the ending to maintain family and community values. So, after lots of stormy affairs and relationships in the beau monde, the destitute and wrecked Garbo is presented in a ceremony celebrating her lover's contribution to engineering, enterprise, public works and the advance of western civilisation through hard work, as the worthy woman behind her man without whom no projects could succeed. The hypocrisy is transparent. In fact Garbo tried throughout to subvert male enterprise through her womanly wiles. Happily the restored original ending gives us a wonderful picture of Garbo as an alcoholic down-and-out gulping down Hennessy cognac (absinthe in the screenplay) in a Parisian cafe terrace. Her ex-lover comes across her. She does not recognise him. He asks if he can help her in any way. She says, yes, you can buy me a drink. Garbo rarely acted as brilliantly as this, a teetotaller teenager of immaculate beauty playing the lush drunk in a consummation that dazzled against all the feel-good morality of the Hollywood code.

Goulding *LOVE* USA 1927
This was Garbo's first (silent) version of the later talking picture of Tolstoy's *Anna Karenina*. The title *Love* was a PR wheeze enabling posters and publicity to announce as a forthcoming attraction "Garbo and Gilbert in *LOVE*". It is a better film than the later talkie. It has more raw emotion and its exclusive concentration on the Anna/Vronsky relationship means that we forget all that Levin philosophy which other

film versions call attention to the absence of. Two factors are outstandingly peculiar. The first is the happy end imposed with *deus ex machina* arbitrariness at the very point in the plot where the tragic momentum appears as wonderfully inexorable as in Greek theatre. The awful and awesome end is so beautifully set in motion as the fates and furies decree that Anna will renounce her love to save Vronsky's career as an army officer, and that Vronsky will be redeemed into the military hierarchy because the love of the regiment is stronger than the love of a mere woman. This double renunciation is logically well-grounded and dramatically powerful. We look forward to being purged by pity and fear. And then what happens? Whoosh! Suddenly we see Anna, Vronsky and Anna's beloved son Seriozha reunited after Karenin's death (sic) in one happy family. A crazy turn of events, as fantastic and unbelievable as Kafka's last chapter in *Amerika* where everyone gets a job in the Theatre of Oklahoma. But then I ask WHY NOT. Why shouldn't Hollywood give us a nice corrective to Tolstoy's blistering religious misogyny whereby the woman taken in adultery must be punished for transgressing against a jealous God whose diktat (Tolstoy's epigraph) is "Vengeance is Mine, saith the Lord." And after all is not the happy ending itself a subversion of the strict mosaic code applied by Hollywood? The second factor peculiar to *Love* is what might be called the perversity of Garbo's sexuality. Garbo's Anna appears to spend almost as much time and energy kissing her son (and perversely usually on the lips) as in kissing her lover. In this context of competitive attention-seeking, the husband is nowhere. There is one particular scene, just before the expected tragic climax, when Garbo bestows fulsome caresses on the face, armpits and buttocks of Seriozha in the bathroom. Torn between Seriozha and Vronsky (she cannot have them both), Garbo appears to be into little boys, and (heaven forbid) into little boys who look like little girls. And that is plural, for she desperately attempts to kiss a passing tousle-headed boy-girl who reminds her of Seriozha. I perversely conclude that, like

Andrew Marvell and Catherine Breillat, Garbo is a sexual puritan - where sex is no easy lay but conflicted, problematic and difficult. She may be polymorphous, she may even be coenaesthetic, but at least she takes sex seriously. Little boys, little girls, what's the difference to the dormant bisexual or lesbian within her. Garbo will not be pigeon-holed. She will not be satisfied by grown men, husbands or lovers. She might have a fling with John Gilbert. She would not marry him. That's the secret of Garbo - her mystique. Like Louise Brooks (and this is high praise) she is a free spirit. And in *Love*, in 1927, her acting proves it. (November 2011)

Clarence Brown *FLESH AND THE DEVIL* **USA 1927**
Clarence Brown on Garbo: "Garbo had something behind the eyes that you couldn't see until you photographed it in close-up. You could see thought. If she had to look at one person with jealousy, and another with love, she didn't have to change her expression. You could see it in her eyes as she looked from one to the other. And nobody else has been able to do that on the screen. Garbo did it without the command of the English language." (Kevin Brownlow, *The Parade's Gone By*, 1968, p.169).

Flesh and the Devil is a clear candidate for Film Society billing & one of the best films ever made. Only just seen it. 1927 was the year of Gance's *Napoleon* and Pabst's *Lulu*. This Garbo (wonderful to relate) bears some comparison with both. *Time Out* is wrong or damns with faint praise. Thus: 1. "Renowned for its electric love scenes - which now seem tame." WRONG. They are far from tame. They match the best of early Buñuel. 2. "An elegant bit of melodramatic fluff." WRONG. The melo elegance, far from fluffy, is undermined, undercut and sublimated into pure poetry. 3. "Garbo is in swooning form." FAINT PRAISE. She swoons and emotes with a Kool panache rarely equalled (Louise Brooks and Ingrid Bergman excepted). 4, "Much ado about nothing really." WRONG. Unless you take NO-THING (like Donne and Shakespeare) to embody the female genitals. In which case Much is more than enough, 5. "But Garbo is as luminous as ever, thanks to Walter Damiel's camerawork." FAINT PRAISE. She is more luminous than ever. Only when you've seen this film do you realise why Garbo was the vamp supreme, the femme fatale par excellence. Compared to this her sound films are stodgy pianola performances, cardboard cut-outs, as mistimed and misplaced in talkies as the silent star in *Singin' in the Rain*.

Flesh and the Devil provokes by its form and content cross-reference to the following iconic touchstones: *L'Age d'Or* 1930; *Wuthering Heights*; *Jules et Jim*; Pabst's *Lulu*; Wagner's *Tristan*; Wilde's *Salome*; Anais Nin. And, a variation on all these, Garbo's film trumps every *femme fatale* cliché with an overall homoerotic *amour fou*. Does this happen anywhere else? Probably, but I can't think of any examples. The homoerotic passion adds spice, suspense and advanced sexual politics to the archetypal threesome motif (do Palamon and Arcite in Chaucer's *Knight's Tale* qualify?). The *menage a trois*, with its utopian solidarities and its smouldering jealousies, recalls *Jules et Jim* (and more accurately if less poetically *Anne and Muriel*, where Truffaut's 2M1F becomes 2F1M).

Then there is a wonderful intertitle: THE TRAGIC, UNQUESTIONING, AMUSING LOVE OF YOUTH - NO ONE HAD EVER LOVED BEFORE. Then we see Garbo rubbing her knuckles together in a solipsist onanism redolent of the many displaced and condensed images of masturbation in *L'Age d'Or*. That luminous intertitle (what a brilliant definition of first love as simultaneously tragic, unquestioning AND amusing) comes after one of the most erotic scenes in world cinema - a slow series of kisses in extreme close-up, intensified literally and symbolically by the prop of the lighting and mutual smoking of a cigarette - oh, those 1927 tubes of tobacco, symbolising decadence and degeneration as in Huxley's *Brave New World*, how would they not be censored or banned by today's politically correct health and safety brigade. And, to add joy to joy, after the eloquent intertitle, we get to see in close-up a reclining Garbo with her lover's head (decapitated by the frame) in her capacious lap. Garbo achieves what Salome failed to achieve, possession of her man's head without having it chopped off, a *Liebestod* worthy of Lulu's with Jack the Ripper, but in *vagina dentata* mode rather than as literal sex-murder. And it is a consummation for the man (the astounded and astounding John Gilbert, highest paid actor in the universe and simultaneously Garbo's erstwhile lover off-set as well as on). The carefully framed tableau tells us that Garbo has total control of her man. She is Vamp as Magna Mater, even (blasphemously) a Mary Mother of God Pieta consoling her immaculately conceived son in post-coital embrace (for him *une petite mort* after the crucifixion of sex, for her the triumph of woman as Madonna and Whore.) And Garbo, as the aptly named Felicitas, fulfils herself in post-Freudian polymorphous perversity: like her contemporary Anais Nin, she claims the human right to have two husbands at the same time. And does. The cigarette (and cigar and pipe) smoke is aesthetically and ideologically over the top in fine expressionist fettle. Garbo smokes, not as if, but because she is on fire. The Racinian euphemism for female libido (*flamme*), reprised with cynical gusto by Flaubert, is condensed into Garbo's imagery of incendiary eroticism. Garbo undoubtedly smokes the most sensuous cigarette in the history of cinema (surpassing even the pornographic genital smoking in one of the Emmanuelle films).

The dvd is excellently reconstructed by Kevin Brownlow and Carl Davies. They do as much brilliant justice to this fim as they did for the 1927 *Napoleon*. It is not clear from her sound films why Garbo was so great. There is a raw Swedish magic in *Anna Christie* and there are some poetic touches in *Mata Hari* and *Camille*, but *Anna Karenina* and *Queen Christina* leave much to be desired in their formulaic Hollywoodenness, and the dismal *Ninotchka* simply proves that the celebrated Lubitsch touch can be the touch of death. But once you have seen *Flesh and the Devil* you understand that Garbo almost alone has the lineaments of the greatest of them all, Louise Brooks, albeit more glacial and less loose-limbed.

And there is comedy in the film, revolving around a very protestant pastor whose occasional alcoholism leads him to think he is seeing double (twins in fact), and who preaches from the pulpit with the fanatical fervour of the ranting sermon in Lockwood's dream in *Wuthering Heights* (70 times 7). At one point (but I invented this in joyful hallucination) the pastor appears to be about to preach from the text "Thou shalt love thy neighbour's wife" (a nice subversion of the Mosaic law). But this diversion which on first viewing I appear to have imagined rather than read, does not prevent the pastor functioning as a sublime super-ego as he fulminates against King David's adultery, leading Garbo to require some smelling salts for an attack of the vapours as she and her lover are forced to listen in the congregation.

The plot is secondary of course, but it is clear, logical, coherent - with of course the added enhancement and complexity inherent in the ultimate overriding Amour being homoerotic (and Garbo indulges momentarily in some semi-lesbian business in her boudoir). In the end after Garbo is almost strangled to death for two-timing beyond the otherwise utopian male tolerance which cements the three in their fantasy menage, her two men are propelled by convention and fate to fight a duel. And then, guess what happens! ... Honestly, you just can't imagine how the wretched film will end. ... Well, the two men's love for each other means they cannot pull the trigger. They and their love survive victorious. And Garbo? ... Well, after a long sulk in her boudoir, she rushes at breakneck speed through the snow to stop her two lovers killing each other, only to slip through the ice and drown - a truly beautiful death for the femme fatale whose last breath rises to the surface of the freezing pond in gorgeous big bubbles.

All this I wrote down on one small sheet of paper in late October 2011.

PS. Further reflection and research gives us the following. 1. Garbo and Gilbert collaborated in a silent version of *Anna Karenina* titled *Love* 1927 which allowed the PR poster to proclaim on a thousand billboards GARBO AND GILBERT IN LOVE. As of course they were, in more ways than one. 2. Gilbert's highly expressionist acting is all done with his EYES. His voice failed the test of the talkies. He might have been the greatest and richest star of the silent era, but in art and in life he was hopelessly at the mercy of the divine Garbo. 3. The tableau at the start of the film should not be overlooked. Three small children are playing their magic games. Emblematically the tiny six year old girl presides as a goddess over the ritual blood sharing of the two somewhat older boys who are engaged in a ceremony of potentially homoerotic blood brotherhood. The atmosphere is solemn, vatic, perverse - and bravely prophetic of what will happen when these kinky kids grow up. The tableau is repeated in flashback at the film's climax. 4. Garbo's biographer notes (what I missed on first viewing) that when Gilbert and Garbo are drinking the communion wine, Garbo deliberately twists the cup to allow her luscious lips to taste traces of Gilbert's saliva left on the rim of the cup. A subtle and lubricious touch that - was it Clarence Brown's idea, or Garbo's? 5. The dvd gives us an alternate ending, trumping the buddy homoeroticism with Gilbert going off to marry Hertha who had always been in love with him but couldn't get to him past Garbo until Garbo was dead. This looks like a happy feel-good Hollywood ending with the immoral bisexual complexities of the plot resolved into a conventional heterosexual happy end to satisfy the censor.

Leontine Sagan *MAIDENS IN UNIFORM* Germany 1931
This film, banned by Goebbels, shows us life in a Prussian girls boarding school. In this feminine space (no men in sight), a totalitarian male authority rules. The sadism and suffering is transcended by the developing attraction between the orphaned Manuela and her one relatively humane teacher

Fraulein von Bernburg. In what has come to be seen as the first truly radical lesbian film, the vibrations of homoerotic friendship transform prevailing social relations, and give us a tragic and revolutionary critique of that Prussian authoritarianism and militarism that prefigures the horrors of the Third Reich.

Hitchcock *YOUNG AND INNOCENT* GB 1937

At some point I was in the crazy position of thinking that this film was half way between Will Hay and *L'Age d'or*. It has the manic plot of a Will Hay film (eg. *Ask a Policeman*, *The Goose Steps Out*). Jokes and pratfalls abound. And then there is between the improbably named Derrick de Marnay and Nora Pilbeam the most unlikely, crazy and amazing Mad Love (*amour fou*). I'd never seen Marnay before. He is stupendously beautiful in that sleek, smooth, unruffled 30s style of leading men. And Nora Pilbeam (you couldn't invent the name could you) is out of this world. She was only 17 or 18 when Hitchcock put her in his film and because she was so young she did not have to submit to Hitch's sadistic directorial methods over-much. And hey, she's still alive now, aged 90! Close-ups between the two leads are extremely close. She seems to be drugged, hypnotised, and yet has the normal appearance of a John Betjeman Home Counties girl (no sign of special beauty or femme fatale). Their love (I don't think they ever get as far as a kiss, still less a clinch) is all-consuming and set against a Buñuelesque absurd world of upper-middle class inanity - mainly in the shape of her father (chief of police) and her five siblings. One of her brothers, a bespectacled public school horror, aged about 12 is a mister-know-all child prodigy and speaks a bit like Peter Ustinov in *The Goose Steps Out* - i.e. like a Russian actor playing a German character learning to speak perfect English. The social scenes are just like *L'Age d'or* - whether a children's party with blind man's bluff, or a dancing soiree. All the children in the film are grotesque in the extreme, freaks masquerading as Home Counties offspring. So, this is one of my favourite Hitchcock films. I never enjoyed the twitching blacked-up murderer - far too much manipulation - but all the rest is wonderful. Indeed, I could even argue it may be Hitch's masterpiece. And remember, though I enjoyed *Rear Window* when it came out, I cannot stand *Vertigo* - it gives me the ...

Renoir *LA MARSEILLAISE* France 1937
This was a real surprise, so much better than I was expecting. It can even be mentioned on the same page with Abel Gance's *Napoleon* (1927). The film carries a fantastic revolutionary fervour with it. And of course this is partly because it tells us about the feelings, actions and heroic endeavours of the Popular Front period - from 1936 when France had a left-wing government under Leon Blum, uniting Communists, Socialists and Radicals. The CGT (Communist Party Trade Union) is in the credits. Class consciousness permeated the whole film, but in the Renoir *bon enfant* spirit of bonhomie, larger than life, with heroic realism etc. Particularly brilliant is the character of Louis XVI, played by Renoir's brother as a kind of idiotic George III who knows that his time is up. This in wonderful contrast to Marie Antoinette who is gorgeously evil with a streak of Lady Macbeth about her. The film only takes us up to the decisive battle of Valmy (1792), before the execution of the Royals. There is no Danton, no Robespierre, no Marat, no Saint-Just - just the ordinary proles and peasants from Marseille who bring their song to Paris. Renoir never joined the Communist Party but he certainly gave artistic oomph to the cause of the Popular Front. And he was godfather to the child of Maurice Thorez (French Communist Party leader). Lise Delamare plays Marie Antoinette. And remember, in 1934 there had been an unsuccessful fascist coup in France, the Popular Front government was as revolutionary as it could be, but also pretty fragile so that the *rapport de forces* between revolution and counter-revolution infuses the whole film. Swathes of the French bourgeoisie supported Hitler, like Marie Antoinette an Austrian. Renoir knows what side he's on. We are inevitably drawn in to the world of Monsieur Veto,

Monsieur Capet and the Austrian queen. And Renoir knows how to tear-jerk in the best possible aesthetic and ideological fashion. Apparently the film went down better in the Soviet Union than in France. And the film ends with a quote from Goethe who was around at the time of the Marseillaise.

Mankiewicz *ALL ABOUT EVE* USA 1950

I have at last got round to watching *All About Eve* which I'd never properly seen before. It took me several false starts before I got into it. It is pretty damned brilliant and justifies its ambitious title (which I'd always doubted). Of course this is a fine example showcasing the older actress (in fact and in theme). I hadn't realised that Marilyn Monroe has a small part as a perfectly formed bimbo. Pity she was type-cast in her early films. Apart from Bette Davis doing some high-class bitching, there is also the wonderful George Sanders playing the sophisticated film critic Addison de Witt whose name aptly recalls the 18thC journalist and arbiter of taste, Joseph Addison, together with the line of wit from Dryden to Pope. Mankiewicz's film is far more classical and composed than *Sunset Boulevard*. And that makes the passion that much more vicious - remember Bette Davis answering a quip by raising her celery stick up in the air in an obscene gesture. As a reminder of Bette Davis in her youthful pomp, as a loose canon with nympho tendencies in the tropics, I have managed to get hold of William Wyler's *The Letter* (1940) (from a Somerset Maugham story). In the mode of sultry-stubborn, no one beats Bette Davis. (29 May 2009)

Losey *THE PROWLER* USA 1951

Just watched this film properly, and also with excellent audio commentary by film noir expert. It is very good. Superficially like *Double Indemnity*, but far more psychologically complex, and with Losey's usual acute sense of class-consciousness. It's also full of hidden clandestine contributions from the black-listed American communists who had to flee their government's tyranny. One of the things Hollywood was henceforth banned from doing was - wait for it - making critical remarks about banks and bankers. Van Heflin is excellent and so is Evelyn Keyes. Not exactly household names, but they execute Losey and Trumbo's hard unsentimental vision with great aplomb. The ebb and flow between good and evil is highly sophisticated and way beyond the conventional Hollywood manichean sense of right and wrong. As usual Losey scores trumps with his insights into sexual psychology and class conflict. (September 2011)

Clouzot *THE WAGES OF FEAR* France 1953
Restored to full length, this is an epic film of tension and suspense to match anything by Hitchcock or Chabrol. We can now fully enjoy the seedy sleaze of a latin-american outpost (Venezuela? shades of Conrad's *Nostromo*), where Yves Montand's only link with European civilisation is his carefully preserved Paris metro ticket. In the freelance world of ex-pat oil workers and tanker drivers, anything goes. Greed is the name of the game. The stakes are high. Crazy risks must be taken. The heroic and sordid struggle to transport the oil is magnificently portrayed, with Montand at the handsome height of his charm. But beware the final twist in the tale. It is almost unbearable. Try it!

Bergman *A LESSON IN LOVE* Sweden 1954
The great revelation in early Bergman was *A Lesson in Love* (1954). I'd never seen this before, and it seemed so sparkling and generous in scope that I thought *Smiles of a Summer Night* (which I'd always had reservations about) could not match it. As it happened, in the course of trawling through the Bergman Collection, this proved not to be true and the 1955 breakthrough iconic masterpiece was in effect better than the earlier one. But, what wit, what perspective in *Lesson in Love*. Eva Dahlburg is magnificent, lets down her hair (usually hoisted up in a severe chignon), and the scene in Copenhagen is something Bergman never does again - a riot in a slum bar with all the Swedes losing their inhibitions among the

liberated dissolute Danes. Harriet Andersson has only a small part as the tomboy daughter of Dahlburg, but her face is exquisitely expressive, especially when she is alone with her grandfather. The Cupid at the end seems like a rehearsal for *Smiles of a Summer Night* and captures the spirit of the comedy brilliantly. Don't miss this one. (20 October 2007)

Agnes Varda *LA POINTE COURTE* France 1954
This is truly a revelation - seeing it now for the first time 55 years later. It was Varda's first effort and she had absolutely no training or contacts. It is a unique film, very different from her other things, yet, as a first film, shows the strong documentary element that is in most of her films. For 1954 it is precociously avant-garde. There are influences and affinities, but these are prestigous and illustrious. Thus Renoir's *Partie de Campagne* (1936) comes to mind - one of Varda's characters says "Parties don't change anything, but they make us feel good". And Vigo - his spirit is there, that magic fusion of poetry and realism that shines out of *L'Atalante* (1934). Also Visconti whose *Terra Trema* (1948) must have contributed to her documentary technique. Also Rossellini's neo-realism, especially *Stromboli* (1950) where a couple's relationship is set against a traditional, even archaic, spirit of place. The film is unique because, without strain or manipulation, it sets a couple's austerely high-mannered courtly love with its literary dialogue against the absolute earthy peasant population of Sete, which was Varda's home town in her youth. (4 June 2009)

Bergman *BRINK OF LIFE* Sweden 1958
We have just seem *Brink of Life*. Bruce was quite impressed on the grounds that it was pretty radical for a male director to take on this gynecological issue as long ago as 1958. And he liked the switching between the three cases of pregnancy. I found it somewhat desultory, as if Bergman's heart were not in it. Competent enough, but more of an academic exercise, a kind of male consultant bird's-eye view of that female

condition from which the ruling gender is inevitably excluded. Compared with the much more vibrant and feminist *Loving Couples* (1964), Mai Zetterling's take on the same subject, women's differing feelings and attitudes to having a baby, Bergman's effort is quite lifeless, still-born, to coin a pun. *Brink of Life* is not much more than a hospital drama, spiced up with Bergman's well-known knowledge of women's problems. Into this everyday story of Stockholm folk with its well-organised social realism, he injects a bizarre Nietzchean notion that the will to live is more important than life itself. The best thing was Bibi Andersson being 'naughty', jigging her body in 60s abandon within the strict confines of a Swedish hospital, as if the dourly spartan 1950s could be shaken off through sheer *joie de vivre*. (10 December 2008)

Pontecorvo KAPO Italy/France 1959
One of the reasons Pontecorvo's *Kapo* has been ignored, despised and rejected is that the great guru Rivette launched a savage attack on it in *Cahiers du Cinema* in 1961. Look up Rivette on *Kapo* on the net. More high-minded reasoned abuse you will not find elsewhere. Rivette's critique is grounded in his take on one travelling shot. Fascinating stuff. *Kapo* is nonetheless a masterpiece, and must not be consigned to the dustbin of cinematic history simply because in Rivette's eyes it falls lamentably short of Resnais' *Night and Fog* (1955). It is amazing how the whole leftist establishment of *Cahiers* maintained a kind of embargo or boycott on Pontecorvo's film on the grounds that because it used actors and manipulated shots in a film about concentration camps it must be rejected by all and sundry for whom *Night and Fog* had become the only authorised (fetishised one might say) approach to Auschwitz. *Kapo* is obviously not as good as *The Batttle of Algiers* (1965), but that is no shame. *Kapo* had me in buckets of tears. Pontecorvo was a communist in the Italian resistance, and it shows. *Kapo* has touches of Eisenstein, and Susan Strasberg is magnificent in a role that combines the suffering

innocence of Dreyer's *Joan of Arc* and Bresson's *Mouchette*. (29 September 2009)

Serge Bourgignon   *SUNDAYS AND CYBELE (LES DIMANCHES DU VILLE D'AVRAY)*   France 1962

Another one of those forgotten gems. It occurred to me on second thoughts that a possible weakness of the film was the crude Freudian symbolism - female lakes and pre-patriarchal pagan name (Cybele), and (worse) the steeple-cock. One of Kruger's problems (following his being shot down in the war) is his sexual impotence, over which his wife is amazingly sympathetic. The vertigo theme, aeroplanes, climbing the steeple, securing the cock, it's all a bit crude, don't you think? Still, it's a great film, though with a horribly sad ending. Its atmosphere comes from some kind of poetic dialectic between the magic Sunday World (cf. Ursula's Sunday World chapter in D. H. Lawrence's *The Rainbow*) and the everyday world of hospitals, marriage, psychiatry and bourgeois norms. Apparently Patricia Gozzi who plays Cybele went on to make a film called *Rapture* (1965), in which also one of Bergman's actresses plays. *Rapture* is described as another long-lost gem, and is therefore naturally unavailable. In it Gozzi plays a tormented 15 year-old (that age of maximum torment). And that year she was 15, just as she was 12 in Cybele. Bourgignon's film skirts skilfully around the innocent young girl's relationship with a disturbed and putatively criminal adult man. In that sense the film fleshes out a similar relationship at the core of J. Lee Thompson's *Tiger Bay* (1959). The evocation of paedophilia, however spurious, is not easy to pull off, and *Sundays and Cybele* is a brittle, spiky and tender success. (12 November 2009)

Cacoyannis *ELEKTRA* Greece 1962

For some reason I've only just seen this film. It had to be ordered from Aghios Nikolaus in Crete, a place I'd visited as a student tourist in 1959. There are people who say this is one of the greatest films ever made. I am inclined to agree. It follows Euripides faithfully but is totally filmic, precise, concise, sober and yet touching the heights of expressive art (cf. Dreyer's *Joan of Arc*, cf. Bresson's *Mouchette*). In my Utopia, every citizen, every student, every child should do the following: watch Cacoyannis's version of *Elektra*, and then watch Jancso's *Elektra My Love* (Hungary 1974). You would learn a very high degree of discrimination, appreciation and critical sense of difference from watching these two films in sequence. Pure classical Greek, sense of conscience, revenge, fate, the gods, human rights, justice, with the emotional impact of a Shakespeare or Emily Bronte. And then the utopian communist song and dance routine with rhythmic horses and naked women circling each other in mesmerising patterns on the great Hungarian Plain, with which authorial trademark Jancso transmutes Greek Tragedy into revolutionary optimism against totalitarian tyranny. I'd have to prefer the Jancso, but only just. Electra is Hamlet with a touch of Lady Macbeth and Oliver Cromwell about her. Complex, no doubt? And probably only Irene Papas (recognised by many as the greatest and most beautiful and strongest and most unknown screen actress since Louise Brooks) could have pulled it off. Her charismatic presence spills over into Helen of Troy in *The Trojans* (1972) and into Clytemnestra in *Iphigenia* (1977), the two other Cacoyannis films in his Euripides trilogy. Cacoyannis obviously keeps more closely to the wonderful dramatic ironies of Greek Tragedy than Jancso. The play with recognition and non-recognition between Electra and Orestes is nail-bitingly suspenseful and unutterably moving. Cacoyannis gives us Papas in close-up to such effect that you want to die upon the midnight with no pain. And Cacoyannis is also more faithful to the Family Romance at the heart of the House of Atreus. Family Romance, as interpreted by Freud, with Family Values, for a Family Audience (no sex, no 'language' i.e. swear words, or violence on screen - it's all off-screen, off-stage, off-scene, i.e. OB-SCENE). The Greeks tried heroically to REASON about FATE. They all have their reasons and present them eloquently in the agora, to the Chorus of Women, to the democratic community. Even Clytemnestra can justify murdering her husband Agamemnon. Did he not sacrifice their daughter Iphigenia at Aulis in order to placate the gods of the wind and a bloodthirsty army. Did he not return from Troy with Cassandra as his own personal slave-girl and expect Clytemnestra to share their bed. There was always an original sin to avenge. And so Orestes and Electra, after they've murdered their mother and step-father, wend their weary way over the Greek pastoral landscape much as Adam and Eve wandered out of Paradise after their Fall, all passion spent. And yet we wanted them to kill Aegisthus and Clytemnestra, just as Blake and Shelley wanted Eve to side with Satan against Adam and God. I had not heard it before. Cacoyannis gives Clytemnestra some excellent feminist logic. "When women are unfaithful they are condemned whatever their excuse, Men never." Chorus of Women: "She speaks the truth. But how vile a truth." *The Trojan Women* is nowhere near as good as *Elektra*, not even nearly as good as *Iphigenia*. Partly because it is in English with a commercial eye to the international (i.e. Hollywood) market. Katharine Hepburn, Genevieve Bujold, Vanessa Redgrave and even the blessed Brian Blessed speak their lines competently as trained actors. But only Papas as Helen in her cage gives us any poetry. So. *Trojan Women* is worthy but wooden, *Iphigenia* a broadly brilliant epic, but *Elektra* is electrically charged. And how can the great Harold Bloom claim that 'conscience' was invented by Shakespeare's Hamlet when it's there in spades in Greek Tragedy. *Elektra* is probably Cacoyannis's best film and probably Irene Papas's best film. Remember: Cacoyannis *ELEKTRA* Greece 1962. Remember Jancso *ELEKTRA* Hungary 1974. See them in sequence - and die. (September 2011)

Bertolucci *BEFORE THE REVOLUTION* Italy 1964
New dvd of *Before the Revolution*. A much more important film than I remember from the old days. Here are some random scraps I noted last week. Formally based on Stendhal's

Chartreuse de Parme 1839, ideologically based on Flaubert's *Sentimental Education* 1869. Film influences mainly Pasolini, Godard, Antonioni. Self-referential. "In 20 years Anna Karina will be what Louise Brooks is to us now." "What is so typical of 1946 is Bogart and Bacall in Hawks' *Big Sleep*." "I've seen *Journey to Italy* 15 times. How can one live without Rossellini." "You say that Resnais and Godard are escapist, but for them style is a moral fact." Adriana Asti is Bertolucci's Anna Karina (and, not coincidentally, following Godard, his wife). Fabrizio (B's hero and alter ego) says: "I wanted to fill Gina with vitality. I filled her with anguish." "I have nostalgia for the present. I don't want to change the present." FOR MY SORT IT IS ALWAYS BEFORE THE REVOLUTION. This film in 1964 makes the definitive break with Italian neorealism. My theory on Bertolucci. Can a bourgeois become a communist? No. The SEX-POL approach goes like this. Following his first master Pasolini (see Pasolini's *Accattone* 1961 & B's first film *The Grim Reaper* 1962), B aspires to be a communist (PCI of Gramsci, Togliatti) in IDEOLOGY and AESTHETICS - so, he will follow Pasolini and not use professional actors. That happens in *Before the Revolution* - that is Politics (POL). But B has fallen in love with and married Adrianna Asti, who, apart from being one of the sexiest women in the world, was also a professional actress. As Gina, she is the centre of the film - that is SEX. So, there is a wonderful contradiction - the SEX and the POL rub against each other and produce that ambivalence at the heart of the revolution as documented by Flaubert in 1848 and Brecht in 1919. In the last resort political utopia collapses. Romance trumps revolution. By way of the discreet charm of the bourgeoisie we are always diverted from (and before) the revolution. In B's film the cross between Pasolini's revolutionary ideology and aesthetics and B's Anna Karina type Muse is what makes the film throb. The tone and message of the film tells us that it will always be before the revolution - cos of LOVE. It is also of course in line with the Fabian tendencies of western communist parties, from the German KPD in 1933 to the French CP in 1968. As the German utopian marxist Ernst Bloch put it - NOCH NICHT. NOT YET. WE ALWAYS LIVE BEFORE THE REVOLUTION - especially if we're married to Adriana Asti, who plays Fabrizio's aunt - try and fit the Incest Motif into all this! Incest and revolution, taboo and danger. Hamlet and Electra. Something rotten in the state of Denmark, Italy, NATO. Ironically B met Adriana on the set of Pasolini's *Accattone* for which he was assistant director. Adriana/Gina is not only Fabrizio's aunt, but also a neurasthenic crazy woman with wild eyes and the most marvellously deranged look ever seen in a screen goddess. Ultimately Bertolucci plays his sex-pol (sex-pot) games (cf *Last Tango* and *Dreamers*) with great sincerity and aesthetic brio. He is another of that Italian breed of sensualist communist aesthetes (like Visconti?) who feed off D'Annunzio as much as they follow Gramsci. Pasolini is the exception, he is more of a real revolutionary as he is more of a real poet than the other noble phalanx of card-carrying comrades. (August 2011)

Vera Chytilova *DAISIES* Czechoslovakia 1966

Chytilova surpasses even the genial Jiri Menzel in her blissful critique of the pieties and austerities associated with the Czech Stalinist regime under President Husak. *Daisies* is an exercise in revolutionary modernism, anarcho-dadaist in spirit and form. 21 deputies objected in parliament to the extravagant waste of food in the film, and Chytilova had to defend her work on communist-moral grounds - i.e. the two female protagonists were spoilt brats to be condemned as so much waste-matter in the body politic of the workers' state. But we know that they are feminist anarchists, living (in terms of the plot narrative) off silly old men who buy them dinners, and (in terms of the poetic texture of the film) calling everything into question with the unquenchable brio of cartoon characters (they eat even photographs of food from glossy magazines). We, the audience, are happily infected by the blessed spirit of nihilism Chytilova has conjured up in those dangerous and exhilarating days of the Prague Spring. First there was Kafka (*Amerika*), then there was Hasek (*The Good Soldier Svejk*), then there was Vera Chytilova.

Alexander Kluge YESTERDAY GIRL West Germany 1966
This is a fine film, nearer to Godard than to Brecht, with a wonderful carnivalesque display of broken devices and images, only obliquely revealing the Nazi continuum from Hitler to Adenauer. The politics of the film are never loudly paraded, but always grounded in the personal life of an individual. (9 May 2010)

Tony Richardson MADEMOISELLE France/GB 1966
Overwhelmed by seeing this film for the first time. It is a masterpiece, the only flaw being the dubbing into English (except for the Italians!). It owes something to Buñuel's *Diary of a Chambermaid* (1964), especially the character of Jeanne Moreau, central to both films. Jeanne Moreau morphs from abject surrealist maid into criminal sadistic slut. Her parts are pure genius. Chabrol's *Le Boucher* (1970) owes something to the subject matter and style of *Mademoiselle*. Jeanne Moreau again in her pomp as village schoolteacher in uneasy relationship with an ex-military psychotic killer. References to Gilles de Rais predate Michel Tournier's novel *Gilles et Jeanne* (1983) by almost twenty years. The touches of Genet in the film are lubriciously glorious shots of the degradingly abject variety - spitting real spittle, licking orifices and protuberances of the face in extreme close-up. Cruelty to animals abounds, notably the crushing of birds eggs (cf. early Breillat). (6 September 2009)

Alain Robbe-Grillet *TRANS-EUROP-EXPRESS* France 1966
Here are some higgledy-piggledy thoughts on *Trans-Europ-Express* which I found mesmerising in spite of it being dubbed into Italian with no subtitles. Compare with *The Image*, Robbe-Grillet's wife's s&m porn classic written ten years before *TEE*. She was an expert in bondage and *TEE* is replete with images of gorgeous girls tied up. 'Tis a very high-class piece of post-

structuralist filth (oops, sorry *nouveau roman*), full of slinky Anna Karina look-alikes. It's like it's made by someone who knows all about Bergman (cf. *The Silence*), even foreshadowing Bela Tarr. The plot of drugs and contraband is undercut by farce and Godardian tricks. It is eerie throughout. It lies between Bergman, Godard, Breillat and Resnais - not bad connections. The soundtrack and visuals are stunning. The triumph of image over plot is drastic. *Time Out* says it is pompous modernism, but then so is *The Waste Land*, so is *Ulysses*, so is Antonioni. Trintignant is sublime throughout. In a way he is beyond Belmondo and Brando, a KOOL to live with for ever, enough strong silent man to last a lifetime. The Robbe-Grillets are in the film, but I don't know their faces. Is the wise un-floozie-like woman with the tape recorder in the compartment our very own Catherine Robbe-Grillet (alias Jean de Berg, alias Jeanne de Berg)? Maybe. *Time Out* is stupid in its lib-dem way, as most of us are most of the time. What we need is an aesthetics of perversity (see Kingsley Widmer on D.H.Lawrence in *The Art of Perversity* to cope with *The Woman Who Rode Away*). Yes, the film is pretentious, it is pompous, and that's partly why it's so bloody good. And, oh, that train, that trans-europe express - you can catch it in Paris at the *Gare du Nord*. From there the destinations include Amsterdam, Stockholm and Moscow. You fancy a combination of Simenon, *L'Avventura*, *Last Year in Marienbad* and some Bela Tarr landscapes, then watch this film. A lot of it seems to take place in Belgium, the home of Simenon, Magritte, Maeterlinck and Jacques Brel. Don't you just love those Flemish folk, especially when they are French-speaking Wallons. (13 December 2010)

Mai Zetterling *NIGHT GAMES* Sweden 1966
I wondered whether you had things to say about this film which we have only just managed to get hold of after 42 years. It seemed utterly fantastic and brilliant. Managed to get hold of her novel of it as well. What amazed us is that Bergman, anxiously waiting to see it in 1966, went on to accuse

Zetterling of obscenity. Shock horror! And why? Well, it was apparently because of the way she'd shown sexual activity between a fully fleshed Ingrid Thulin (one of Bergman's regular actresses) and the 13 year-old only just pubescent boy - one of Bergman's regular boy stars from *The Silence* (1963) and *Persona* (1966). So, it was alright for Bergman to do kinky sexual things with his actresses, but not for his colleague Zetterling (who'd been in professional and personal touch with Bergman since her appearance in the 1944 *Frenzy*) to mess with a teenage boy! This led to me finding on IMDB the following comment which delighted me. Lara Jacobsson, Stockholm, 10 September 2002. On *Frieda* (1947): "Outstanding English language effort by the great Swedish actor/director Mai Zetterling (Any one who have seen her brilliant film *Night Games* will agree she kicks Bergman's sorry ass!"). Is there any sign of the following lost Zetterlings? *Dr Glas* (1967), *Amorosa* (1986), *The Woman Who Cleaned the World* (1994). She died while making this last one. Have been watching my Zetterlings again. There's a lovely line in *Loving Couples*: "There is no love, just beds and dirt and slime." This is the woman's view as supremely laid out in *Night Games*. It was a view which Bergman, mere man, could not share. Hence his back-handed compliment (of obscenity) delivered to his kindred spirit and Swedish sister. (12 September 2008)

Bresson *MOUCHETTE* France 1967
Arguably Bresson's greatest film, this portrayal of an inarticulate marginalised schoolgirl surrounded by alcoholic degenerates and provincial Catholic pieties achieves an intense poetic purity. The depressing miserabilism of an anomic society is transcended by Bresson's scrupulous cinematic grace. The grace belongs to a profound humanism beyond the divisions between Christians and atheists. Unable to sing correctly in her music lesson, Mouchette finds the right note when comforting an epileptic mental debile in a lonely shed during a symbolic 'cyclone'. In sullen revolt against all attempts to recuperate her, she finds salvation in a suicide

which brings tears of joy to the alarmed viewer's eyes. This must be one of the ten best films ever made. The only films which can with some justice be related to *Mouchette* are Buñuel's ferociously subversive *Los Olvidados* (1950) and Agnes Varda's *Vagabond* (1985). Only Varda could have succeeded in carrying on the spirit of Mouchette in her rebellious deviant Mona (Sandrine Bonnaire).

Losey *BOOM* GB 1968
Brilliant sustained Tennesse Williams (TW) script letting Losey shine. Viewed 19 June 2011. Everything is brilliant, including Noel Coward, Joanna Shimkus, Dwarf, Dogs, costumes, setting, music. It has the verve, high seriousness, parody, self-irony to such a degree as to contribute to the culture of surrealism, to that sublime state of the marvellous-absurd. Poetry that is. At 46" Burton intones "Church bells are waking up..." and we hear the voice of *Under Milk Wood*. Burton and Taylor can be compared to Tristan and Isolde, that Wagnerian ridiculous-sublime, that fix of love=death, that old Liebestod Rag. At 55" Burton's voice is at its zenith, Taylor is majestic. The props are kinky-kitsch - a monkey, a loquacious parrot, a dwarf as faithful retainer. BUT Burton and Taylor are THEMSELVES - they appear to be not acting. At 60" Burton tells Coward that he is "the heart of a world that has no heart", almost a homage to Marx's observation that religion is the heart of a heartless world. Liz Taylor is MRS GOFORTH - going forth comes to signify not only becoming a world celebrity and a woman with a multitude of husbands, but also DYING. At 105" Burton kisses Liz. Liz: "I usually let it be known when I want to be kissed." This film transcendentally re-enacts the Burton-Taylor relationship with oomph, knowingness, self-irony and panache. Real glitz, real glamour, real *weltschmerz*, like that Shakespeare sonnet (I lie with her and she lies with me wordplay). Blackie (Mrs Black, Shimkus) is perfect as the norm, that normality, that common sense from which the whole film departs with such utter extravagance and illusion. The TW syndrome, romance

cynically subverted - and yet without illusion there is no life. BOOM - is the noise of the sea, the noise of death, of eternity, and like the Boom in the Malabar Caves of *Passage to India*, it is the noise of the Unsayable, of the mystic beyond reason. It is perhaps verbalised as "the shock of each moment of still being alive", a motif that is repeated more than once. Burton (in character/plot) is a Poet. He has the Welsh voice of Dylan Thomas. You hear *Under Milk Wood* as he speaks. That voice is his greatest gift, just as Liz Taylor has a face and body to launch a thousand ships and mount the topless towers of Ilium. "Sissy Goforth is not ready to go forth yet." Liz is like Cleopatra - she has imperial longings. She is also (like so may TW women) a neurasthenic par excellence and a hypochondriac to the nth degree. Amazingly the film has touches of *L'Avventura* about it - the mystery, the meaninglessness, the impossible quest, the search, the setting even, a rocky island. "Your body has more warmth than most men have." Burton/Taylor here act at the summit of their powers. 122" She says "Is this a time for kissing?" ... and kisses the Angel of Death, for that is Burton's Wagnerian alias. Liz is not only the world's greatest hypochondriac, she also has vertigo, living as she does at the top of that steep-cliffed crag. Almost a touch of *Black Narcissus* here, a peculiar kind of etiolated, sublimated eroticism. And Liz is obsessed with diet and pills. Liz: "Come to my bedroom. I have lots of art treasures in my bedroom ... (long pause) ... including myself." It's pure kitsch. Language in this film is measured, stylised in TW's best mode, the better to reveal the titanic love-death struggle between the couple. This film is hilarious as well as wonderful (like *L'Age d'Or*). "If you have a world-famous figure ... why be selfish about it?" As if she is being interviewed for a Hollywood magazine. And then all that Death Talk. Not go forth and multiply, but GO FORTH and DIE. And she does, spitting blood in high consumptive camp, a veritable Dame aux Camelias, a true disciple of Keats and Kafka, her hankie becoming a paper rose (TW's words no doubt). As if that were not enough, we get an Assisted Suicide

Theme in Burton's last speech to his dying partner. And the last word is BOOM. So now we know. It is not a French School Party with Sophie Marceau (BOUM). It is death, infinity, life, mystery, the unknown. The TW play is "The Milk Train Doesn't Stop Here Any More", produced on Broadway. A friend reports that TW thought this script was the best of his to be filmed (better than *STREETCAR*?!). *BOOM* was made in Sardinia and Rome.

Bergman *THE PASSION OF ANNA* Sweden 1969
I had a very fruitful morning watching *The Passion of Anna* from 7 to 9. Mellow September air wafted in through the open front door. The film actually moved on from *Persona* - with Bibi and Liv carrying on the agony. Idea of the month: Passion is both Desire and Suffering (Liebestod, Life versus Death etc). Liv has the passion, appears to believe in Life (against the others who are broken, cynical and manipulative). But it is possible that her passion, which appears so sincere and authentic, is itself a mask to cover her failure (she was driving the car which crashed, killing her husband and child). Strong stuff - with the positive and negative dialectically enacted with an absurdist ending smacking of black humour - but all a delight to watch. According to DVD Times, the English dvd has a short scene of a dog hanged on a tree, cut by the BBFC. Why is Pudding Island so paranoid about animals and children - the only sacred objects left on this benighted island? (9 September 2007)

Fassbinder *WHITY* West Germany 1970
Just seen this. It is one of Fassbinder's best. Strangely enough it is not without affinities with Russ Meyer's *Black Snake* (1973) - in content that is, not in *mis en scene*! Hanna Schygulla at her best, and that's saying something. The thing was so strong I had to take it in bite-size bits. Oh yes, the blonde wife of the white plantation owner was a bit like Anouska Hempel in *Black Snake* - i.e. a cool racist white trash sadist and Brigitte Bardot look-alike to boot. Fassbinder's theatre of cruelty excels

with the most-ever lashes of the whip on poor Whity (the black bastard of the family), the most-ever standing-up kisses on the mouth from Hanna, and the most-ever slaps on the face I have ever seen on film. I was in stitches of laughter, both of delight and derision. The film is obviously *sui generis* unique, a western with a House of Atreus script and touches of the Strindbergs all over the place. All the whites ask Whity, Fassbinder's long-term gay lover and the blackest character in the film apart from his wonderfully blacked-up mother and household cook, to kill all the other whites. And so he does, leaving no one, except of course Hanna, the saloon Kitty who plays the biggest and most beautiful white-trash whore the other side of the Mississippi. Hanna has fucked every one. Whity has killed every one. In the only possible sublime ending the couple embrace and dance in the desert to the sound of the music which is hauntingly mesmerising throughout. I am now going to lie down in a darkened room. PS - the French subtitles were easy enough to follow as people tended to speak slowly or not at all! (15 February 2008)

Jires *VALERIE AND HER WEEK OF WONDERS* Czechoslovakia 1970

Themes: fantasy, play, mischief. Valerie: sexual awareness following her first menstruation does not destroy her serenity. Images of Valerie are of unchanging beauty, innocence and mischief. Links: Blake, *Alice in Wonderland*, Prevert. Tcho: vampire feeding on chickens and young girls. A phallic-shaped sharp-toothed weasel. The repressive power of male authority. A reassuring father figure. A potential lover. A vicious rapist.. A nobodaddy, father, priest and policeman. Orlik: Tcho's son. Valerie's brother and boyfriend. Actor, artist, poet, minstrel. Grandma: clockwork doll, with bible and rosary. Looks after Valerie. Prefers missionaries to actors. Is also Elsa, a vampire and victim of Tcho. Is also Valerie's mother. Is also aggressive threat of female sexuality, offering lesbian temptation. Topics in the film: All are sexual beings. Sexuality is masked by repressive structures of authority and religion. Play as disorder versus ordered behaviour. Art versus morality. Childhood versus adulthood. Actors versus missionaries. Poetic surrealism versus socialist realism. The Happy End: A haunting lullaby, reminding me of (a) the end of Kafka's *Amerika*, and (b) the Cindie song at the end of *The Edge of the Park* (uncut). (a) is dialectically ironic, i.e. a consummation devoutly to be wished, a satire and celebration of the American Dream, the Hollywood Dream Factory and Hollywood Babylon, and a piece of black humour. (b) is a disturbing commentary on the rape, slashing and murder of young girls in a banned video nasty. And yet, ultimately: In *Valerie* there is no irony, no satire, only an aesthetically achieved utopia of escape from the Russian tanks. Discuss?! I did not see any of this at first viewing. You've got to pay attention, open the doors of perception, let Los in, banish Urizen, and then you'll discover one of the most amazing pieces of imaginative cinema ever committed to celluloid. As the genial Jonathan Rosenbaum puts it: "This film is a collection of dream adventures, spurred by guiltless and poly-sexual eroticism. Virtually every shot is a knock-out.". The actress plays Valerie as a 13 year old having her first period, and is herself 13. The story is based on a poetic novel by Nezval, a communist surrealist from the thirties till his death in 1958 (even under Stalinism!). The film was hugely influenced by the set designer and mother of the Czech New Wave, Ester Krumbachova. She is responsible for the feminist vision beyond Jires's usual male fantasies. She was Nemec's wife. Angela Carter was apparently greatly influnced by *Valerie* and its vampires. Valerie's week of wonders may be only a week, like the Prague Spring, but has its roots in Blake's innocence, via Prevert's surrealism, plus the genuine (non-escapist) naive, like Douanier Rousseau. (September 2008)

Alexander Kluge   THE OCCASIONAL WORK OF A FEMALE SLAVE West Germany 1973
The importance of this film has been acknowledged, as a piece of marxist-feminist agit-prop arising out of the everyday life

of an ordinary couple (see Ed Howard in *Only The Cinema* 28 April 2010). The film is marvellous, with its Engels and Brecht wittily and modestly displayed. The only problem for the squeamish (or we'd better say the sensitive female spectators) is that it shows a real abortion in close-up, near the beginning. I can only suggest closing your eyes (not leaving the cinema to be sick on the pavement, as has happened). It is arguable whether the abortion sequence is necessary. The heroine, Kluge's sister, Alexandra, is not having the abortion, she is simply a part-time nurse being exploited by an unscrupulous doctor performing illegal operations. Abortion had not yet been decriminalised in West Germany (though it had in East Germany). I think it probably is important to include the graphic detail, as it might demythologise the bigotry and panic surrounding the issue. In any case the film as a whole is an aesthetic and ideological feast. And it chimes with Fassbinder's magisterial critiques of the West German economic miracle. (9 June 2010)

Makavejev *SWEET MOVIE*
Yugoslavia/Canada/France/Wet Germany 1974
Certificate 16 (France).
Banned by BBFC 1975, DVD (USA) 19 June 2007. Carole Laure - Miss Canada, Miss Monde 1984. According to Ebert she walked out of the film, so disturbed was she by the Otto Muehl scenes. She also sought legal suppression of certain shots (would that be the chocolate masturbation?). Laure was asked by Makavejev to slit a sheep's throat and refused. She was mainly a singer, very famous in Canada. She had an absent father and a mother who committed suicide. Pierre Clementi (heavily disguised) was the Potemkin Sailor (cf. his roles in Buñuel's *Milky Way* and *Belle de Jour*). Anna Prucnal (Anna Planeta, Captain Ann, Marxist paedophile and mad killer) was a Polish singer and actress working in Paris. For appearing in this film she was banished from Poland for 15 years. Anna's father was a Jewish Gipsy murdered by the Nazis. Sami Frey (*Bande à Part*), extremely heavily disguised,

was El Macho, the Latin singer and lover at the Tour Eiffel. Mr Kapital was played by the famous Canadian actor John Vernon. Otto Muehl, leader of the Vienna Aktionists and the Therapie Sex Kommune (see documentary *Slaves in Paradise*), later denounced the film as "downright kitsch"! Muehl's films of the late 60s and early 70s can be accessed on the internet. The 38 IMDB user comments on *Sweet Movie* are mostly full of admiration, though none of them quite gets to the bottom of things. One Brazilian bloke calls the film eschatological - I think he means scatological! Ebert (surprisingly) admires the film but ultimately rejects it as cold and lacking in Catholic humanity. The striking musical score is by a Greek friend of Theodorakis apparently. Excellent choice of super-virgins, Miss Southern Rhodesia, Miss Congo, Miss Canada. Excellent pro-Canadian joke with Miss Canada revolting against Mr Kapital. Excellent pro-Serbian joke with Miss Yugoslavia refusing to obey instructions. The film was apparently banned in Canada (but not in France?). Makavejev's *Mysteries of the Organism* (1971) had been banned in Yugoslavia in spite of its non-aligned position (neither Moscow nor Washington). Erotic/pornographic highlights in *Sweet Movie* include naked woman in chocolate soup totally exposed (combining hard-core taboo with satire of commodity-fetishism, therefore intellectually and sensually stimulating an amalgam of art and porn); and the marvelously degrading striptease over the cool kiddies (making a point that children have a right to be represented in a context of polymorphous perversity that has nothing to do with sex-abuse-panic, so ridiculously controlled in Pudding Island by the so-called Children Act). Makavejev seems also to have achieved that combination of the marvelous and the ridiculous, the passionate and the absurd, the high and the low, the cortex and the cunt, which was the concern of the Surrealists. As Amos Vogel (quoting Otto Muehl I think) writes: only intelligent pornography can cure our genital panic.

CAPSULE REVIEWS

Chantal Akerman *JEANNE DIELMAN* **Belgium 1975**
Reputedly Akerman's chef d'oeuvre, this is the successful minimalist film par excellence. Nothing, but nothing happens (until right at the end), so why and how are we riveted to the screen? One reason must be that the eponymous heroine is Delphine Seyrig. She plays the lead, she is on the screen all the time, in her small flat where she performs household tasks, sends her son off to school and entertains men as a part-time prostitute. We never go through the bedroom door. We get two hours of Delphine Seyrig, aged 41, keeping things clean and tidy. Behind her are those mysterious iconic roles in Resnais' *Last Year in Marienbad* (1961) and Buñuel's *The Milky Way* (1969). Now she is a husbandless Brussels housewife performing mundane tasks, mainly over the kitchen sink. At the end of these two hours Jeanne Dielman's grip begins to relax. She starts dropping a couple of things on the floor. The slow fuse of suspense quickens, and this film which is the *ne plus ultra* of minimalism *a l'etat pur* (as they say in Latin and French) still withholds its hammer-blow of an ending. All I will say is that it never flags (though the viewer might), that there is a hilarious scene with a baby which you cannot not laugh out aloud at, and that the end is as strikingly wonderful as the end of Catherine Breillat's *Perfect Love*! Extras: Self-interviewed, Akerman does a Godard, revealing only what we all wanted to know - yes she is a Polish Jew. Of course she couldn't be simply Belgian with all that talent. She has to be a member of that chosen race which of all the peoples in the world has risen from the ashes of Auschwitz into the utopian workshop of great art. But there is also a Behind the Scenes (as they call it in Hollywood), photographed with amateurish obstinacy by Sami Frey himself. Here we have the marvelllous spectacle of our Chantal, short, squat and plump with short dark hair trying to direct the tall, blonde, ethereal and utterly superior Delphine Seyrig. Seyrig still has the voice from *Last Year in Marienbad*, arcane, delphic, disembodied, as she peels the spuds, boils the kettle, makes the beds and does the shopping. And Delphine wants to know how and why, she

wants motivation, she wants psychology, to be comfortable in her movements and gestures. And Chantal just grins, like the Cheshire cat, not really knowing what she wants, 'cos she's the young artist with minimalism in her soul. It's as if our Chantal is taking mischievous pleasure in not getting Seyrig to understand, and then also in getting her sublime actress to perform mundane tasks in the kitchen. And then, out of the blue, Delphine Seyrig utters a brilliant manifesto of feminist aesthetics. Notice well. She says "All women are feminists. Otherwise you should kill yourself." Our Delphine, of course, when she was 14, had no other way than to wear make-up, attract men and play the divine diva, but she thinks that if she were 13 now (1975) she would give all that up and become a real person, not a femme fatale on a male pedestal - and in a final touch of realpolitik - "Perhaps". Not many people have seen Akerman's most ambitious film. Why? (12 April 2009)

Brownlow *WINSTANLEY* GB 1975
In 1649, just as the absolute monarch Charles I was being executed, the first commune was established by Winstanley and his Diggers in Surrey. This film recreates the rise and fall of that commune with almost antiquarian attention to detail. The radical politics here celebrated is coloured with the spirit of 1968, as the gentle hippie protesters attempt to influence the Cromwellian authorities, are disturbed by an incursion of punkish Ranters, and eventually cruelly dispersed by local landowners and presbyterian clergy.

Richard Fleischer *MANDINGO* USA 1975
This is amazing as you say, on racism and miscegenation. It's not at all an exploitation movie, or disgusting as it was often called. It's a moving and serious investigation of slave culture. It was presumably hidden from us because it was seen to be in bad taste and not appropriate for politically correct liberal-humanists. Did you like the ending - the only time the slaves threw off their abject passivity and fought back? For those who like fights, the fight between the two slaves was pretty

spectacular, and ideologically contextualised. In sum, *Mandingo*, fearless in its shameless cult of perversity, had touches of those two other films we watched which provoked strong feelings about racism, Fassbinder's *Whity* (1970) and Russ Meyer's *Black Snake* (1973). *Mandingo* (1975) completes an amazing trilogy. (13 March 2010)

Louis Malle *BLACK MOON* France 1975
Greatest film seen this year. Pure magic. Owing a lot to *Alice in Wonderland*, and with a 15 year-old actress Cathryn Harrison, who was Rex Harrison's granddaughter, and much later married one of R.D.Laing's sons. *Black Moon* is up to the high standard of the Jires-Krumbachova *Valerie and her Week of Wonders*. It has the most wonderful munching unicorn, a bed-ridden grannie with a pet rat, Joe Dallesandrio and Alexandra Stewart (Malle's erstwhile flame pregnant with his child) cavorting in the park, and much more besides, especially lots of naked little children playing with sheep and pigs, and to cap all these improbable wonders, the singing of Tristan's *Liebestod* by really solemn serious little children. In this Malle film you cannot believe what you are seeing. So, once again the question arises - why did this film bomb publicly and critically, why have we had to wait a whole generation to enjoy its creatively polymorphous perversities? (18 July 2009)

Peter Weir *PICNIC AT HANGING ROCK* Australia 1975
Just watched a documentary on *Picnic at Hanging Rock*. Peter Weir the director reminded me of both Peter Brook and Peter Watkins (quite a trilogy of Peters). In manner and speech very engaging, sensitive and articulate. Peter the Rock. On the 'mystery' of the book and film, two opinions stood out above the mystery-accepting consensus. Thus. Patrick White had rung Weir up and said of course it was all about Lesbianism. And the very artistic-looking artistic director reckoned it was about some woman's business that was beyond the male imagination. What no one mentioned was the affinity with Sagan's *Maidens in Uniform*, especially with reference to the

Headmistress in both films being a dessicated phallic woman of fascistic proportions. Both women Heads are left stranded failures in the end of both films. (1 July 2008)

Karoly Makk *ANOTHER WAY* Hungary 1981
Operating in the space opened up by Marta Meszaros' *The Two of Them* (1977), Makk pursues the theme of friendship between women. The free-spirited journalist Eva represents a 'double perversion' (Makk's own phrase): she is both lesbian and political dissident in the years following the 1956 Hungarian uprising. Makk's film is a poised, sparkling and trenchant study in nonconformity as Eva struggles against both the dead hand of Stalinism and the dead hand of her friend Livia's marriage - with tragic consequences. Jadwiga Jankowska who plays Eva won best actress prize in Cannes (1982). Both actresses had to be imported from Poland in the absence of any Hungarians willing to play lesbian parts. Western audiences tend to read this film for its sexual politics, but in the context of the advanced thaw in Stalinism taking place in Hungary in the 1970s and 80s (a thaw which would lead inexorably to the fall of the Berlin Wall), *Another Way* has also to be read as a critical reflection of that (utopian) progress towards socialism with a human face. For Makk, sisterhood and lesbianism are as much metaphors as subjects in their own right.

Margarethe von Trotta *GERMAN SISTERS (DIE BLEIERNE ZEIT)* West Germany 1981
Just revisited this film. Where Trotta, a robust socialist feminist, got the Von from God knows. In case you haven't seen it, it is one of the strongest films I've seen. It appears even stronger after seeing the Fassbinder political trilogy gathered around the Baader-Meinhof phenomenon. Barbara Sukova plays the Gudrun Ensslin character. Trotta uses the Bergman *Persona* super-imposition trick, to great aesthetic and ideological effect. Julianne, the feminist journalist, is visiting Marianne, stuck with Baader-Meinhof types in West

Germany's newest high-tech high-security prison. Their faces are superimposed via the glass barrier through which they must speak to each other. The dialectic between the sisters, their enormous solidarity and difference, mostly in the film a tragic hostility, is wonderfully embodied in the Bergmanesque image. Amazing stuff. That Trotta was the sexy chambermaid in Fassbinder's *American Soldier*, then married to Schloendorff with whom she co-directed *The Lost Honour of Katherina Blum*. She seems to have ended up in Paris. I reckon *German Sisters* is even better than *Rosa Luxemburg*. Why is it not known in Hollywood Babylon? Especially as it is a fine accessible political film (*Time Out*), with plot, flashbacks, family history, personal and political. The epilogue, with Gudrun Ensslin's small son being almost burnt alive by children who thought his mother was an evil terrorist, could be seen as a redundant *longueur*, but it certainly makes you feel and think. Incidentally, when Julianne is trying to find out whether her sister really committed suicide in prison, she is told by a dominant male that all that stuff belongs to the 70s, and that the things to stir people now (1981) are Islam, the energy crisis and the Third World! Mightily prophetic. (23 February 2008)

Mike Leigh HOME SWEET HOME GB 1982

This is an accomplished satire on domesticity and dysfunctional family life. But don't you think that his characterisation of social workers lapses into trite caricature beyond anything he ever did to the ruling class? The woman social worker was cringingly offensive and at a pinch accurate, but the male social worker spouting official textual jargon from those quasi-marxist manuals of the 70s was so over the top that one got the impression that Mike Leigh really hates social workers with a venomous irrationality worthy of a Swiftian persona. 'The Mechanical Operation of the Spirit' in *A Tale of a Tub* comes to mind. Since the film ends with an endless parody of leftist case-con logorrhoea, I wonder whether Leigh, like Swift's persona, is not himself deranged! (25 April 2009)

Losey LA TRUITE France 1982
Did we know that Losey worked with Huppert? I didn't. Here she is aged 29 looking 15 playing a simple peasant girl. She can do that as well as pretty well damned everything else. As Frederique she wears a t-shirt with *PEUT-ETRE* on the front ... and ... wait for it ... *JAMAIS* on the back - a SCUM-like manifesto of the metaphysical cock-teaser-cum-ultra-instinctive feminist. Losey had wanted to make this film in the 60s with Brigitte Bardot but couldn't raise the money. And so Bardot morphs via a generation of feminist revolution into our Huppert, as pert and cunning in her naive persona as a character out of a Voltaire novel on the discontents of western civilisation. At 52" she bares her tits to a fat old dirty peasant in the barn - for money. There's an uncanny oblique connexion between this film and Blier's *Les Valseuses* (1974) if only because Isabelle Huppert and Jeanne Moreau are in both. Huppert is a 16 year old sexual rebel in both. Moreau is killed in both films, bludgeoned to death by a jealous husband in *TROUT*, committing suicide with a pistol shot to her vagina for existentialist reasons in *VALSEUSES*. Huppert and a bevy of peasant lovelies parade their sexual charms in their CLUB OF CAREFREE GIRLS. Huppert has another ideologically charged t-shirt with *CHASSE GARDEE* on the front and *CHASSE INTERDITE* on the back. The girls lift their t-shirts, show their tits to the shrine and stick pins in the dirty old man's picture, two in his eyes, one in his groin. Transferred from La France Profonde to Cosmopolitan Tokyo, Huppert carries on her games with rich international capitalists (globalised fish farms are the name of the game) - removing her kimono to stand stark naked before us all. Oh, I forgot to say that the opening scene shows Isabelle squeezing the semen out of the trout into a bowl for breeding purposes - an innovative way of capturing the attention of jaded cinema goers. At 122" Huppert and Moreau form a sisterhood diptych that is as central to the film as the diptych Liz Taylor-Mia Farrow in Losey's *Secret Ceremony* (1968). The older more

mature Moreau tells Isabelle that "Today heterosexuality and homosexuality mean nothing ... You're either sexual or you're not." Their sisterhood hints at a militant feminist film - in 1982 all men are crap, fishes to be fished in a fish farm. But there is a more conventional thriller plot to the film with lots of action, jealousy and murder. The ending on first viewing is problematic. In spite of the revolutionary/nihilistic consciousness of the women, nothing actually changes. We simply move from a peasant economy to a vast globalised conglommerate - Fish Farm International as American, Norwegian, Japanese and French plutocrats enjoy the fruits of their capitalist enterprise. AND poor old Jeanne Moreau is slaughtered in Trotsky fashion by her worthless husband - a real creep played by Jean-Pierre Cassel. What does it all mean? We all know Jeanne Moreau is beyond compare. And we all know Isabelle Huppert is the greatest living actress in the world. She is mercurial - compare her in *Les Valseuses*, in Chabrol's *Ceremony* with Sandrine Bonnaire, second best actress in the world, in Ozon's *Huit Femmes*, in Chabrol's *Violette Noziere*, in Chabrol's *Affaire de Femmes*, in *The Piano Teacher* - never quite the same face, always different, a genius, playing all the tormented women of the universe, and apparently happily married with three chidren in real life... etc etc. BUT did we know that the blessed Joseph Losey had both Huppert and Moreau in his film just two years before his death. That man was always older than he should have been, all his films made between his forties and his seventies. But then that's because he was working in the theatre as a young man with Brecht in the days of Roosevelt's New Deal before those premature anti-fascists of the American Communist Party were infiltrated and blacklisted by the Unamerican McCarthyite terrorists who forced Losey, Chaplin et.al. out of the land of the free. So *The Trout* gets an A- from me.

Istvan Szabo COLONEL REDL Hungary/West Germany 1984

The key to Szabo's relationship to his material is this. Given that he worked for the Hungarian equivalent of East Germany's Stasi and was a first class filmmaker, we must conclude that Szabo was Mephisto and Mephisto was Szabo. It all fits in. In this perspective *Colonel Redl* is a tour de force. The Ruthenian Redl, having sold his little ethnic minority austro-hungarian soul to become a secret agent in the service of the imperial authorities in Vienna, Arch Duke Ferdinand charges him to find a scapegoat to cover the political problems of the Empire. He is told not to touch the Austrians (too much part of the establishment), or the Hungarians (respected secondary part of the dual monarchy), or the Czechs (too spikily rebellious), or the Jews (don't want to annoy the international community), or the Serbo-Croats (far too combustible, especially in Bosnia/Sarajevo), so the only race left in the massively ramshackle Austro-Hungarian Empire to target is the Ruthenians, and that ends up being Redl himself. So, suicide. So Sarajevo, Redl's boss, the Archduke assassinated. So the First World War. This is a wonderful study of a moribund empire. Funny that Szabo calls it a liberal empire, given that the Archduke sees the main enemy of his regime as Liberalism. Perhaps it all links up with Kafka and Hasek who lived and wrote in Franz Joseph's Czech lands - liberal totalitarianism, a suitable case for comic-cum-surrealist treatment (unlike Hitler's Germany). Szabo is a solemn man, not quite in tune with those insubordinate absurdists Kafka and Hasek, Nor does he have the subversive poetic lyricism of Jancso. Still, Colonel Redl has a very neat plot full of brutal ironies as the net closes in on our Ruthenian outsider. Hoist with his own petard, the logical end of Redl's rise to the top is for him to top himself in a parody of Christian service and sacrifice. Szabo is an excellent analyser of the police state, and in all his great films, especially the *Mephisto* trilogy, he illustrates the compromises, complicities, betrayals that mere mortal flesh must make to survive in the totalitarian states of middle-europe. (28 December 2010)

CAPSULE REVIEWS

Mike Leigh *4 DAYS IN JULY* **GB 1985**

This is arguably the best thing Leigh has ever done, far surpassing the oh so worthy work of Ken Loach, and leaving the wretched *Hunger* in the sewer of its own formalism. This is Mike Leigh's genius, to steer a course between formalism and art with a tendency. It is unbelievable that most of us have had to wait 24 years to see this masterpiece (yes, I have just seen it for the first time). It is different from anything else he's done. The age-old Irish Question has never been better addressed (and with Shaw, Yeats, O'Casey, as well as Loach, looming influences behind him, that is praise indeed). Highlights must be the two songs – 'The Sash My Father Wore' for the Orange people (as powerful as the Horst Wessel song for the Nazis), and 'The Patriots' Game', sung for the Green people by a heavily pregnant Nationalist Molly Bloom type character, in bed, to her disabled husband. There was the right balance between the two factions, but no liberal objective humanism. We know that Leigh is on the side of the Catholic mother, who named her baby with the Irish version of Margaret. We know he is less enthusiastic for the Protestant mother who names her baby Billy, after her UDA husband and the original King Billy, that 1689 deliverer from the bondage, who mounted his horse, chased away the ghastly James II at the Battle of the Boyne, and guaranteed our English civil liberties. Yes, this film was distinguished because it worked through real ordinary people, their faces, their speech-rhythms, their being locked into the necessity of their respective causes. Don't forget. Get hold of Mike Leigh at the BBC. (25 April 2009)

Marco Bellocchio *DEVIL IN THE FLESH* **Italy 1986**

Have you seen this film? It's an adaptation of the Radiguet novel, updated to an Italian setting at the time of the Red Brigades. It has the most convincing fellatio in a mainline film I have ever seen - starring Maruschka Detmers, a stunning Dutch actress who easily matches Emmanuelle. She has that open, transparent and sincere face which is as Dutch as a

143

Dutch interior, with no lace curtains, naked and unashamed. Her blow-job is straight out of Rembrandt or Vermeer. (13 March 2010)

Kahane *THE ARCHITECTS* East Germany 1990

Thanks Richard for putting me onto Kahane's *The Architects*. I thought it was fairly average as film, but historically it was a unique piece of work. It was the last film made in the DDR, and while it was being made the East Germans were haemorraging to the West via Hungary, and the Berlin Wall was about to be demolished. In the real world, fiction is taken over by documentary reality, but Kahane has to stick to his DDR script. So, unintentionally, by force of circumstance, the reel of the film melts into the real of history. As Kahane puts it, 'Real life had a better plot'. When the film was finished, no one wanted to see it, 'cos it was out of date, and everyone was busy converting East German marks into West German marks. The absurd piles upon the absurd. Ignored by the public, the film won a prize at the last DDR film festival. And so, the film was the victim of changes it had sought to trigger. Apart from all that, the film addresses the analogy between cinema and architecture, as projects subject to delay, revision, compromise. "Tomorrow was happening yesterday" sums up the amazing conjuncture behind the production of *The Architects*. Poor old Kahane and his reform-minded communist comrades had then to find their feet in a unified Germany, and his film was not shown on TV until 2003, and then only on a provincial channel. I ought to watch the film again to see if you can detect on the faces of the actors any trace of the knowledge that their project was being undermined by external events, (4 November 2009)

Kirchell *BERKELEY IN THE SIXTIES* USA 1990

This is a well-organised, comprehensive documentary survey of the central planks of the American counter-culture, from the Free Speech Movement on the university campus, through the anti-Vietnam War protests, Women's Liberation, Black

Power and Gay Liberation. The documentation is not only just wonderfully militant, but also incorporates strong doses of self-criticism about what was done and what was not done. The remembrance of things past by participants in the struggles adds a salutary sense of personal and political development over a generation. (17 April 2010)

Sautet UN COEUR EN HIVER France 1992

Some remarks on the paucity of reality in French bourgeois cinema with special reference to the Sautet/Auteuil clique. Ever since I identified Daniel Auteuil as a star actor in Michael Haneke's *Hidden*, I have wondered what he stands for, how he operates, and what it all means (given that I found *Hidden* politically and aesthetically repugnant). Having bought Sautet's *Un Coeur en Hiver* with the aim of watching Emmanuelle Béart in one of her early films. I was confronted with Auteuil in an even more significant role as a puke-making man of conscience, a veritable Prince Hamlet of heroic indecision, masquerading in our enlightened generation as the feminised mind. My immediate conclusion was that this film was made by someone who either knew or chose to know nothing of Buñuel, let alone the SCUM Manifesto. It is a truism that the whole of western civilisation is founded on wilful or accidental ignorance of these two radical sites of the sex-pol imagination. But there was more to it than that, or at least middle-class refinements and nuances were more self-evident in Sautet's film than in Haneke's. These qualities were brazenly paraded on the dvd cover of 'this award-winning classic of modern French cinema', as 'cool and elegant' (*The Guardian*), and 'oozing quality'(*The Independent*). What a treat for the British left-wing intelligentsia: Daniel Auteuil embodying the essence of bourgeois kitsch. Auteuil is the caring sharing, restrained and conflicted, politically correct male of the species, a veritable *Guardian* reader (or in his case *Le Monde*). Concern with a big C is etched on his forehead. But that Concern (a favourite word incidentally of those bourgeois politicians who promise everything and deliver nothing) is in reality Guilt and Hypocrisy. Auteuil oozes sincere hypocrisy (a far greater flaw in human nature than the more common hypocritical sincerity). Confined by the Gentility Principle (cf. Alvarez on *The New Poetry*), Auteuil cannot admit what is written on his silly face in close-up, i.e. that he wants to fuck Béart. That this modesty comes across as caring and concerned (is he aspiring to be a New Man?), is partly due to the ghastly character in the film who is actually fucking Béart's character, a man whose excessively mechanical sanctimoniousness embodies the most obnoxious traits of bourgeois intellectual self-satisfaction. This creature, redolent of Restoration Comedy and Moliere, a powerful player in the world of violin restoring and musical performance, stinks of officer-class hypocritical sincerity. After all he possesses the body and soul of the most sexy and artistic woman in all Paris. A truly ghastly scum-bag that bloke who wears Béart's cunt on his arm. And plot-wise he is the only *raison d'etre* for Auteuil to be consumed with jealousy. But, just a moment, I hear you say, you have misconstrued, you have like Diogenes lost your marbles, is not Daniel Auteuil the perfect specimen of bourgeois normality and bourgeois morality, a man for all seasons, a role-model for our time? Well, I'll let you choose. For me, his normality is the normality of Mayakovsky's Bed-Bugus Normalis to which we all aspire because we have failed to be revolutionary enough. As for Béart, she is simply the Eternal Feminine. Forget Helen of Troy whose face launched a thousand ships and burnt the topless towers of Ilium. One movement of Emmanuelle Béart's eyelash provokes phallic erections in all around. She acts with her face, with no need to display those naked charms which form the subject-matter of *La Belle Noiseuse*. A Béart glance, that divine pout, does the trick. Auteuil's face (as in *Hidden*) is so full of false consciousness, masquerading as conscience, sensitivity and general willy-wet-legs whimsy that it takes on the shape of a naked prick. He's forgotten to put on his underpants. He is a Pickwickian Prufrock in liberal-humanist-unesco-humanitarian-aid-amnesty-international disguise. Hence the power of his appeal to the thinking woman. The give-away line: Auteuil to Béart (who questions whether he is listening to her): "No, I love to watch you talk." Béart, at least, has some common sense, when she tells Auteuil: "If it was to get at your friend, you should have fucked me". Yes, but Auteuil has no real friends and can't fuck. Fucking is what the violin restorer impressario and Svengali does to Béart, his restored sexual instrument. As Béart says to Auteuil "You have no imagination, no heart, no balls." Daniel Auteuil appears to have missed out on the Dada movement. He combines a Buster Keaton deadpan face with the most mobile darting eyes ever committed to the silver screen since the days of Cary Grant. The final twist of the knife. "Daniel Auteuil est habille par Christian Dior." Well thank God for that! (26 June 2010)

Patrick Keiller *LONDON* GB 1993

A gem to prove English cinema is alive and well. Behind the genteel documentary format and dead-pan commentary (beautifully delivered by the impeccable Paul Scofield) lurks a vicious critique of Thatcherism and all its works. Without apparent irony (thanks mainly to the Swiftian device of the persona, a kind of latter-day Robinson Crusoe, content to observe the surface of things), the sweetness of a banal travelogue turns into a sour vision of a lost world. Composed of a series of (often still) camera shots of unlikely and unprepossessing scenes, buildings and places, this film owes a lot to the tradition of the *flaneur* (originating with Baudelaire and perfected in the early 20thC in Louis Aragon's *Paris Paysan* and Walter Benjamin's *Arcades*). What Haussmann did to Paris and Thatcherism to London was not absolute, and Keiller's camera broods lovingly over the debris.

Mary Harron *I SHOT ANDY WARHOL* USA 1995

Thank God for Mary Harron who dares subvert the post-modern cool of Andy Warhol and all his hangers-on. The punk heroine is Valerie Solanas, sole author and distributor of that most extreme feminist declaration, the SCUM (Society for

Cutting Up Men) Manifesto (1967). Solanas it was who took a pot-shot at Warhol. And in this film she weighs into the shadowy unreal post-hippie Warhol set with dazzling crazy feminist brio. She is hard and real, angry, witty and wise, and above all spikily paranoid in a world of pretentious sixties zombies. A more than worthy successor to Frances Farmer. Like Frances, Valerie was committed to a radical cause. Like Frances, Valerie ended up committed to a lunatic asylum. That can happen to communists and feminists in the USA. *I Shot Andy Warhol* gives us a brilliant take on the sexual politics of 1968, superstars galore, an enervated Andy presiding over his factory, and a score by John Cale.

Vera Belmont *MARQUISE* France 1997
I have done extensive research into Marquise Therese du Parc, an actress who married an actor and slept with Moliere and Racine and danced for Louis XIV. She is played by Sophie Marceau in Vera Belmont's costume drama film *Marquise*. The film is particularly stunning in showing the arrogant sang-froid of a showgirl plucked from the taverns of Lyon by Moliere's travelling company. Becoming the woman for whom Racine wrote *Andromaque*, she is shown forgetting to put on her knickerbockers before doing an intimate cartwheel dance in front of the King's nose. And her freewheeling libertine spirit adds considerable zest in the form of a pipi-kaka dimension to this august and well researched historical drama. Louis XIV's morning shit is accompanied by scores of servants and arse-wipers; and a courtly lady standing up by a pillar, on being asked what she is doing, says with casual aplomb, "I am taking a piss". All in all this is a very superior costume drama, a fascinating reconstruction of the theatrical world of Corneille, Moliere and Racine, and one of Sophie Marceau's most accomplished efforts. Of course, since *La Boum* (1980), Sophie's precocious genius has always seemed so effortless. According to Vera Belmont, Sophie Marceau was allowed not to attend rehearsals, so self-assured was she. (2 January 2010)

Pawlikowski *THE STRINGER* GB/Russia 1997
Well, everyone admires *Lives of Others* - except me. So, assuming I was too high-brow, I am going to have another look at it. I happened to see *The Stringer* in the same 24 hour period, and I did get very manichaean about a comparison between the two. *Stringer* has practically no publicity on the net - most missed it when it was on BBC2 recently. I watched it next morning while my car was being serviced, and was convinced it had all the qualities *Lives of Others* lacked - wit, grip on the realities of the post-Gorbachev oligarchs, and subtle (or even crude) symbolism against the wretched neo-capitalists who gambled away the infrastructure and culture of the Soviet Union's heritage. Pawlikowski's film was Rabelaisian, Swiftian, and all in Russian, made for the BBC way back in 1997 I think. Whereas the Stasi film was Hollywoodian - pro-American by innuendo (hence its Oscar) with the most ghastly musical score evocative of the most tedious formalism. And, like *Hidden*, it psychologised the political in a way that has become fashionable under the influence of post-modernist chic. *Stringer* by contrast carries its heavy political message with gorgeous ludic levity. (30 September 2007)

Lukas Moodysson *SHOW ME LOVE* (aka *FUCKING AMAL*) Sweden/Denmark 1998
Agnes (Rebecca Liljeberg), the 'dark-haired smart loner' is absolutely fabulous, locked in her own sovereign self, emanating teenage angst and poetically luminous lesbianism. Elin (Alexandra Dahlstrom), the 'bitchy blonde babe', is superbly realistic and confused as she oscillates between tribal zombiedom and a tentative capacity to look for and find something new in and for herself. Yes, this film has the 'freshness and surprise' signally lacking in Larry Clark's *Kids* (1995); and yes, the boys and parents live in the dumbed-down everyday world of shit that surrounds us all. This film is utterly without sensationalism, sentimentality, or liberal

humanist apology. Like Vigo's *Zero de Conduite* (1933), *Fucking Amal* is a revolutionary call to arms. When Agnes and Elin kiss in the back of the middle-aged man's car, there is a frisson of mad love, a joy that raises orgasmic tears. When Agnes and Elin literally come out of the closet (the school toilet) there is real sexual politics (so much more believable than the ridiculously trite sensational ending to *Thelma and Louise*). Hollywood changed the title of this film and Hollywood feeds pap and crap to our English youth. This film invites us to lift our eyes to the hills. And it has had a salutary influence on later projects, including the almost equally fresh and surprising debut film from Celine Sciamma, *Water Lilies* (2007).

Laurent Cantet *HUMAN RESOURCES* France 1999
This film stands half way between *I'm Alright Jack* and *Germinal*, but is arguably more sensitive and militant than either. It is nothing less than a communist film for our time. Cantet (unfashionably perhaps) chooses a CGT trade unionist as his militant heroine (a communist *pur et dur*) rather than someone from FO or the CFDT (socialist organisations). The film takes place in a factory, the conflicted hero is a bourgeoisified prole promoted to HR manager, and Cantet's work is far more moving and emotional than Godard's cartoonish *Tout Va Bien*. Factory occupation is the order of the day, updating the political tactics of 1936 and 1968. There's a nice little review of the film on the World (i.e. American) Socialist Web (a Trotskyist 4th International site). The film is saturated with those unfashionable values of class-consciousness, class-struggle and class-war, all registered by the device of the Human Resources angle at the human and humane level, with family and factory commitments wonderfully intertwined. And (university teachers and managers generally please note) the plot is all about the use and abuse of questionnaires! In these days when managerialism and all its tricks go without saying, it is both

surprising and pleasing to come across an intelligent radical film which carries on the spirit of Chaplin and Eisenstein.

Francois Ozon CRIMINAL LOVERS France 1999
This achieves what Trier's *Antichrist* signally fails to deliver. It is a witty, gay evocation of cannibalism, babes in the wood, and primeval horror. (18 February 2010)

Kimberly Peirce BOYS DON'T CRY USA 1999
'Does Lana know Brandon is a girl? She knows, yet she doesn't know, because she doesn't want to know.' (Roger Ebert). I agree with Ebert. This is a great film, not because it is about a transsexual, a lesbian, a cross-dresser or any other politically correct cliche of sexual identity, but because it is about a girl who thinks of herself as a boy. This 'sad song about a free spirit' (Ebert) is also a utopian protest against the psychotic sexism and homophobia of average American manhood. And yes, it did really happen, in rural Nebraska. Both Chloe Sevigny (Lana) and Hilary Swank (Brandon) are stunning in this portrayal of the scrambled mess that makes up American social, family and sexual relations. The desire for something else ends up in the most horrifying violence. Welcome to the USA.

Bergman THE IMAGE MAKERS Sweden 2000
The Image Makers is a great Bergman film, comparable to *After the Rehearsal* and *Saraband*. It's a chamber piece, like *After the Rehearsal*, but with some of the serious family angst of *Saraband*. It is brilliantly constructed like a well-made play, and is the only Bergman film I have seen where the young enfant terrible actress swears like a trooper. The Nobel Prize winner novelist is played by what they call Sweden's most famous stage actress, Anita Bjork - aged 77. She is fantastic. How can you be so brilliant when you're 77? The young actress is Elin Klinga. The dialectical fireworks between the two - tenderness, cynicism, hostility, attraction - are marvellous to behold. *The Image Makers* is truly hot stuff. The

young actress fucks like a rabbit, the old novelist has never had sex. As Bjork says to Klinga: 'You don't write what you know, you write what you want to be'. Shades of Emily Bronte I thought. Another insight from the old-timer: 'Art is to transform life's filth'. And there's more than a touch of Dreyer about Bergman's film - the question of resurrection. Elin Klinga is not quite as flauntingly sexual as the young ingenues in *After the Rehearsal* and *Saraband*, but she's even more successfully histrionic (and, for the anoraks, she is the granddaughter of Anders Ek, the tragic hero of *Sawdust and Tinsel*. (15 February 2008)

Mary Harron *AMERICAN PSYCHO* USA 2000

Thank God for Mary Harron who dares subvert Bret Ellis's macho-fantasy of guns, girls and gore into the very black humour of another Scum Manifesto for cutting up men who cut up women. Perhaps only the woman who gave us *I Shot Andy Warhol* could have taken on the task of turning the pornographic story of everyday Wall Street yuppiedom's trip down psychotic lane into a feminist film. Designer-chic misogyny has never been so brilliantly sent up. Don't believe those critics who argue this film is about 80s Reagonomics and therefore dated. It is about man-made language. There is no word for the opposite of misogyny or phallocrat. After all, how can anyone hate men? Luckily for us Mary Harron did not use Leonardo DiCaprio for her scary hero (he thought his fragrant image might suffer considerable financial loss). Instead she found the well-named Christian Bale (a Welshman to boot!).

Catherine Breillat *A MA SOEUR* France 2001

Another feminist diatribe from the maker of *Romance* will not please the politically correct liberals who dictate the taste of the chattering classes. Breillat at her best is always perverse. And some critics have appreciated that *A Ma Soeur*'s nasty ending is not so much a willful *deus ex machina* as a logical and liberating trope which completes the thesis that even in these enlightened days love in the experience of women is too often indistinguishable from rape. In the long *cinéma vérité* sequences of sexual activity, we as spectators (or voyeurs) are forced to be complicit in the utterly realistic 'love-making' between the 15 year-old Elena and the 20 year-old Fernando. Our own sexual desires and behaviour are graphically called into question, aided and abetted by the critical eye of Elena's 12 year-old sister Anais (the eponymous 'fat girl'). Breillat comments: "Elena asks Fernando to lie to her, then she actually lies to herself. That need for a myth of love is a mental rape. At 15 there's no loss of dignity in having had sex, but there is a loss of dignity in having to lie." Whether you accept Breillat's thesis or not, this film is always thought-provoking and is guaranteed to shatter the received ideas and illusions of all who have struggled theoretically and practically with that strange conflation of brutality and liberation which characterises sexual politics in our epoch. (Posted by John 2 March 2011)

Peter Watkins *THE COMMUNE* France 2001

This amazing film is accompanied on the dvd by a typical Watkins passionate polemic, shot in a park near Vilnius, Lithuania where the old statues of Marx, Lenin and Stalin have been stored. Watkins looks forward to a time when there will be a Globalisation Park, full of TV screens, Hollywood blockbusters, McDonald Fast Food outlets, and, of course the film director's persecutor and bete noire, the BBC - all of them to be consigned, like their redundant communist predecessors, to the dustbin of history. Funny though, there's a paradox here, because Watkins abominates above all what he calls Monoform, and he knows that he is unable to break out of that Monoform even when addressing us on his dvd. You know, I met him a couple of times in the UK (Aberdeen and Hull) and enjoyed long conversations with him about his work. He is a dyed in the wool melancholy pessimist. It always amazes me how he summons up the energy and faith to make all those innovative, revolutionary, epic films. Suffice to say that *The Commune*, with its scrupulous attention to historical detail and its creatively anachronistic evocation of present-day class-struggle in France, is a worthy companion to that film in which Watkins excels himself, *Edvard Munch*. (29 June 2008)

Richard Curtis *LOVE ACTUALLY* GB 2003
For the attention of Mark Kermode. I am writing because your remarks to Simon Mayo on Radio Five Live coincide with remarks I have just made to someone who simply asked me why I liked *Love Actually*. I felt I must rise to the occasion of such serendipity by sending you my remarks, mainly because, if I remember rightly, you were unable to rationalise your liking. Since I share your dislike of the Curtis fellow and enjoy (usually) your Radio Five Live intransigence, allow me to tell you why I liked *Love Actually*. Just looked at first five minutes after heavy session on *Wild Strawberries*. So, I like *Love Actually*, 'cos it's the England we know and hate. Because it's ironic and scattered with obscenities that belie the jolly old hypocrisy of Perfidious Albion (aka Pudding Island). Because Richard Curtis (albeit a purveyor of Cow and Gate crap) is no fool and was probably educated at the same schools and universities as me. Because it's a feel-good film that takes the piss out of feel-good films. Because the word "actually" is what all English bourgeois people say in every sentence of their humdrum lives. Because Nighy (whom I hate as an actor and person) takes the piss out of pop music and disc jockeys. Because the nauseatingly smooth luvvies, Hugh Grant, Colin Firth, Emma Thompson, Liam Neeson (to name but the ones I've heard of), and the ghastly floozie and would-be Hollywood show-off Keira Knightley are all there to see in all their stupid glory. And, above all, because Hugh Grant (as Tony Blair) puts down and does one-up-manship on that nauseous ex-Methodist Bush. Nice piece of British patriotism that (of course the reverse of the actuality) - appeals in equal measure to Left and Right. PS Incidentally there's a real odd piece of anachronistically unintentional irony in the first five

minutes, when Emma Thompson says in an off-hand way to Liam Neeson: "Oh, I forgot that your wife has just died."[NB Liam Neeson's wife, Natasha Richardson, died in an accident in 2009]. No copyright on my reasons for liking a Curtis film. But it, and you [Kermode], give me light relief from my Easter duty of watching the Chantal Akerman box set. Yours most sincerely, John Hoyles, Hull Film Society.

Claude Miller *LA PETITE LILI* France 2003

A film that is not what it pretends to be. It pretends to be a clever updating of Chekhov's *Seagull*. Its production values as such are adequate and aesthetically pleasing. It is actually a vehicle to present the gorgeous physical attractions of Ludivine Sagnier, which are manifold enough to raise the dead and tickle the moribund. Typically the America program notes highlight the opening scene as one of the steamiest sexual encounters in film, and fetishise the Chekhov connexion to satisfy the intelligentsia. Much could be said of the transformation of Chekhovian tragedy into a latter-day feel-good film. But the bottom line is that the film is wonderful if you want to ogle Ms Sagnier, and rather pitiful if you want some Chekhov that is more than a warmed-up dog's dinner. Of course I might have got it all wrong with my twisted taste. Miller is a good director though he is somewhat self-deprecating in calling himself 'conventional'.

Marziyeh Meshkini *STRAY DOGS* Iran 2004

Brilliant second film from Samira and Hana's mum. She has learnt from Samira's *Apple* and Hana's *Buddha*. This is Afghanistan seen through the wide eyes of a seven year-old orphan girl. (18 February 2010)

Sally Potter *YES* GB 2004

Dear Sally Potter, I am moved to contact you after viewing the dvd of *Yes* last night in our regular film society meeting. We were truly dazzled by your film and want to let you know how brilliant we found it. We had a choice between some

Ozon, some Kluge and some Antonioni, but because it was April 23rd (St George, Shakespeare, *England's Dreaming* etc.) we voted to see a proper English film to celebrate our national day and to prove to ourselves (hopefully!) that Truffaut's badinage about English Cinema being a contradiction in terms was not true. We just loved the cleaning lady - that must be one of the best beginnings in world cinema. We just loved the haunting yet often invisible rhyming verse. And we just loved the last Communist in Belfast. And we were totally persuaded by both ideology and aesthetic, radical and true. Situations (as Sartre would put it): Brilliant use of Harrison *V* style in the kitchen sink episodes, only wider, broader with greater variety of regional and national accents and age-group. Haunting echoes of poor old T.S.Eliot's attempts to write plays in verse (*The Family Reunion*, as well as *Murder in the Cathedral*), and of translations of Aeschylus and Sophocles. Bizarre echoes of Roy Andersson's *Songs from the Second Floor*, that daring to be kinky/silly *mis en scene* (eg the husband's dance). Gorgeous homage to *A Brief Encounter* in your reworking of a much more serious brief encounter. A touch of Denis Potter daring to be silly to get the vision thing. Overall a poetic reworking of material that could have been done differently by Mike Leigh and Ken Loach. This gave me a little echo of Tony Richardson's *A Taste of Honey* where the poetic vision lifted the film above its naturalistic setting. This amounts for me to your attaining Voyante status, like Virginia Woolf at her best, like Rhoda in *The Waves*, like the great Emilys - Bronte and Dickinson. It is that magic that transmutes the raw material of our world (so richly documented in your themes). It would be invidious to pick one out, but what really shook us up was the confrontation between Western Feminism and Eastern Anti-Colonialism, and especially that wonderful dwelling on the attraction and repulsion of the sexualised half-dressed American blonde icon. Wonderfully evoked dialectic between Taliban and Hollywood. What we don't understand is why this film is not better known in the country and world at large. We want to shout out: English cinema is not dead, there is Ken Loach, there is Mike Leigh, and there is Sally Potter. I do hope this message gets to you. We are in a provincial corner, but we love good cinema and we love you for making it. Sincerely, John Hoyles on behalf of Hull Film Society (last communists in East Yorkshire).

Susan Streitfeld *FEMALE PERVERSIONS* USA 2004
Just watched this film attentively on the computer. It is a great film, absolutely magnificent. Tilda Swinton is superb, must be her best performance ever. The whole thing has a manic yet controlled intelligence. I just love the pussy lipstick ('Le Minou Rouge'), the 'Licence to Flirt' badge, 'You're a Woman, You've got the Curse', 'Show off your Assets', Maddy to Eve: 'Will that give you the Big Daddy Dick you've always wanted?", 'First thing you've got to remember is it's all about Power, you've got to be everyone's Dream' (striptease woman), and above all this: Eve: 'I blew it. I'm not married.' Maddie: 'What does being married have to do with being a Judge?' I've ordered the book from Amazon, it is reviewed as large and rambling, with some incoherence, but overall brilliant and thought-provoking - over 500 pages. Why is this film (and book) not acclaimed as up to the standard of Bergman and Fassbinder? That itself is a perversion. I'm still unable to comprehend (or explain) the use of the word 'perversion'. What the film purports to tell us is this: 'In a perversion there is no freedom only a rigid conformity to a gender stereotypy.' I feel we need a woman to enlighten us.

Jessica Nilsson *ALL ABOUT ANNA* Denmark 2005
This is a brave if misguided attempt to do woman's porn in a straight story line. Jessica Nilsson was hired by Trier's Zentropa to set up a centre for producing such cross-over films. Superior to what Orwell's Porn Sec in 1984 was churning out, it is full of interesting and annoying contradictions. Thus the leading actress did not want to show her private parts and operates the Marie Forsa method of

having sex on camera but with the naughty bits hidden from view. The sex is open, raw and frank enough. Viewers may however take most delight in a cameo lesbian scene with the intellectual French porn star Ovidie who went all the way to Denmark without having to do more than heavy petting. (14 July 2010)

Vittoria   ONE BRIGHT SHINING MOMENT: THE FORGOTTEN SUMMER OF GEORGE MCGOVERN   USA 2005
A really bad mouthful of a title. But this is a heart-breaking analysis of how the Democratic Party redeemed itself after the 1968 Chicago Convention debacle, and incorporated the brightest themes and hopes of the counter-culture at the 1972 Miami Convention, only to lose it all to the fiendishly evil Tricky Dicky (Richard Nixon). Compare Milton's *Paradise Lost*. In 1972 McGovern and his re-formed utopian Democratic Party were too enthusiastic to be well-organised. McGovern's Miami Convention speech (one of the greatest in American history, they say) was broadcast at 2am. No one saw it! So you see, the Society of the Spectacle rules, and if you don't get your TV scheduling right, you are cast into outer darkness. 1972 - one of the ads that propelled Tricky Dicky Nixon to power was a jingle that went like this: "DON'T CHANGE DICKS IN THE MIDDLE OF A SCREW - VOTE FOR NIXON IN 72." 1972 - Gore Vidal opines: "I was brought up in the ruling class. They hate the people." God bless America. Vote posh - you know it makes sense. (18 April 2010)

Jasmila Zbanic ESMA'S SECRET (GRBAVICA / LAND OF MY DREAMS) Bosnia-Herzegovina 2006
This is a powerful film, economical and well-organised. It adds much to the stuff I already have on the Bosnia Rape theme. There is Dizdar's startlingly original and paradoxically feel-good *Beautiful People*, where the English doctor cannot get his head round the byzantine quarrels in the Serbo-Croat Balkans, and simply cannot understand why the rape victim

doesn't want her baby. Making comedy out of atrocity - that's clever. And there is of course the Bosnian Rape Poem in *The Vagina Monologues* - a strong piece of lyrical feminist agit-prop. The mother is brilliantly done and the 12 year-old daughter is terrific and never over the top. After all those dazzling artistic Serb films, it is salutary to find a Bosnian (Muslim) take on the war. Aren't those Sarajevo muslims just the most secularised and multi-cultural we ever get to see in this Talibanised world. The film was funded by Croatia, Austria, and probably Germany. It got its prize in Berlin. And as someone erring on the Serb side in these matters, the Zagreb-Vienna-Berlin axis was for me somewhat irksome. A better title might have been 'To Sarajevo with Love', in recognition of its affinities with *Hiroshima Mon Amour*. It is after all a sensitive, personal, humane film, devoid of tribal partisanship. The personal is of course political in the feminist sense, far from the internecine squabbles of Balkan men. (27 May 2008)

Catherine Breillat *UNE VIEILLE MAITRESSE* France 2007

Watched the new Breillat three times. For me it is among her best. I rate it with *Une Vraie Jeune Fille* and *Romance*. The sex in the film is gorgeous, enhanced by sweet disorders in the dress - for it is what is loosely termed a costume drama, one of Breillat's only literary adaptations, following quite faithfully the scandalous 1851 text of the ultra-conservative Barbey d'Aurevilly. Breillat makes both protagonists androgynous. The close-ups are sublime. Asia Argento is a miracle, going over the top and getting away with it as the greatest femme fatale since Louise Brooks. There's a triptych when they are in a unique sexual position, at right angles across each other's bodies, left her gloriously hirsute armpit, centre her eyes and lips, right the man's fetishised foot in extreme close-up, I kid you not. The framing device (at start and finish) is nicely constructed with Michael Lonsdale and his ancient mistress indulging the foibles of the young generation from their 18thC pre-revolutionary libertine perspective. And the device of the grandmother getting the young lover to tell his story of the femme fatale and the sober fiancee in extensive flashbacks is well handled. And she belongs to the world of Laclos, the world of dangerous liaisons, of sophisticated cynicism, yet tempered by some intervening romanticism. My only concern was how to believe Marigny was sincere in the protestations of love for his new wife Hermangarde. I didn't recognise her as Roxane Mesquida, the cock-teasing sex-pot from *A Ma Soeur*, so disguised was she in blonde wig and pinched pious features. Apparently Breillat and Barbey d'Aurevilly intended the dialectic between wife and mistress to be even. In the film however Asia Argento's fleshly charms are so exquisitely flaunted that there can be no contest, except of course that the marriage is one of economic convenience. Barbey d'Aurevilly was an ultra-catholic monarchist libertine. His book was banned. His supporters included Flaubert and Baudelaire, whose books were also banned. Breillat had a history of being banned. But here at last she comes out into the delicious sunshine of a Republic of Letters that is in the best tradition of French culture - and all that achieved under the handicap of partial paralysis following a really bad stroke. (2 September 2008)

Karslake *FOR THE BIBLE TELLS ME SO* USA 2007
American Christian homophobia at its evil best. The other side of the counter-culture. The New Hampshire first gay Episcopalian bishop had to wear a bullet-proof vest. They shoot faggots over there. (17 April 2010)

Peter Kosminsky *BRITZ* GB 2007
Britz was a four hour fictional documentary on the vexed question of the place of Moslems in British society. Excellent on Channel Four, now out on dvd. Attacked on IMDB for being treasonable, it invites you to sympathise with a female suicide bomber. I agree in a way, 'twas very subversive of *Daily Mail* values. Have you seen Britz (wordplay on the Blitz, I assume)? 'Twill advance discussions on the vexed issue of

lyrical terrorism (a young Moslem woman was recently charged with terrorism for writing a lyrical poem). In my opinion (am I being ironical do you think?) *Britz*, like the Blitz, is an enemy subversive of the British State, and should be banned. It asks us to choose (or side with) one of two positions. Do we support the Yorkshire Moslem sister who becomes a suicide bomber in London? Or do we support her upright brother who works hard against racial prejudice to get a job as a British secret agent? Everything's in that film, including scenes in Rawalpindi, rendition torture, forced marriage, and anti-terrorism laws in the UK. Kominsky's work is even better than the similar fictional documentary *Sex Traffic*, a Canadian co-production which accused American agencies and UN officials of organising the sex trade - from Moldava, via Romania, Serbia, Bosnia, Albania, Italy, England. Another sorry tale to whet the palate of arm-chair voyeurs who like their strong sensations to be tasted at arm's length. Britz, even more than *Sex Traffic*, is a radical reminder of the bloody mess we live in and which we call civilisation. (5 January 2008)

Celine Sciamma *WATER LILIES* France 2007

Latest from me is that *Water Lilies* is a first-rate film, comparable to *Fucking Amal*, only more subtle and nuanced. It is also comparable to *A Ma Soeur*, indeed in a creative way derivative of that masterpiece. It combines lesbian touches (carefully developed with geat sensitivity) with the Breillat thing about mad love being discrepant with losing one's virginity, the challenges of being too beautiful or too ugly as a teenage girl, plus the brilliant characterisation of the central protagonist who is neither obviously beautiful nor obviously ugly (unlike her two best friends against whom she is the piggy in the middle). She is, rather, sensitive, inwardly stubborn, cool on the outside, hot on the inside, with a seriousness which transcends the trivia of schoolgirl bagatelles. When you start watching the film you think it's going to be a pedestrian rom-com about the trials and tribulations of a synchronised swimming team in a French school. It soon becomes deeper and more interesting. The scene where the team leader, so popular and attractive that she has the reputation of being mature and sexually experienced, gets our heroine to help her lose her virginity, is a unique example of the solemn and the absurd meeting under the bed sheets (hence off-scene, because not seen, but we see the sheets moving). (2 October 2009)

Sokurov *ALEXANDRA* Russia 2007
Film Society Report. I need to correct the bad experience we had with Sokurov's *Moloch* by serving as advocate for *Alexandra*. Certainly *Moloch* was for me a damp squib, and *The Sun* 2005 was hardly any better. I guess his so-called trilogy on Hitler (*Moloch* 1999), Lenin (*Taurus* 2001), which I've not seen, and *Hirohito* (*The Sun* 2005) are just failed experiments, marred in my view 'cos they are depoliticised whimsies marked by a stagnant minimalist formalism - understandable historically of course given that Sokurov was somewhat persecuted under the Soviets (like Tarkovsky and Paradjanov). But *Alexandra* is something else. It's a fairly gripping film in which the minimalism is put to good use, squaring with the central character's stubborn plod through the army camp. In a nutshell it's a war film. But the film never mentions Chechnya, though it is clearly demonstrating the effect of the Chechnyan War on the Russian soul. And Sokurov, in his interview, never mentions Levinas, and yet the whole weight of the film is an application of the philosophy of Levinas as it relates to war and killing, i.e. you cannot kill if you make eye contact with the enemy. I've always thought Levinas was an old Jewish moralist, resurrected to justify the humanitarian ideology so fashionable since Bosnia. Indeed I believe the wretched Bernard-Henri Levy espouses this so-called New Philosophy in his books and stands against leftist intellectuals. Even as I copy this passage the news is that President Sarkozy led the invasion of Libya (March 2011) prompted by the said Levy. The whole thing reeks of Unamuno's liberal neutrality over

the Spanish Civil War, and more universally Julien Benda's *Betrayal of the Intellectuals*. Still, the new politics and the new philosophy is important, is fashionable, is being practised. So, although it was I think Nizan (the independent communist) whose *Watchdog* refuted Benda from the left, it is perhaps instructive to analyse a recent film which embodies Levinas so thoroughly. Sokurov himself states that those who put the political before the humanitarian are criminals. And this is the message of *Alexandra*. Only, as one might expect, it is a message grounded in the forms and faces we see in the film. And it was actually filmed in Chechnya, with the threat of terrorism ever present to the whole film crew. 'There is no place in the world where there is no war', says the composer of the film's musical score - he was aiming for a kind of Requiem for Beslan. So, let's give Sokurov another chance to redeem himself. Let's put *Alexandra* on the Film Society menu. The central character, grandma of one of the soldiers, played by a famous opera diva, evoked Mother Courage. In this her first film role she is magnificent. (6 November 2010)

Dennis Gansel *THE WAVE* Germany 2008
This is the terrifying experiment that went out of control, based on the work of Ron Jones in the USA. Gansel presents his film as a didactic educational effort to warn German youth of the dangerous attractions of autocracy (i.e. neo-nazism). It's a well-made film full of suspense as the students go beyond their role-play as lovers of autocracy to becoming full-blown neo-nazis. Their teacher is a well-intentioned anarchist who cannot control the forces he has unleashed. Highly entertaining and thought-provoking. The kids/students are very convincing. The lesson is loud and clear. Or is it? When does acting become action? I guess *The Wave* is a didactic parable. The realism did seem stretched at times. But hey, tinpot fascists abound - especially in school playgrounds. Witness 9 year-olds whose ultimate bullying insult is "GAY!". I think the mass psychology of fascism is everywhere endemic - especially in our society of the spectacle - in TV game shows,

audience applause, and the assumption that we all share the same banalised taste. So, horse-racing is fetishised, horse-eating is taboo - at least in Pudding Island it is. Totem and Taboo, as Freud wrote, is all around us. We are little savages under the crust of civilisation. The repressed will return. The sleep of reason is more than a Goya painting. In Latvia they celebrate the end of World War Two and Hitler by decorating Waffen SS officers. And I remember the Billy Graham Rallies, mass hysteria for Jesus. (10 May 2010)

Mike Leigh *HAPPY GO LUCKY* GB 2008

Saw new Mike Leigh film *Happy Go Lucky* last week in multiplex shithouse. What are we to think of Poppy, the happy-clappy primary school teacher, who unfortunately sounds and looks and acts like the wretched Alison Steadman in *Abigail's Party*. At first I thought Poppy was a repressed psychopath, but, no, she was apparently just a happy poppy, facing all of life's little problems with the happy-go-lucky twitching felicity of a fresh social worker cum infants teacher. The two blokes who chaperoned me to the multiplex had similar reservations, but expressed them less trenchantly. The driving instructor was the only person I identified with - he was a grumpy old git, a woman-hater with psychopathic tendencies and a touch of the nightwatchman's apocalyptic rant in *Naked*. (2 May 2008)

Jane Campion *BRIGHT STAR* GB 2009

Who killed John Keats? Well folks it wasn't Jane Campion. Her *Bright Star* is well above average and measures up to her best work (*Sweetie*, *Angel at My Table*, *Holy Smoke*). Some notes I made watching it early this morning. The film appeared self-assured and modest at the same time. It was always wanting to be watched. It did some justice to Keats and was sufficiently daring to provoke tears. At first I thought it was carving out some territory between Pickwick and Alice, between whimsy and vision. The stitching (graphic fact and metaphysical metaphor) was however *sui generis*. The stitching was nerdy, obsessive, domestic hobby-horse, at once safeguard of economic independence and of strategic virginity/frigidity in the material world of young women like Fanny, as well as a symbol of creative manufacture and suffering (women's work). It was Kate Millett in *Sexual Politics* who signally put her finger on the phenomenon of 19thC strategic frigidity (see her discussion of Sue in Hardy's *Jude*). Campion, a savvy woman, knows her stuff. But what was that strange initial close-up image? It looked like a sharp knife about to plunge into some flesh-like material. Some viewers may have been distracted by this enigma into thinking of the last image in *The Trial* by Franz Kafka (like Keats a TB victim) when Joseph K ends up knifed in a ditch. Who knows? As for the whimsy, it could be justified as grounded in the everyday activities pertaining to early 19thC Hampstead Village - stitching to earn some money, keeping up with London fashion, listening to an orchestra playing Mozart. We think that life has moved on from that, but has it? Why were the Brawnes speaking French? To sound posh, like the aristocrats in *War and Peace*? Toots, Fanny's younger sister, is a hoot, and greatly helped Campion turn a corner of NW3 into Wonderland. Toots was a curly redhead who resembled the alienated deviant Sweetie and the young Janet Frame in *Angel at my Table*. And she was an angelic brat in the best tradition of the cute gamine (cf. Chaplin's films). The field full of washing and the blown curtains were wonderful to behold. A tea break. So, Mr Brown was Keats's real spouse, always there (except when he spawned a bastard baby with the gorgeous Irish maid Abigail, which prevented him from looking after Keats at the end). Always there, trying to get rid of the wretched Fanny whose fleshly presence he regarded as a threat to poetic inspiration. And Brown was the *homme moyen sensuel* (like Joyce's Bloom), the practical worldly Boswell to his impossibly visionary Dr Johnson. Brown was also for me, by coincidence (or objective chance as the surrealists had it) a kind of prosaic opposite to the poetic Keats - reminding me of that other Mr Brown in Joyce's 'The Dead', whose lugubrious presence at the

Christmas festivities symbolises the Belfast Protestant minority among the green Catholic Dubliners. Brown is Orange! A dismal commercial type at odds with the lax merriment of those green Dubliners who are already dead. An unnamed Mr Brown also appears in that other story of Irish paralysis in *Dubliners*, 'Eveline'. He is from Belfast, knows the price of everything and the value of nothing. He makes money building boring modern houses for Protestant entrepreneurs. And Fanny is a tease, but only because she has to be given the sexual politics of the age. Coyness comes with flirting. And Fanny, as Keats would put it, teases out of thought. Keats was just as coy. He struggled manfully with the female body (as when he only just manages to get his woman undressed in 'The Eve of St Agnes'). The phrase 'ripening breast' ripples through Campion's film. What a phrase - redolent of that mellow fruitfulness to come in the ode 'To Autumn'. Proust, observing Albertine's naked sleeping body is teased out of thought by those small breasts which seem to have been added like fruits to the androgynous body. And it is not enough to say, well, he would wouldn't he, he was gay. Heterosexuals like Keats can see the same mystery. And so, Keats is stuck between a rock and a hard place, between Mr Brown and Fanny Brawne. Kafka and Keats both begin with K. And both died of TB. Fanny was Keats's Belle Dame Sans Merci, in one of the greatest poems ever written. FB is Fanny Brawne. FB is also Felice Bauer, Kafka's impossible fiancée. Hampstead Village NW3 has a poor neighbour, Kentish Town. Keats looked into Chapman's Homer. I have looked into Campion's *Bright Star*. I am as pleased as Keats was. Jane Campion has stitched us a great film. (14 March 2010)

Soderbergh *THE GIRLFRIEND EXPERIENCE* USA 2009
Soderbergh is not a great director, but can do interesting stuff. Sasha Grey also acted in another straight film in 2009, *Smash Cut* by the Canadian Lee Demarbre. So it's not clear that *GFE* was her first outing into legitimate cinema. Anyway one was made before the other but was released after the other I

believe. Sasha is the only one who can act in *Smash Cut*, which goes against the purpose of the film, which is to have fun making a bad film with bad acting. Still Sasha features in the extras quite abundantly, and she is very modest, obedient and brave. As for *GFE*, tis cool, esoteric, opaque. Very cool. Sasha eats a lot in posh restaurants, munching otherwise than in her porn day job. *GFE* resembles *American Psycho* in style and content. But with the woman as agent, not victim. Above all *GFE* made me think of Daniel Defoe's *Moll Flanders*. Cos there is the same emphasis on sex and business as transactions. Defoe deals with a prostitute at the time of the 18thC South Sea Bubble, Soderbergh with a high-class call-girl at the time of the Wall Street Crash (1998 that is, not 1929). In both Defoe and Soderbergh there is the sense of adventure, venture, venture capitalism, risk-taking, speculation, calculated risk, the monetary value of sex, even the sexual value of money. In both there is the question of identity, the playing of roles, exchange, clients, enterprise, business, careers, life as a series of transactions, the importance of appearance, clothes, decor, make-up. All of which raises questions about sex and economics, commodity-fetishism in modern society. Soderbergh is clever, and perhaps lucky in associating Sasha's search for a niche market with the Wall Street crash. Ebert has a very bright piece on all this on IMDB. The ending is a puzzle to me. Why is her last client an old Jew whose trembling while embracing Sasha's almost naked body is very moving suggesting a reality beyond the routine transaction? And there is talk of gold and diamonds (presumably because the money market is most unsafe and the banks are bankrupt!). Well, there is one other point to make. Sasha Grey, by coming out of her own porn ghetto, creates an effect (clearly desired and engineered by Soderbergh) whereby the un-porn becomes by strange alchemy a new porn, a sublimation devoutly to be wished, as if the 1934 Hays Code had just been imposed. Sasha is clearly the same woman we can see in her porn films, and this creates a frisson that is quite palpable, as well as a rare revelation that not all porn stars are dumb bimboes. The woman can act, and will presumably go on to direct. Finally, it has to be said that Sasha more than holds her own in the twin audio commentary with Soderbergh. If anything Sasha's intelligence outshines Soderbergh's plod. The film is no masterpiece, but, because of Sasha it is fascinating, very low key, quiet and yet far-reaching.

Trier *THE ANTICHRIST* Denmark 2009
"Contains no material likely to offend or harm". Thus the BBFC on Sally Potter's *Gold Diggers*. Hooray! What other complex art film has received such a Kansas-pleasing accolade. As for the Von Trier, well .... I was expecting something worth writing home about, and was particularly interested in Charlotte Gainsbourg's prize-winning performance and the presumably ludic-cum-ironic-cum-faux - metaphysical world-view of the Great Dane. My attention was not compelled in this film and was forced to suppose that our Charlotte won a prize because she is a French national icon, for she was no better than her mum in her dad's kinky film *Je t'aime moi non plus*. Jane Birkin was good in that one. Having had high hopes I have only negative things to say about *The Antichrist*. And this was compounded by the dvd extras, where the Great Dane came across as a stammering Billy Bunter with the speech rhythms and mentality of a maiden aunt. Is this a reality or a pathetic persona. I don't know. This is Trier's equivalent to Moodysson's *Hole in the Heart*. So - a misfired attempt to shock everyone with some of ·the tired nostrums of pseudo-horror movies. So - lots of meandering mush (from *The Blair Witch Project*) punctured by only two graphically revolting shots - one a close-up of a nasty wolf (scared the shit out of me), the other a close-up sequence of scissors clipping the clitoris (which was quite daring, but left you asking questions about the prosthetics - therefore no better than the castration in *Ai No Corrida* or Breillat's prosthetic penis in *Sex is Comedy*.) The dvd extras were invariably formalistically specialised contributions - and that even includes Charlotte's cool comments on how emotional

nakedness was more traumatic than physical nakedness. And then the credits - like the lighting of the lamps in Eliot's *Preludes*, ridiculously routinely massive, as if the whole universe had contributed to the wretched bagatelle. And the film! Why Anti-Christ? Where? How? I saw not the scintilla of an idea which had anything to do with either Satan or Christianity. There were some paltry references to antique misogyny (eg. *Malleus Mallificorum*), but none of the narrative oomph and ideological paradoxes of *Breaking the Waves* or *Idiots*. The metaphysical intention failed utterly. So that it was possible for me to find Dafoe do a far superior performance in *Tom and Viv* than here. And, photographed at Cannes, Dafoe looked like a vacuous chump from the silent era with a silly Harold Lloyd hang-dog visage. And so of course the Richardson woman in *Tom and Viv*, though constrained by a more conventional narrative, was performing better, and was more interesting than the wretched Charlotte. Who could have thought that the couple in *Tom and Viv* tell us more about this waste-land of a world and ourselves than Trier's capriciously ponderous spout! Poor Charlotte - a genius in *Charlotte for ever* and *L'Effrontee*. My nasty anti-celebrity mind wonders whether her decline owes something to her marriage to the abysmal Yvan Attal! So, it seems that *Antichrist* is marketed as a horror movie - that perhaps explains why the bouffant Exorcist-loving Kermode likes parts of it. But, oh BBFC, your knickers are, as always, in a twist. "Contains strong real sex"? Perhaps my eyes are dim I cannot see I have not brought my specs with me. But this sounds like Clinton's definitions vis-a-vis Monica Lewinsky. All I saw was Charlotte naked on her back doing a very manic wank. This had some dramatic relevance to the plot, but was piss-poor as real sex compared with the fierce naked dance Zulawski got Valerie Kaplinsky to do in *La Femme Publique*, or (wank-wise) what Claudine Beccarie does in Davy's *Exhibition*. All I can say is that, after watching *Antichrist*, should you require therapy, you should do what I did, watch Tilda Swinton in *Female Perversions*. Now there's a film that mixes materialism and metaphysics on the sexual politics front.

CHAPTER NINE: SCRAPS

Agora and Hypatia

Yes, the *Guardian* reviews do make Amenabar's *Agora* (2009) interesting, especially if Hypatia's persecutors are linked with Taliban types. Something like that is evident in Charles Kingsley's *Hypatia* (1863). With my book-reading sisters, I decided that Kingsley was prepared to confront those early Christians in his novel, because he, as a Christian Socialist and proto-feminist, had more in common with the pagan neo-platonist lecturer Hypatia than with the ghastly Talibanic forbears of his own Christianity. Hypatia was murdered in Alexandria's market-place (agora, in Greek) by a lynch mob of early Christians. When the Christians took power in Rome, they had already made Hypatia a non-person, wiped her from the pages of history and replaced her with an invented saint, St Catherine of Alexandria. tortured by nasty pagans on the legendary catherine wheel. This substitution of a mythical Christian Saint for a real pagan woman means that to do justice to the heroine of *Hypatia* and *Agora*, all the Catherines of this world should rename themselves Hypatia. (23 April 2010)

Another Kind of Cinema

Jean-Andre Fieschi on Straub in Richard Roud's *Cinema: A Critical Dictionary* (1980), p.969: "A kind of cinema could be imagined which would sell nothing, which would not consider the spectator as a customer, which would not lure him, nor flatter, nor despise him, nor seduce him, would not rape him, or put him to sleep, a kind of cinema that would be the exact opposite of advertising." (10 May 2010)

Artur Aristakisyan's *Palms*

Palms is out now. Its director is a Russian anarchist hippie visionary, with a real practical woman companion looking after his place in the system. He is against the system, all systems, with a Jewish mother and Armenian father (thereby a double victim of genocide), raised in Kishinev (Moldovia). And look out for his second film, a documentary on Moscow hippie commune, *A Place on Earth*. His style links with *Los Olvidados*, *Down and Out in Paris and London*, Bataille and Genet. (5/9/2007)

Asia Argento *Scarlet Diva*
So astounded was I by Asia Argento - interview on her *Scarlet Diva* dvd - wow, wow, wow - then audio commentary on her first film as director - that after you left me today the stuff was so strong, exciting and brilliant that I could only manage the first 40 minutes. I was knackered with pleasure. Best commentary ever seen by me. What she reveals is obscene in the sublimest sense of that word. That would be worth discussing in a proper Film Society - half way through the film she says things she felt when in suicidal mode, but which are belied by the absolute abject beauty of her eyes, lips and armpit, lipstick smeared over her face as she licks her own armpit in front of a mirror, filmed by herself with no one else present thanks to digital camera. The aesthetics of female display and male gaze transcends the intentional fallacy of confessional suicidal misery. Beauty is truth. Keats knew it. And he was so young. Would a woman see what I have seen? (1 October 2009)

Autumnal Films
Mai Zetterling's *Girls* (1968) was a revelation. Utterly fantastic, with wonderful montage between Lysistrata as a Greek play, and 60s Women's Lib. Like *Loving Couples*, it needs to be seen several times. Can't understand why it's only available in the USA. As for *Night Games* - that will be like waiting for Godot. Since *Girls* (*Flickorna*) we have watched *Autumn Sonata* - for the third time in my case - so I am now convinced it and *Persona* are the best of all Bergman. Also we saw *Haxan* (1922), cobbled together in Copenhagen for a Stockholm company.

Banned and lost for generations and rediscovered in a cupboard in a Swedish mental hospital. Am still waiting for conversation about comparison between *Lives of Others* and *The Stringer*. The German film is a bit like Haneke's *Hidden* - over-psychologising of the political, with false solemnity and over-reliance on technical suspense effects. Really, *Lives of Others* told me nothing about the DDR, nothing about the cross-over between sex and politics, and simply paraded a Hollywood gloss with ghastly post-modern music. Whereas *Stringer*, a film in Russian by an anglicised Pole for the BBC, deals, with great wit, symbolism and nonchalance, with the Russia of the post-Gorbachev oligarchs. (24/9/2007)

Bergman and Fassbinder
Joyce said Swift was stern and Sterne was swift. Fassbinder is stern and swift! If Bergman is golden, Fassbinder is black. If you like the idea that Swift is black and Blake golden, then Bergman and Fassbinder are the contraries without which there is no progression. They carry the Swift/Blake dialectic into new territory. (16 December 2007)

Bergman's Last Things
The great revelation at the end of the Bergman Collection season was how brilliant his last two films were - *After the Rehearsal* and *Saraband*. The first was even tighter than *Winter Light* and had the exquisite Lena Olin in it. *Saraband* had the breadth and depth of his previous great family sagas, and a brand new actress Julia Dufvenius, caught in the family romance (i.e. incest) and unable to become independent. So, really, these last two films are almost up to the standard of *Persona* and *Autumn Sonata*. And I'd never seen them before. There's a lovely extra documentary of the almost decrepit Bergman directing his obviously last film with *Saraband*. Do not miss it. (20 October 2007)

Bergman's Women at Mai Zetterling's
Got a nice birthday present from Lena in Malmo - a dvd

documentary about three of Bergman's actresses meeting up thirty years later in Mai Zetterling's house in the south of France after Mai's death. It's *Lines from the Heart* (*I rollerna tre*) by Christina Olofson. Ageing is so uncanny when you haven't seen the faces since they were young. How much more generously tender and spookily honest when those three women are Bibi Andersson, Harriet Andersson and Gunnel Lindblom! (9 September 2007)

Best and Worst Bergman
Persona was today's Bergman - it must be his best, he cannot do more than that. And only two years after the abysmal *All These Women*, a film really as bad as they all say. Indeed no one seems to have disagreed that *All These Women* is clearly Bergman's worst film. Well, even the greatest genius has his Achilles heel. Since most of you will not have seen that contradiction in terms, a Bergman turkey, you may like to know that there is in it one somewhat droll line: "The basics of cello playing is the parting of the legs."

Bigelow Phallic Woman
No, I didn't see *Hurt Locker* and don't want to. The publicity has been incessant. As you say, an oscar winner means a crap film. I heard the woman was right-wing and reactionary. Also it fits into those formalist performance technical films, like *Hunger* (how to hunger-starve in Northern Ireland) and *Hidden* (how to keep a racist secret from surveillance cameras), where ideology and politics are expunged in favour of minimalist navel-gazing (body-torture, bourgeois guilt, bomb dismantling fetishism). All this adds up to one thing: Kathryn Bigelow is a phallic woman. All her stuff is action, macho, asking how, never why. So, she may be a woman braving the slings and arrows of a male profession, but she is, like Thatcher, a man in a woman's clothing. So, thank God, you have seen *Hurt Locker*, agree with my prejudice (oops, world-view). (13 March 2010)

Brisseau's Erotic Chic
Les anges exterminateurs (2006), the new Brisseau, is a lesser work than *Secret Things*, but a second viewing may get you thinking as well as excited. Of course you have to digest the obligatory tableau of naked wanking nymphs. Their chief activity does not stretch beyond rubbing themselves and each other down below. So, what is the intellectual content behind the flesh? Is it Blake's 'only a curtain of flesh on the bed of their desire'? Are we to believe what women say about their sexual desire and experience? Can we know what is real, what simulated, what fake, what fabricated, what made up? When is sex love and love sex? Are we teased out of thought by the mysteries of the organism? Is sex a mystery, or a fix? An art or a drug? And can you do art-porn without bad faith? As many questions as the thinking man or woman can ask. Is it a mind-blowing blow-job?

Bruce defends Varda in Guardian
Dear Sir, I felt I had to protest about Peter Bradshaw's luke-warm four-star review of Agnes Varda's new film *The Beaches of Agnes* in today's paper, in which he perpetuates the marginalisation of Varda by calling her 'a fellow traveller' with the French male 'new wave', completely overlooking the pioneering experimental film *La Pointe Courte* (1954), which in fact launched the new wave. I expect more from the *Guardian's* film authority. Is it symptomatic of the film culture in pudding island? Yours sincerely, Dr Bruce Woodcock, Hull Film Society. (2 October 2009 - unpublished!)

Chabrol on Abortion
Chabrol's *Story of Women* (1988) evokes the atmosphere of his earlier *Violette Noziere* and directly addresses the issue of abortion in Vichy France. Isabelle Huppert is as good as she gets as Chabrol's version of Vera Drake. Only, it's far more tragic even than Mike Leigh's film. And a bitter alienated Huppert, seeking an illegal abortion which under Vichy law carries the death penalty, utters the immortal lines

(unparalleled in Chabrol's work): "Hail Mary, full of grace, thy womb is full of shit." (12 November 2009)

Christine Pascal 1953-1996

Can anyone help find films by Christine Pascal (1953-96), a great friend of Catherine Breillat (and of Isabelle Huppert and Isabelle Adjani), who committed suicide after struggling to make Breillat-type films which were rubbished by the French cinematic establishment? The main one is *Felicité* (1979) - a kind of companion piece to Breillat's *Tapage Nocturne* (1979). Breillat says it was a better film than her own. As rare women directors, they were competing for funds from the male mafia. Breillat was jealous that her soul-sister got money easier than she did. Both were severely attacked by the male mafia for giving bold cinematic expression to women's sexual desire. Breillat was shattered by CP's suicide, claimed that CP was more of a soul-sister to her than her actual sister Marie Helene, and dedicated *Romance* to CP. Pascal's other films as director were *Zanzibar* (1989) and *Adultere Mode d'Emploi* (1995). This last film was made while she was suffering severe manic-depression, hospitalised, and subject to radical self-censorship, because she did not want a repeat avalanche of criticism such as had buried *Felicité*. In anorexic suicidal mood, she cut her own film. Christine Pascal was from Lyon and got into films via Bertrand Tavernier (also from Lyon). She was also an actress obsessed with her figure who courted popularity and appeared in lots of relatively rubbish films (according to Breillat). (9 December 2010)

Fassbinder's Political Trilogy

Have now completed my Bergman and Fassbinder marathons. You must see *Germany in Autumn*, (1978) as well as *Mother Kusters Goes to Heaven* (1975), and *The Third Generation* (1979), a trilogy of films on Germany, its history, and with special reference to terrorism in the 1970s. The communist in *Mother Kusters* is played by Karl Heinz Bohm, son of the great conductor, who played the dashing handsome prince in Romy

Schneider's *Sissi* films, and the baby-faced serial killer in *Peeping Tom*. That way Fassbinder keeps us guessing whether the communist leader is good or evil! Hanna Schygulla is Fassbinder's Liv Ullmann - both are strangely meek when interviewed recently. All their fire is in their acting. (5 January 2008)

Horrible Herzog
I cannot take to Herzog. The Kinski/Amazon stuff seems like an unintentional parody of the *Boys Own Paper*. I wanted more of Manaus and Iquitos, less of German *sturm und drang*. There were more Amazon style cities in the Luticia (a real place) of *Cannibal Holocaust* which I much preferred to the Kinski kitsch. Herzog (unlike Wenders and Fassbinder) is mostly a dead loss, though *Stroszek* and the Büchner have some power. The only bit of Herzog that gripped my groin (and he does dabble in the visceral) was Kinski's long slow kiss with Isabelle Adjani, that pouting cock-teaser whose mouth prevented poor Kinski from noticing the dawn (fatal to vampires) in *Nosferatu*. Surely an understandable mistake since no man for sure could tear himself away from that femme fatale. As they say at the end of Peter Jackson's inordinately otiose *King Kong*: "And Beauty killed the Beast". A consummation devoutly to be wished. (17 September 2008)

Joe Sarno and Some Swedish Sex Stars
In my infinitely spare time I have been researching the genre known as Retro Seduction - worth a module for students perhaps. Until last month I was unaware of the existence of Joe Sarno, an American who worked in Sweden and Germany as well as in the States. He is no mere trash merchant and his speciality is a peculiar form of epic eroticism which has all the oomph of pornography without the ultimate graphic details so much in demand today. The three principal stars in this Retro Seduction genre are: Christina Lindberg b.1950, Marie Liljedahl b.1950, and Marie Forsa b.1956. Christina has the reputation of being the Queen, and the two Maries are known

as the Princesses. I find Lindberg liberated and cool, Liljedahl is the pouting Swedish Lolita, but that Forsa is the supreme star. Sarno worked a lot with Forsa, 'discovered', then 'uncovered' her. She had the reputation from the age of 16 of being 'covered' by all and sundry on the set, male and female. But she guarded her career prospects by making a contract that though she would do sex in front of the camera, her films would never show her private parts, and would therefore pass the censor as mere soft porn. But there has never been harder soft porn, and Sarno has the knack of delineating sexual pleasure on Forsa's face. She can dilate her nostrils with more specific expression and sexual power than any porn star. There is a condensation and displacement from the genitals to the facial muscles. And those eyes! Well, Sarno's films seem now to be available. I recommend *Inga*, *Vampire Ecstasy*, *Baby Love* and *Butterflies*, all from the 1967-75 period. He usually avoids dubbing by using German and Swedish actresses who can speak English. (8 October 2010)

Jordanova on Makavajev
Dear Professor Dina Jordanova. We have only just got hold of Makavejev's *Sweet Movie*, and I wanted to thank you for your brilliant dvd introduction to this film and its relationship to Makavejev's previous sex-pol masterpiece *WR Mysteries of the Organism*. Your mix of aesthetic and ideological analysis, your attention to detail and the bigger picture of Balkan politics, and above all your ability to combine an approach to the sexual content with an appreciation of the film's avant-garde modernism - all this was way beyond what we have come to expect from a dvd extra. What I love about Makavejev is not only the taking Wilhelm Reich and Otto Muehl seriously, but also his ability to combine passion with irony, utopia with dystopia. I guess that is a Balkan (perhaps especially a Yugoslav/Serbian) trick, and as you say, no one else has done it so well - he must have been a closet surrealist. Best wishes for St Andrews cinema studies. Yours sincerely, John Hoyles. (25 August 2007)

Kafka Films
The film versions of *The Castle* (Haneke) and *Amerika* (Straub/Huillet) are not at all first-class. Unlike *The Trial* (Welles) they merely call attention to their originating texts. (16 January 2008)

Kluge
Have been revisiting early Kluge (like Varda, an unacknowledged inspirer of the New Wave). That is, *Yesterday Girl* (1966) and *The Part Time Work of a Female Slave* (1973). They both figure Kluge's sister, Alexandra, almost a German Anna Karina, but obviously with more marxist-feminist gravitas. (9 May 2010)

Marta Meszaros and the Communist Utopia
Have just finished watching Meszaros *Diaries* 2 and 3. She doesn't half lay on the old agony, so much more solemn than her mercurial erst-while husband Jancso. The whole trilogy reminded me so much of teaching Koestler's *Darkness at Noon*. He was Hungarian. So bleak. What an infernal history. Points of contact between Meszaros and me:
1. A Russian mocks Hungarian angst. They are mortified with anguish, unlike the Poles. They are even more melancholic than the Portuguese.
2. Death of Stalin. Oh my God, that was well done in the film. That mood even spread to the empty classroom in Kingswood School, Bath, where I wrote an elegy on the death of Stalin (happily the ms is lost).
3. Women in charge. Like Magda. When we crossed the border into East Germany in 1961, the customs post was controlled by a woman. For us, quasi-communists, that was a relief and sign of liberation after the unpleasant officials on the West German side of the Iron Curtain.
4. Budapest Film School - the first in the world, even before the USSR. The 1919 Revolution had Lukács and Béla Balász in it as cultural commissars. Lukács was removed to Rumania along with Nagy after the failure of the 1956 uprising, but was

allowed back later. Visited his house by the Danube in 1984, saw his books, he had lots of Penguins.
5. Radio Moscow call sign. Listened to this clandestinely at KS Bath.
6. October 1956 - on leave from National Service in the British Army for the weekend of the Hungarian (and Suez) events. On our AER (Army Emergency Reserve) base near Bedford we had black soldiers from Kenya training to fight the Mau Mau, and the Glasgow reservists from Red Clydeside were refusing to be sent to Suez to fight Nasser and regain the Suez Canal, nationalised by the dreadful Egyptian colonel. Compared to all that we have it easy in Pudding Island where Koestler came with his para-psychology to escape the rigours of continental totalitarianism. Meszaros stayed on in Hungary to create with Jancsó, Szabó and Makk a school of cinema unsurpassed in central Europe. (18 March 2008)

Marvellous Melville
A text from Melville: "The uphill road to failure is a very human thing." There's lots of cheap Melville dvds out with some excellent commentaries by Ginette Vinceandeau (Warwick University Film School). My favourite is *Bob le Flambeur*, in which the debut performance by the under-age nymphette Isabelle Corey is mesmeric. She puts the lascivious Adjani to shame. Incidentally the Alain Delon hero in *Le Cercle Rouge* is called Corey. And I've an idea that the magic nomenclature appears in earlier American films (Dieterle's *The Last Flight* comes to mind). The conjunction in 1961 (*Leon Morin Pretre*) of Emmanuelle Riva and Jean-Paul Belmondo is astoundingly risky given that Belmondo came straight out of Godard's *Breathless* and Riva out of Resnais' *Hiroshima Mon Amour* (both from 1959). It works in a strange way and got the seal of Catholic approval 'cos Belmondo (a fine upstanding priest he makes) refuses to have sex with Riva when Riva really wanted it (and she, poor thing, a lapsed communist with Jewish connexions to boot). Melville was not popular in left-wing circles then, which may have been the reason I was

not taken to see it at the time (when I was living in Paris) 'cos all my friends were communists and Jews. (17 September 2008)

Mike Leigh on Abortion and Adoption
I hesitate to say anything against Mike Leigh, our greatest director (our fat of the land, and not Lean). But I think he gets mixed up with the law. Thus, in the extras to *Secrets and Lies*, he nowhere suggests that there might be a debate about the law allowing adopted children to search out their birth-mothers. He simply seems to accept it as the law. On the other hand, with *Vera Drake*, he suggests that his film should open a debate on abortion, as if there could be a debate about something that was a criminal offence before it became legal. He surely wouldn't suggest that there should be a debate about homosexuality, when, like abortion, that thing was either a criminal offence, or (as the world and English left-liberalism progressed) decriminalised. This may be an otiose carp (maybe I've missed something), but it did strike me as illogical and lazy, and indeed wrong, as if Leigh was trying to be a middle-of-the-road pragmatist over issues which to progressive leftists must be cut and dried. But hats off to Mike Leigh for tackling head-on, in abortion and adoption, two of the contentious issues of our time.

Missing Bergman
The missing Bergman is *Face to Face* (*Ansikte Mot Ansikte*) 1976. Liv Ullmann is a psychiatrist. A man tries to rape her and she suffers a nervous breakdown and develops disturbing visions. Thanks to the attentions of Erland Josephson, a gynecologist, she recovers from her mental illness. Predictable fare from the old nordic maestro, one might think. But, according to Roger Ebert, Bergman was not in control of his material. Could he have been having a momentary collapse into his feminine self? Our Liv, on the other hand, was, beyond and behind her director's back, in touch with the existential fear and trembling that Bergman had so often tapped into. So, while

the master was drifting, his most faithful Muse was giving the performance of her life! Sounds intriguing enough, but it is unobtainable. Why? (20 December 2009) PS it has appeared since thank God.

Neeson and Nesbitt: Ulster, Green and Orange

I found something wrong in the much heralded tv film *Five Minutes of Heaven* - on the Ulster troubles. For me, Liam Neeson looked like an Irish Republican (shades of Michael Collins, shades of the eminent revolutionary statesman, shades of the highbrow intellectual), and James Nesbitt looked like a Loyalist (an angry, bitter prole). So I was hopelessly confused by the characters, plot, message etc, 'cos in fact they were the opposite! Neeson was the UVF man and Nesbitt the IRA man. This was either stupid, or too clever by half. Stupid because it is well known that Nesbitt was a Paisleyite Orange man and Neeson was brought up as (and still is) a Roman Catholic. Clever, if this swap was deliberate on the part of the sophisticated makers of the film in their attempt to appear as liberal-humanists with the objective non-partisan line of 'a plague on both your houses' - in which case this film falls into the current trend of depoliticisation (eg *Hunger, Hidden, Lust Caution, Lives of Others*, no wonder they are so many!). All these films - addressing such epic topics as the Bobby Sands Hunger Strike, the Algerian War, the Japanese Occupation of China, and the Stasi in East Germany - are highly praised, highly wrought aesthetically, and highly effective in knocking the politics out of our consciousness. Not so much a conspiracy, I guess, as a sign of our times. PS - Incidentally, according to Wikipedia, both Neeson and Nesbitt hail from Ballymena. But Neeson was prevented from gaining the Freedom of Ballymena offered to him when the DUP Paisleyites objected!

Nelly Kaplan's *Nea*

We have discovered Nelly Kaplan. *Nea* is a scandalous erotic thriller starring Sami Frey, he who danced the Madison with

Anna Karina in *Bande à Part*. It's about a child prodigy, so sexually liberated that she has written The Great Erotic Novel. In between masturbating and composing her filthy book, she cultivates a publisher (Sami Frey) who agrees to get her into print, as long as she becomes his lover so she can get more erotic material for her creative writing. The film seems to be marketed as soft-porn trash for us anglo-american consumers. But it is a clever and fascinating celebration of a 16 year-old girl who like Catherine Breillat, has ideas in advance of her age and station in life. And it's by Nelly Kaplan, a racy feminist genius, born in Argentina, destined to work in Paris at the Cinematheque with Abel Gance, about whom she made a couple of documentaries. (5 September 2008)

Queen Farce
I have not yet seen *The Queen*. Best review of it I could find says: "The outpouring of grief for Diana is ridiculous - the Queen knows it, knows full well that the woman was a frivolous twit, and yet she has to betray her aristocratic vantage point and cater to fifty million emotionally spastic subjects, all for the sake of her Q ratings." (Nick Pinkerton, "Blue Blood" in *Reverse Shot*, New York). As with the Alastair Campbell play, the only way to take this stuff is as farce - there can be no question of tragedy, heroic drama etc. It is simply farce, with Diana, the Queen and Blair as ridiculous characters who should be voted out of office.

Russ Meyer Master of Trash
Just seen *Vixen* and *Black Snake*. Wow, this is just not Russ Meyer as he is known. Look up Ebert's review of *Vixen*. Ebert, in his role as seedy Catholic voyeur with the bloated choirboy look, was deeply involved in the idiosyncratic erotic effusions of the great Russ Meyer. At one time they were kindred spirits. It's totally irrelevant but I can never separate the magisterial Chicago critic from his namesake who was social-democratic head of the Weimar Republic when the communist Rosa Luxemburg was murdered. *Black Snake* is even more

unusual than *Vixen*, if not quite so brilliantly composed. Indeed, see what's in the film: Black Power, plus Slave Revolts, with British Sugar aristos, and Haiti-type French-speaking gay wogs, all under the aegis of a Brigitte Bardot look-alike with sadistic tastes (actress born in New Zealand would you believe?). The plot motifs can hardly be verbalised, let alone interpreted. An embarrassment of riches is the phrase that comes to mind. There is a kind of politically correct *deus ex machina* at the end, claiming that the whole frenzied film is all in aid of the Civil Rights Movement. Wow, wow and wow. See *Black Snake* even if you think Russ Meyer's a load of garbage. (16 January 2008)

Sam's Choice
I showed three great films to Sam this weekend and asked him to rate them in order. He came out with 1. *Yes* (Sally Potter), 2. *Whity* (Fassbinder), 3. *Sweet Movie* (Makavejev). Which surprised me. I had them in the opposite order. Anyway Sam was truly impressed by Sally Potter. He also requested two Will Hay films: *Ask a Policeman* (which had my young nephew Toby in stitches 25 years ago) and *Old Bones of the River* (with its insouciant assumption that British imperialist racism can be taken for granted and played for laughs). (2 June 2008)

Sexual Murder and Cinema in Weimar Germany
I recommend Maria Tatar's *Lustmord: Sexual Murder in Weimar Germany*. Lots of stuff on Dix, Grosz, Doblin and Fritz Lang (especially on *M*). Good stuff on Wedekind, but strangely nothing on Pabst's *Lulu* (*Pandora's Box*) 1927. Tatar is a highly articulate feminist who almost converts me from my perverse position on Louise Brooks and Jack the Ripper. Her evidence, especially in the areas of painting and graphic art, is overwhelming as a dossier on the most extreme phase of psychopathic misogyny in modern European history. That is convincing. My own view on the film *Pandora's Box* is that Wedekind's Lulu in the shape of Louise Brooks welcomes her

death at the hands of the handsomest actor to play Jack the Ripper as a consummation devoutly to be wished, as a Wagnerian *Liebestod*. Incidentally Tatar's epigraph to her book is this brilliant quote from the film director Brian de Palma: "I don't particularly want to chop up women, but it seems to work." (13 April 2010)

Shoah makes me laugh
Just finished watching Claude Lanzmann's *Shoah* - for the second time. The dvd is great, 'cos you can find anything you want via the very detailed index. There is one bit I must show Sam, 'cos it made me laugh out loud. An old Nazi woman tries hard to remember the old days when she was a young German colonist in Poland. She is, as a die-hard racist, unable to distinguish between Poles and Jews. Poor old Lanzmann, in the process of interviewing her, is flabbergasted. The episode gives us a wonderful insight into the German mentality. (27 May 2008)

Szabo according to Brian
Brian Hoyle to Dr Hoyles: "Oddly enough I have also been on a Szabo binge. I agree, *Sunshine* and *Taking Sides* are rather excellent. I could have maybe dropped the subplot in the latter, but the confrontation between Furtwangler (check out his *Tristan and Isolde*, sublime) and the Yank was spellbinding. Both Keitel and Sgarsgard were excellent, and it was one of the few truly adult films of recent years. *Sunshine*, however, is a genuine epic and contains some amazing imagery. The trilogy is also brilliant, especially *Redl* and *Mephisto* (*Hanussen* is slightly weaker, but much better than Werner Herzog's shit stab at the same story). But I must make a plug for another little known Szabo masterpiece, *Sweet Emma, Dear Babe*. Made in the early 90s in Hungary, it remains one of the finest responses to the fall of communism cinema has to offer. Two female language teachers, who specialise in Russian, find their services no longer required, and so they teach themselves English and stay one week ahead of their new students, while

trying to deal with the confusion of the new "free" regime. The two actresses (one Hungarian, one Dutch) are wonderful, and it makes a great double bill with Makk's *Another Way* - although Szabo's film is in a rather minor key. It's on DVD from Amazon. Finally, did you know that Szabo was co-opted by the Hungarian equivalent of the Stasi to testify on fellow artists and filmmakers? He claims he never said anything that would incriminate, and actually used his position to help other filmmakers. Jansco for one would not condemn him. This has always made me look at *Mephisto* in a different light. Is it Szabo's own story?" (24 December 2010)

Tilda's Lipstick Traces
Wow, we ought to compile a book of Hull Film Society trivia. My favourite is: What lipstick did Tilda Swinton wear in *Female Perversions*? Answer: Same as her high-powered female executive companion, *Minou Rouge* (trs. into anglo-saxon as *Red Pussy*). Hence the impossibility of individual difference/identity in a world controlled by monopoly commodity-fetishism, such as L'Oreal. Make-up is manufactured. As the John Lennon song 'Woman is the Nigger of the World' puts it, of men's corporate cultural control over woman: "We make her paint her face and dance". Susan Streitfeld is rehashing in a more sophisticated fashion the old commonplace of two women discovering that they are wearing the same dress (tee-hee, aren't women silly creatures). All this is wonderfully ironic since the highly idiosyncratic Tilda Swinton specialises in acting *au naturel* in both her other films that come to my mind, *War Zone* (real-life pregnant), and *Young Adam* (armpits unshaved). Unfortunately, practically no one else since the early films of Jeanne Moreau, manages to resist the totalitarian blandishments of L'Oreal (Paris, New York, London) and its deoderising pharmaceutical running dogs. (11 February 2010)

Trivia of Trivia: Lascaux is Glasgow
My contribution to the most trivial of trivia is this. On a dvd of

Francois Leroi's 1993 *Emmanuelle* series, produced in Holland, there is reference in the dialogue to the cave paintings of Lascaux. The Dutch subtitle gets mega-lost in translation. Lascaux is subtitled Glasgow! (21 February 2010)

Truffaut Revisited April 2011
Have just watched all 23 Truffaut films in chronological order. I over-rated him in the past. I always judged he was better overall than Chabrol and Malle, and that he only just fell short of Godard, Buñuel and Bresson. I now reckon he only made three great films and that his overall output otherwise is no more interesting or enjoyable than the works of Joe Sarno which I've also just seen in chronological order. Indeed Sarno is consistently better than Truffaut! So the only Truffaut films I admire are *Jules et Jim* 1961, one of the best films ever made, definitely in my top ten; *Les 400 Coups* 1959, a brilliant revolutionary debut for both Truffaut and the New Wave; and *Les Deux Anglaises et le Continent* (*Anne et Muriel*) 1971, a wonderful sequel to *Jules et Jim*, both films being inspired versions of two novels by Henri-Pierre Roche. One is tempted to say that Truffaut had one great autobiographical film bursting to get out, and two literary adaptations of Roche's peculiar texts, the one stimulating Truffaut to the heights of freethinking utopian bliss, the other getting him to express his conflicted views on Passion and Puritanism, England and France, love and lust. The first a sublime comedy in spite of the tragic ending, the second a fascinating tragedy with lashings of the human comedy as a bonus. There is a second division of Truffaut films which are moderately good - *Tirez sur le Pianiste* 1960, *La Peau Douce* 1964, *La Mariée était en Noir* 1967, *La Nuit Americaine* 1973, and *L'Histoire d'Adèle H* 1975. Most of the others are pathetic. But not, I hasten to interlope, his debut short with the delectable cyclist Bernadette Lafont, *Les Mistons* 1957, or the film about making films, *La Nuit Americaine* (*Day for Night*) which in its energetic *joie de vivre* bears comparison with Fellini's *Eight and a Half*, or Fassbinder's *Beware the Holy Whore*. Truffaut, unlike Godard,

was interested in neither sex or politics. So his take on sex comes from Roche's novels and is only really deep and explicit in *Anne and Muriel*, in which he felt very uncomfortable with Muriel's confession of lesbianism and masturbation. He never really liked getting beyond, or above, ladies' legs. That did not stop him bedding his leading ladies, including Pippa Markham who played Muriel's sister Anne. So Truffaut only occasionally rises to luminous realism or lyrical beauty. The rest of the time he is way down on the ground of facile sexual politics, servile whimsy and cheap Restoration Comedy type devices and desires. And he can't or doesn't do irony. Some have assumed there must be irony in his Don Juan film *L'Homme qui aimait les femmes* 1977. Otherwise it would be unbearably unacceptable. But, no, no, no! Truffaut was *un homme moyen sensuel*, a serial sexist. When Toubiana, sometime editor of *Cahiers du Cinema* (after that journal's depoliticisation) repeats *ad nauseam* in his pedestrian commentaries on the dvds that Truffaut really put women before men in his life and art, we have to say HUMBUG.

Varda and Chabrol: Real Life and the Cinema
I was planning to ask questions about *Partie de Plaisir* by Chabrol, But it's too difficult. Suffice to say, it is either his most unpleasant and/or his most maligned film. I couldn't make head or tail of it. It was extremely annoying. Maligned could mean malevolent, and that could mean male-violent, the male wanting, willing, evil (a counterpoint to Eve as Evil). Then I read it had been compared to *Le Bonheur* by Agnes Varda. That started the brain cells racing. Both, then, are critiques of masculinity. Though Peter Cowie, and many others no doubt, took the Varda as a celebration of the sexual revolution. And I took the Chabrol as a nasty piece of phallocratic prejudice. The other factor thrown into the melting pot of this comparison is the observation that in both films the actors are related in real life. Thus in *Partie de Plaisir*, Paul Gegauff (Chabrol's longtime scriptwriter) plays the male lead, with his real-life ex-wife Daniele Gegauff and real-life

daughter Clemence Gegauff. Just as in *Le Bonheur*, Varda gets Jean-Claude Drouot to play himself, as do his real wife Claire Drouot and their children Sandrine and Olivier Drouot. What effect does this have on how we receive the films, if any? Is it immaterial, or does it have consequences (unintended or otherwise)? Extrapolating out of the films into life, we learn that the Drouot family lives happily ever after, and not as in the film with suicide, accidental or on purpose. The real-life couple are not affected by Varda's savage but subtle feminist critique of practical sexism. They survive into middle-age unscathed by the revelation that men are smooth bastards. And, in a reverse situation (hostile rather than harmonious), we learn of the Chabrol actors that Monsieur Gegauff (clearly a screenwriter of genius if problematic as an actor) is a few years later stabbed to death by his second wife (in real life, remember). Did he deserve to be stabbed because of his sexist behaviour in the film? !!! Well, what can all this mean? Varda clearly undercuts the real *bonheur* of real life with a brilliantly understated expose of how man's happiness is built on woman's misery. But Chabrol seems to be coldly presenting the Gegauff character as a normative husband whose wife (real ex-wife, remember) is a passive piss-pot who does what she's told and is bullied with a domestic violence rarely seen on screen. And yet all the women in Chabrol's film are seen through the male gaze as wretched creatures who cannot please men even when they act as doormats. 'Hope not for mind in woman' seems to be Chabrol's mantra. Well, maybe this can be construed as a critique of masculinity, but it doesn't come across like that to me on first viewing. I am tempted to conclude that Chabrol is giving vent to a nasty misogynist tendency of the first order. How have I gone wrong? Or is there a subtle ironic dialectic in the Chabrol which I have missed, just as Cowie missed the hard feminist clout in *Le Bonheur*? (24 October 2009)

Wajda is Polish
Polish is the word - it skews Wajda's work, usually for the

better (as in the War Trilogy of 1954-8 with which he emerged as a genius of world cinema with *Ashes and Diamonds* as an undoubted masterpiece.) But, in the case of *Danton* (1983), for the worse. So, Robespierre is Russia. Depardieu as Danton, screaming his way hoarse to the guillotine, is Poland. False analogy. And then, if Wajda's *Katyn* (2007) is profoundly memorable and a worthy correction to a historical injustice committed as atrocity by Stalin, that film never quite shocks us into a sense of evil absurdity as does the *Katyn* footage in Makavejev's much earlier and therefore much more daringly iconoclastic *Sweet Movie* (1974). (8 February 2010)

Wardrobes
We were collecting cinematic examples of wardrobes. We had watched Polanski's *Two Men and a Wardrobe* (1959), that freshly inventive short exercise in the theatre of the absurd in which everything is at the same time meaningful and meaningless. What immediately came to my mind were the two films with which I started and finished my university course on Cinema and Totalitarianism, *The Cabinet of Dr Caligari* (1919) and *WR Mysteries of the Organism* (1971). The happy chance juxtaposition of Caligari's cabinet and Reich's orgone box could not be an accident. Both boxes were magic coffins leading to killing or resurrection. Vertical or horizontal, these wardrobes are bewitched and bewitching, places of secret magic powers, which can lead to murder and Hitler (see Kracauer's book *From Caligari to Hitler*), or sexual health and a cure for cancer. To which one of our members, John Wheatcroft offered the following addition: "To extend our little wardrobe thematic discussed over lunch, I would put forward *Chatollets Hemmelighed* 1913 (*The Secret of the Cupboard*), directed by Hjalmar Davidsen, but more interestingly written by Carl Theodor Dreyer, of all people." (11 February 2010)

Zetterling Matters
Scrubbers arrived this morning. Have you seen her other films

as director? *Loving Couples*, *Night Games* and *Girls* are just brilliant, as good as Bergman. I want Mai Zetterling, Agnes Varda and Catherine Breillat to meet up and sock it to the ghastly patriarchal nobodaddy universe. *Scrubbers* is miles better than *Scum*. The *Scum Manifesto* is better than *Scum*. It is simply a sign of the paucity of reality in this Hollywood-ridden country that poor old Mai Zetterling is so neglected. Basil Dearden's *Frieda* (1947) has Mai Zetterling starring. It's a great English film. Did you know that Zetterling had many (surely not ten) abortions, which explains the imagery in *Night Games*? Her autobiography, *All These Tomorrows*, is a good read. (16 August 2008)

CHAPTER TEN: TOP TENS

Top Ten Films

1. Buñuel *L'AGE D'OR* France 1930

2. Bresson *MOUCHETTE* France 1967

3. Vigo *ZÉRO DE CONDUITE* France 1933

4. Truffaut *JULES ET JIM* France 1961

5. Gance *NAPOLÉON* France 1927

6. Eisenstein *IVAN THE TERRIBLE* USSR 1944-6

7. Chaplin *THE GOLD RUSH* USA 1925

8. Jancso *ELEKTRA MY LOVE* Hungary 1974

9. Bergman *PERSONA* Sweden 1966

10. Makavejev *WR MYSTERIES OF THE ORGANISM* Yugoslavia 1971

Next Top Ten Films

11. Dreyer *THE PASSION OF JOAN OF ARC* France/Denmark 1928

12. Godard *WEEKEND* France 1968

13. Kurosawa *DODESKA DEN* Japan 1970

14. Chytilova *DAISIES* Czechoslovakia 1966

15. Antonioni *L'AVVENTURA* Italy 1959

16. Varda *CLÉO DE 5 A 7* France 1961

17. Watkins *EDVARD MUNCH* Norway 1974

18. Vertov *THE MAN WITH A MOVIE CAMERA* USSR 1929

19. Pontecorvo *THE BATTLE OF ALGIERS* Algeria/Italy 1965

20. Oshima *AI NO CORRIDA* Japan 1976

Top Ten British Films

Michael Powell *PEEPING TOM* 1960

Tony Richardson *A TASTE OF HONEY* 1961

Ken Russell *ELGAR* 1962

Peter Watkins *CULLODEN* 1964

Julien Temple *THE GREAT ROCK'N'ROLL SWINDLE* 1979

Derek Jarman *THE TEMPEST* 1979

Mike Leigh *NAKED* 1993

Pawlikowsky *MY SUMMER OF LOVE* 2004

Ken Loach *AE FOND KISS* 2004

Andrea Arnold *FISH TANK* 2009

In chronological order. This almost off the top of my head by instinct and memory. I would like to cite two fantastic films which might be excluded as they feature Russian and Norwegian languages: Pawlikowski's *STRINGER* and Peter Watkins *EDVARD MUNCH*.

Top Ten Shakespeare Films

1. Max Reinhardt *A MIDSUMMER NIGHT'S DREAM* USA 1935

2. Orson Welles *FALSTAFF* (*CHIMES AT MIDNIGHT*) Spain/Switzerland 1966

3. Kosintsev *HAMLET* USSR 1964

4. Kurosawa *THRONE OF BLOOD* (= Macbeth) Japan 1957

5. Jarman *THE TEMPEST* GB 1979

6. Kozintsev *KING LEAR* USSR 1970

7. Kurosawa *RAN* (=Lear) Japan 1985

8. Peter Brook *KING LEAR* GB/Denmark 1970

9. Orson Welles *OTHELLO* Morocco 1951

10. Julie Taymor *TITUS* USA 1999

This in order of merit. To be considered when seen: Tony Richardson *HAMLET* 1969, Peter Brook *HAMLET* 2002, Julie Taymor *THE TEMPEST* 2010. And don't forget Chabrol *OPHELIA* 1963, a fascinating version of *Hamlet* (with affinities to *L'Age d'or*).

Top Ten Erotic Films

1. Oshima *AI NO CORRIDA* Japan 1976

2. Breillat *ROMANCE* France 1999

3. Makavejev *WR MYSTERIES OF THE ORGANISM* Yugoslavia 1971

4. Metzger *THE IMAGE* USA/France 1975

5. Brisseau *LES CHOSES SECRETES* France 2002

6. Brass *CALIGULA* USA/Italy 1980

7. Thorsen *QUIET DAYS IN CLICHY* Denmark 1971

8. Davy *EXHIBITION* France 1975

9. Sarno *ALL THE SINS OF SODOM* USA 1968

10. Nilsson *ALL ABOUT ANNA* Denmark 2005

THANK YOU

Many thanks to Bruce Woodcock, my agent and guardian angel, for getting this scrapbook off the ground. Thanks also to charismatic film directors I have known, Peter Bacso (Budapest) and Peter Watkins (now of Vilnius, Lithuania); to teachers and critics who have led the way, especially Brian Birch (Hull Adult Education), Catherine Breillat (Paris), Linda Williams (Berkeley, California), Amos Vogel (New York Film Society), Sandy Flitterman-Lewis (Rutgers), Roger Ebert (Chicago), Neil Sinyard (Hull), Brian Hoyle (Dundee), Melanie Williams (UEA), Dina Jordanova (St Andrews), Patricia MacCormack (Cambridge) and Paul Hammond (whose BFI book on *L'Age d'or* I have so shamelessly cannibalised); and to those friends and companions who have helped along the way, Cine Tamaris (Paris HQ of Agnes Varda), Malcolm Watson (for his Zulawski blogs), Richard Capes (for his Prague University Film Courses) , Sam Ellis (Huddersfield), Lena Blohme (Malmo), Teresa Brill (Sheffield), Dominique Hoyles (Sheffield), Lucienne Latour (Chambery), and last but not least Alice Hoyles, my granddaughter, who introduced me to Sophie Marceau in *La Boum*, and who (aged 11) taught me how to blog.

POST SCRIPT

A scrapbook is inevitably of its time, in this case around 2010-2011. Change and decay in all around I see. Our feelings and opinions are experimental. They are not set in stone. They are, in Montaigne's words, *divers et ondoyant*. And then, there is always, thank God, the Shock of the New. For me, since this scrapbook was assembled, the great discovery has been Andrzej Zulawski. His most striking films (with their starring divas) are: *L'Important c'est d'aimer* 1975 (Romy Schneider), *Possession* 1981 (Isabelle Adjani), *La Femme publique* 1984 (Valerie Kaprisky), *L'Amour braque* 1985 (Sophie Marceau), and *Szamanka* 1996 (Iwona Petry). Zulawski has been well served by the astute English critic Daniel Bird. Well done him.

APPENDIX "Looney Tunes and Gratuitous Excess"
Malcolm Watson (Hull Film Society) reviews five Zulawski films

POSSESSION (1981)

Zulawski said in an interview in 1996 that "Cinema is an instrument of megaforce to shake, to break barriers, to show you something you couldn't imagine possible." Well, *Possession* did that for me. I've seen nothing like it. Even if *Time Out* said that the 1981 film was "Turkey of the year, though the main ingredient was pure ham." Oooo, missus.

The thing was demented and made no sense. Psychosis on the screen. No rules. Intense, perverse, epic in its examination of love, loss, agony, rage, jealousy, separation, faith, God, madness, and horror. A comedy horror, for all that, ("I'm just checking the windows", chefs coming out of the kitchen to overwhelm Sam Neill, the taxi driver's "Certainly, sir" with a gun at his head, dandy Heinrich's karate moves and ridiculous pronouncements, the motorbike crash, the man in the pink socks) in lurid colour, with the camera itself whirling around and about, circling, swooping, floating, flying... Scenes shot in two halves, cutting from him to her, to him to her. No explanations. Unexplained job. Interview by unexplained Board. Unexplained man in pink socks. Unexplained monster. Unexplained car crashes and shootouts with police. Unexplained apocalypse, unexplained doppelgangers, who are opposites of each other. The couple's ordered and modern home beginning to disintegrate. Order to chaos. Clothes in the fridge, food in the bedroom cupboard.
  Heinrich leaves his immaculate pristine ultra-smart house for the 1st floor pit which is filthy and bare, with a squelching monster on a disgusting mattress, body parts in the freezer.

Green-eyed calm and blue-eyed hysteria. Banal home life, kitchens, bathrooms, bedrooms, making meals, bathing the child, putting him to bed, taking him to school. The child is the centre of normality and order and quiet. Submersion. He wants to be submerged in normality. Except for his nightmares about his mother. Random. Supernatural. Somebody says something about "piercing reality" which might be a metaphor for the film, but once you pierce reality, what do you get??? Epic seizures, monster miscarriages, lost souls, wandering souls. "I am the maker of my own evil. What I miscarried was Sister Faith and what was left was Sister Chance." Adjani mumbling, beseeching before an impassive Jesus Christ looking down on her. Electric carving knives and self harm. Murder in half a dozen varieties. An alien creature that is Mark's doppelganger, who looks at him as he dies. Chopped up meat. A film drowning in liquids, bathwater, blood, pus, milk and foodstuffs on the subway passage wall, vomit, bodily fluids, squelching slime, "Almost." "He's not finished, you know." The weird, English-as-a-second-language diction, which somehow perfectly fits the madness.

And what does Possession mean? Possessed by demons, by the devil, or evil? By love, jealousy, madness or rage? Material possessions in people's houses? Man and woman, husband and wife, or indeed children, as possessions? The soul possessing the body, or the body possessing the soul? Who possesses whom? **Can** a person possess another? There's a very famous print (example of erotic art called shunga) by the Japanese master Hokusai called *The Dream of the Fisherman's Wife* which shows an octopus performing cunnilingus on a pearl diver with a little octopus kissing her mouth and fondling her nipple, very like the artwork for the film poster/DVD cover. The text alongside details an erotic conversation between all three including little boy octopus (!), in which the maiden mumbles and groans like Adjani and says at one point "Oooooh, boundaries and borders gone! I've vanished!!!!". Rodin (a noted eroticist) and Picasso (ditto) among others were influenced by this and did their own versions. And there's an Italian opera called *Iris* by Mascagni in which the heroine recalls an image of an octopus coiled around a smiling young woman and a Buddhist priest saying "That octopus is Pleasure... That octopus is Death!.

In some small ways, reminiscent of Lars von Trier, or Bergman, or Cronenberg, or Lynch (- there was a Zulawski film Fest in New York in 2012, presented by the Polish Cultural Institute of New York, when Zulawski's *Szamanska* and *The Important Thing is to Love* were prefaced by the premiere of Lynch's music video called *Crazy Clown Time*, apparently). And the whole thing ends with the kid between two doppelgangers, the creature who is Mark's double (and the finished monster?) banging on the door and the green-eyed Adjani ignoring the banging, looking up and listening to the Apocalypse, or nuclear war outside, as the boy screams "Don't open it! Don't open it!" before runnning away and submerging (drowning?) himself in the bath. "Don't open it?" Well, Zulawski just did.

LA FEMME PUBLIQUE (1984)

La Femme Publique was another flamboyant, chaotic and hyperactive Zulawski job, nicely summed up by your and Bruce's 4-word Thursday review "**Gratuitous and Erratic Excess**". It's *Hellzappopin'* without the gags. This time, a revival of the old chestnut of a film within a film, or play within a play (from Shakespeare and Jonson to Strindberg, Bergman, Billy Wilder, Vincente Minelli and Tornatore, Truffaut etc etc) and continuing the Dostoevsky link (a shooting of *The Devils*). How autobiographical is it, re the Czech exile in Paris, the mad director pushing his actors beyond their limits? Kaprisky becoming famous after her debut? The film is once again propelled by impulses, not thoughts, but is a nice examination of acting (- including bad acting) and reality, inhabiting and being inhabited, (gender) roles, speech patterns, poses, attitudes, costumes, masks... It's also about manipulation and control, but again delivered via hyperbole, frenzy, delirium. It's intense, fluid, and bonkers. And deliberately highly theatrical, down to the cast taking a public curtain call at the end. Kaprisky follows another trajectory from ingenue to growing assurance, to femme fatale, with men about her dying or killing themselves, but once again, is this really emancipation? And once again, the obsession with doubles, mirrors and splintered selves, the preoccupation with terrorism and religion ("the huge spider in the wardrobe"), and the focus on sex, mess, shouting and screaming, breaking things, heavy breathing, drink, and roughhouse violence. Not to mention shootouts and exploding car crashes! It is frenetically energetic and surprising, but this one is also a crazed love letter to film itself ("Cinema is bubbles of light in the darkness") and the acting profession. Like Bergman, he loves actors, even if he treats them like dogs. Maybe because I'm no longer a Zulawski virgin, I found this less of a knockout than *Possession*, but very well worth the ride.

L'AMOUR BRAQUE (1985)

I'm beginning to like *L'Amour Braque* best of the 3 Zulawskis so far. The chaos is more pointed and more revealing, even if we're battered with the usual hysterics, pain, suffering, desperate necessary endurance, spastic terpsichore, mad music, ultra-violence, flying cameras and lurid colours. The film is characteristically fast, too fast, maybe, to take in the slew of ideas and the whirling, epileptic, Tourette's Syndrome poetry that flies at you from first to last. It is also absurdly comic. But all the talismanic ingredients are still present, love and death, love as insanity, the femme fatale, doom, sex, blood, fighting, nudity, neon, primal screaming, shouting and manic laughter, overwrought dialogue, breaking glass and crockery, overacting, silly voices, silly accents, ridiculous costumes, masks, absurdity, streets, stairs, corridors, shootouts and cars on fire. But what gives it structure and a mad kind of sense are the Dostoevsky and Chekhov threads (as well as the numerous cultural references - Bakhtin, Monod's Chance and Necessity, Bacon, Kafka etc) that stitch it all up. And maybe even *Othello*, with the two male character left with the body of the murdered beloved? As well as the two commentators, the little guy with the moustache (as in *La Femme Publique*) who obliquely suggests plot references and cultural clues, and the world-weary policeman character who poetically explains what is going on.

The film, like *The Idiot*, is nonsensical, anarchistic, surrealistic, and a scathing critique and piss-take of the powers that be and the very idea of control and order, because everything is always precisely at the point of breakdown. The extreme aggression and extreme passivity and extreme suffering mirror Dostoevsky's novel, in which Prince Myshkin and Rogozshin meet on a train in the second paragraph, are in love with the same woman and pursue her in a mad hallucinatory melodrama until Rogozshin kills her and Myshkin goes mad. Nastasya is violent, relentless, furious, and mad. Myshkin considers himself lower and worse than everyone. He is a Holy Fool whose goodness turns everything bad. He breaks a vase in an epileptic fit. The Good Man is an Idiot. While writing the novel, Dostoevsky was also beset by illness, ever more violent fits, the death of his daughter, fantastic money worries, his repeated gambling addiction losing him his advances and ever more borrowed money, and writing in a condition of insanity. He had no idea of a firm plot, wrote a dozen versions in a frantic hurry, and ended up tearing up pages even as he was writing them. No wonder the book, like the film, is full of self-disgust, pride, madness, and frantic drama. Zulawski was reportedly regularly on cocaine benders throughout the 80s. Cf Kafka's self-loathing, self-distrust, ultra-sensitivity and pain, and his own ulcers, TB in his larynx, sleeplessness, shortness of breath, back pain, skin irritation, panic about hair loss and failing eyesight, and extreme sensitivity to noise.. And curiously, in Kafka's reports of dreadful industrial accidents, "all those young girls in chinaware factories who keep falling down stairs with huge piles of dishes in their arms"! Dostoevsky said that bizarre and strange and odd things happen all the time. The newspapers are full of them. He said "The fantastic constitutes the essence of reality". But nobody takes any notice. In Zulawski's film, "normal" people just wander by without a glance, or look on, or shrug, amid the total chaos around them.

And *The Seagull* famously has a play within a play. Nina ("I am the soul of the world in the future"), the second- rate and fading actress, is forced to tour with a second-rate company. Which lets Chekhov and Zulawski explore highly theatrical Dramatic Theory, and performance as madness, like Bergman's film of mad theatre troupes. Though I found Sophie Marceau's reprise of the other actress's "orthodox" delivery of Nina's speech to be even less convincing than Kaprisky's rehash. Chekhov's play is famously all about the unspoken, all comment and no action, people not saying what they are really thinking. As opposed to Zulawski's polar opposite compulsion to show everything that people are thinking, turning everything inside out, so that EVERYTHING is feeling. down to people using flamethrowers to set other people (and the screen itself) on fire.

Tcheky Karyo played Mickey the gangster. He's had a long and varied career, having been in Besson's *La Femme Nikita* and *Jeanne d'Arc*, the Bond film *Goldeneye*, and Mel Gibson's *Patriot*, as well as playing Van Gogh, Moliere, Nostradamus, etc in some 50 films, as well as acting in classical and contemporary theatre.

L'IMPORTANT C'EST D'AIMER (1975)

"Was ever woman in this humour woo'd?
Was ever woman in this humour won?"
                                        Richard III

Well, maybe because it was more restrained (even loony Kinski is relatively restrained), with a more focused narrative, and oozed emotionalism rather than the unbounded, mad expressionism of the later films, this was to me tremendously affecting in a different way. Zulawski might be Romantic, but here he was being equally unsentimental (except in relation to his love of fragile actors as a special, transcendent, essential breed, with whom, like Bergman, he is transparently, and somewhat soppily, in love). Schneider was never more beautiful and intense and tortured, and was to live only another 7 years before her heart attack (or suicide, some say) at the ridiculously early age of 43. She won a César for her performance and thought it her best film. Zulawski called Testi "a moron", and Kinski "clinically mad". In 1999, Almodovar dedicated *All About My Mother* (all about performance) to three starry actresses playing actresses in a crisis of ageing and terror, Gena Rowlands as Myrtle in Cassavetes's *Opening Night* (1977), Bette Davis as Margo Channing in *All About Eve*, and Romy Schneider as Nadine in *L'important, c'est d'aimer*. Not hard to see why.

The important thing is to love, but in Zulawski, love is always an utter bloody mess, even if it is all-consuming. Love equals pain, so equals masochism, and torture. "If I stop it, I'll do harm. If I don't, I'll do more." Everybody is in some sort of emotional or financial debt, everybody owes something to the other (or thinks they do), and consequently everybody exploits or is exploited in a vain effort to expunge the debt. Nevertheless, **unusually** (at least in the 4 films I've now seen), Zulawski is surely and unironically emphasising the necessity of/for love, with Schneider finally softly repeating "Je t'aime;

Je t'aime"... (to the bloody, prostrate, almost dead Jacques) revisiting the opening scene, when she is playing the actress who simply cannot say "Je t'aime; Je t'aime!" to the bloody corpse, no matter how many times the director screams at her to do so.

The usual swirling camerawork makes us the incessant roving eye following every detail of the lives of the three people who are respectively, the tortured taker of an image, the tortured subject (or the image itself), and the tortured collector of images, in a film that obsessively catalogues the entire process of capturing, of keeping, of making eternal the fleeting moment. Nevertheless, all the usual Zulawski tics are here; multiple deaths (the doctor and morgue attendants are very busy), promiscuous sex, transvestism, disgust (-"Man is the worst he can do. Look in the mirror"), sudden violence, philosophy (Thomas Aquinas etc., and the alcoholic bookseller philosopher has some of the best lines), poetry (Rimbaud), sudden surprising jump-cuts, dramatic theory, the theatre (-"Don't give them what they want. They don't know what they want"), performance versus reality/life, the play within a play, stairs, doors, corridors, breaking crockery, revisiting old café haunts, directors pushing actresses beyond their limits, booze, kitchens and bedrooms etc (- though I don't remember any car chases/explosions in this film!). The lyrical (repetitive and occasionally ridiculous, but somehow apposite) music was by Georges Delerue, who did the music for *Le Mépris*, which is reprised here; and Nadine's suicidal clownish husband who "can't live for her" says that he can't bear her pity, which is "terminal" for a relationship, inevitably followed by "mépris", scorn or contempt.

The same husband obsessed with stills and posters (James Dean, Clara Bow, Zorro, Yvonne De Carlo, etc) , on which Jacques and Nadine collapse near the end, lies deathly still in the coffin as Lady Anne's dead husband in the play within a play, *Richard III*, and says "I was good, wasn't I?". A play (with a mad-eyed Kinski channelling a wild Larry Olivier as Richard) in which the "hero" villain Richard kills the husband of Lady Anne, the object his lust, but also her father, and later, when he is tired of her and lusts after another, kills her too. Richard dies in a sea of blood (compare the OTT bloody maquillage of the photographer at the end) the object of his lust's husband dies, and she dies. What's Zulawski saying here about the consequences of lust or the necessity of love? I don't know and I don't really care.

Anything else ring a bell? Last lines of Doctor Donne's *Elegie: On His Mistris*:

> ...oh, my love is slaine; I saw him goe,
> ..I saw him I,
> Assayld, fight, taken, stabb'd, bleede, fall and dye.
> Augure me better chance, except dread Jove
> Think it enough for mee, to'have had thy love.

SZAMANKA (1996)

More *Looney Tunes* (who mentioned *Last Tango in Warsaw*?), but this time, according to Zulawski himself, we have "a film without a mask", and it's considerably different from the other 4 so far. Further, it contains no play within a play, and, contrary to what Bird says, no theatrical/dramatic theory, or concentration on acting per se. I also take issue with Bird about the film being about angels and demons, and God and the Devil (- if so, who's who, and who cares?). But it **is** about the search for God, if you consider this some sort of mystical quest for enlightenment, via sex, drugs and doing what you like (instead of rock 'n' roll). We're into "Do what thou wilt" territory with Aleister Crowley and the Thelemites, or the Franciscan monk Rabelais and the Abbey of Thélème in *Gargantua and Pantagruel*, or Colonna, the Dominican monk, who 130 yrs earlier wrote *Hypnerotomachia Poliphili* contrasting

Reason with Will or Desire (Thelemia), and the hero Poliphilo opting for Desire - and whose beloved vanishes-, or Sir Francis Dashwood and the Hellfire Club, etc etc... All with links to sex and the theme of liberty v restraint, and to Egyptian religion. The urge to do the opposite of what society tells you, the individual, the rebel as the lunatic but enlightened one. Zulawski, however, in his perversity, histrionics and hyperkinesis, is looking for God via the Primal Scream, or more properly, the Primal Fuck, contrasting madness and civilization. With Z., on past form, you'd think madness and demonic lust might just win, but here he's surely saying both madness (or the energy of the non-rational, or instinctual) and civilization are both wanting, and mad sex is never enough to return to God. And even God is a void, because "All Gods are Gods of Death", as somebody says in the film. But we poor souls are destined to spin round on the carousel, *La Ronde*, for eternity

So this is not profound, or provocative, or subversive, rather profoundly nihilistic. There is NO place for love in the entire film. And despite the screenplay being by the Feminist Catholic Manuela Gretowska, it is hardly feminist either. Unless you consider that the depiction of woman as eternally deranged, all-consuming and inevitably fatal is some sort of feminist statement. The professor dies, his brother dies, his ("normal") fiancée dies, his hard-up colleague dies, the gangsters attacking him die, her colleague/failed lover kills himself on his motorbike etc.. This, more than the other films, is deliberately thoughtless ("Thought may be a glandular emission, an audible hiss..."), intended to get to "the naked soul", whatever that is, which Zulawski has hitherto been looking for in the act of acting. I'm not sure he knows what he's doing here. Man's fulfilment/ Nirvana via the Primal Urge? The director as shaman? (Z. has visited Siberia, the Caribbean, West Africa and Jamaica and has said that "Shamans are the greatest actors ever"). Satire on post-Communist 90s Poland in a complete mess, inhabited by gangsters, cretins, the ignored toiling masses, desperate visionaries? Or what?

Familiar tropes abound: sex, madness (formally in the psychiatric hospital and informally just about everywhere else), fights, smashed crockery, stairs and tunnels (above and below = light and dark, heaven and hell?), trains, guns, gangsters, debt, toilets, mincemeat, bodily fluids, violent deaths, the meaningful LOOK that forever enchains, the Cross and the face of the Virgin as in *Possession*, ever there, as within Z himself, to plead with. As ever, much to love in the film; constant surprises, fearless depictions of sex and desperation, Korzynski's excellent soundtrack of electro-synth, airy strings, choral voices, and insistent drumming (which all runs counter to expectations - lyrical strings relating to spiritual relationship to shaman/mummy and industrial/electronic synth/drumming to sex with loopy Lilith), dialogue -"Do you have faith?" "Fuck off", and a very appealing (to me) confection of anthropology (-"Where's Anthropology?" "Anthropology is everywhere"), psychiatry, engineering and industry via the university. I liked (the inferno? of) the steelworks. Setting this in Nowa Huta must have been a deliberate piss-take of both Communist and post-Communist regimes. A purpose-built Soviet industrial utopia, the only town in Poland deliberately built without a church until the future Pope Paul II built a cross and organized protests, scene of riots, strikes, demonstrations for years, the centre of anti-Communist resistance, Solidarity activity, once a model of future prosperity and innovation, now a desperate, polluted shithole. The works was called The Vladimir Lenin Steelworks. Though having worked on a blast furnace, I have no idea what the girl and her colleague were supposed to be doing there, and, I assure you, nor does Zulawski. And the cinematography was more artful and accomplished, with the bodies like landscapes, and the deep, lurid colours and liquid blacks, despite the silliness and Grand Guignol.

However, *Szamanka* was for me a falling off, and an indication of some tiredness, things becoming a bit wearing, and beginning to appear thin and hasty, with little new or different to say. I don't think this is just because it's the 5th film we've seen. The finale, with Michal's death at the hands of the girl, was predictable after the first half- hour. Iwona Petry's frenetic spasticity and gurning was ferocious all right, but began to ferociously piss me off. Her "kooky" exuberance ("Look, I'm mad, me!") got to be a pain in the arse (literally, as well, for her and him) pretty quickly. The *Wasp Factory* brain-munching (echoing the scoffing of the cow's brains at the beginning) was (unintentionally, I'm sure) comic. The munching of the hallucinogens of psylocybin and fly agaric was a bit too lazy a device to connect to the shaman, whose own excavation from the pit and examination in the lab was also ultra-cavalier and comic, the cadaver looked like an ultra-cheapo papier-maché job from the local joke-shop, the Wilson, Keppel and Betty sand dance walking like an Egyptian routine was feeble, the rats in the slaughterhouse/meat factory mincing machine ditto, the incessant non-stop motion running, leaping, jumping, dashing out of cafés where no food is ever eaten and no drink is ever finished all annoying. The only still things were dead people, end even the bloody shaman came to life, to spout some gibberish that might have come from *The Mummy* or *The Mummy Returns*. The radioactive McGuffin in the chocolate box was unconvincing, deadly, but patently non-apocalyptic, with no effect on subsequent events (unlike as in eg *Kiss me Deadly* or *Repo Man*) even if loosely and contrarily compared to the blinding light illuminating the shaman's coming back to life.

I wonder if Zulawski is familiar with Josef Skvorecky's novel *The Engineer of Human Souls* (1977)? Czech, not Polish, but a hugely literate examination of exile and Eastern European politics, where nothing is unmentionable, which includes, love, farce, scatology, factories, sabotage, literature and jazz, dreams, love and death. There are 2 instructive quotes among the 5 epigraphs before he gets started on the novel which might be relevant to *Szamanka*: "Truth lies in nuances." Anatole France, and "To Generalize is to be an Idiot. To Particularize is the Alone Distinction of Merit. General Knowledges are those Knowledges that Idiots possess." William Blake. Discuss.

INDEX

Addison, Joseph 116
Adenauer, Konrad 125
Adjani, Isabelle 53, 54, 176, 177, 180, 197, **199-200**
Aeschylus 156
Akerman, Chantal **32-35, 135-136,** 155
Almodovar, Pedro 204
Alvarez, Al 146
Alvarez, Santiago **59-60**
Amenabar, Alejandro **171**
Anderson, Lindsay 58
Andersson, Bibi 20, 24, 27, 119, 130, 174
Andersson, Harriet 118, 174
Andersson, Roy 156
Andrew, Geoff 77, 79
Anger, Kenneth **59**
Antonioni, Michelangelo 7, 52, 89, 123, 126, 155, **193**
Aquinas, Thomas 205
Aragon, Louis 147
Argento, Asia 159-60. **172**
Aristakisyan, Artur **171-172**
Arnold, Andrea **194**
Asti, Adriana 123-4
Attal, Yvan 169
Aurevilly, Barbet d' 159
Austen, Jane 83
Auteuil, Daniel **145-147**
Bacall, Lauren 123
Bacon, Francis 202
Bacso, Peter 197
Bakhtin, Mikhail 13, 202
Balasz, Bela 179
Bale, Christian 152
Bardot, Brigitte 130, 140, 184
Bataille, Georges 30, 94, 171
Bates, Alan 39, 40
Baudelaire, Charles 147, 160

Bauer, Felice 166
Beart, Emmanuelle **145-147**
Beauvoir, Simone de 62, 94
Beccarie, Claudine 169
Beckett, Samuel 46, 99
Bellocchio, Marco **143-144**
Bellour, Raymond 67
Belmondo, Jean-Paul 126, 180
Belmont, Vera **148**
Benda, Julien 163
Benjamin, Walter 68, 147
Bergman, Ingmar 7, **20-27,** 69, 74, 96, 99, **117-118, 118-119,** 120, **126-127, 130,** 138-9, **151-152,** 157, 172, **173, 174,** 176, **180-181,** 191, **192,** 200, 201, 203, 204
Bergman, Ingrid 109
Berkley, Elizabeth 89
Bernini, Gian Lorenzo 14
Bernstein, Sidney **59**
Bertolucci, Bernardo 88, **122-124**
Besson, Luc 203
Betjeman, John 114
Bigelow, Kathryn **174**
Birch, Brian 197
Bird, Daniel 197, 206
Birkin, Jane 168
Bjork, Anita 151-2
Bjornstrand, Gunnar 26
Blair, Tony 154, 183
Blake, William 60, 122, 131, 132, 173, 175, 210
Blessed, Brian 122
Blier, Bertrand 140
Bloch, Ernst 124
Blohme, Lena 173, 197
Bloom, Harold 122
Blum, Leon 115
Bogart, Humphrey 123
Bohm, Karl Heinz 176
Bonnaire, Sandrine 76, 128, 141
Borden, Lizzie **64, 74-75**
Boswell, James 165

Bourgignon, Serge 120
Bow, Clara 205
Bowen, Michael J 100-101, 104-5
Bradshaw, Peter 175
Brando, Marlon 88, 126
Brass, Tinto **196**
Brauerhoch, Annette 67-68
Brawne, Fanny 165-6
Brecht, Bertolt 50, 80, 123, 125, 13, 141
Breillat, Catherine 8, 10, 29, 33, 34, 35, **36-38,** 79, 90, 104, 106, 109, 125, 126, 135, **152-153, 159-160,** 161, 168, **176,** 183, 191, **196,** 197
Breillat, Marie-Helene 176
Brel, Jacques 33, 126
Bresson, Robert 120, 121, **127-128,** 187, **192**
Brill, Teresa 197
Brisseau, Jean-Claude **175, 196**
Bronte, Emily 121, 152, 156
Brook, Peter 137, **195**
Brooke, Rebecca 101-102, 104
Brooks, Louise 109, 112, 121, 123, 158, 184
Brooks, Mel 53
Brown, Clarence **109-113**
Brownlow, Kevin 109, 111, **136**
Brownmiller, Susan 94
Buchner, Georg 177
Bujold, Genevieve 122
Bunuel, Luis **11-19,** 28, 31, 40, **57-58,** 86-7, 97-8, 125, 128, 133, 135, 145, 187, **192**
Burton, Richard **128-130**
Bush, George 154
Cacoyannis, Michael **39-41, 120-122**
Cale, John 79, 148
Campbell, Alistair 183
Campion, Jane **65, 76-77, 164-166**
Cantet, Laurent **150-151**
Capes, Richard 197
Cardenal, Ernesto 60
Carter, Angela 47, 132
Cassavetes, John 204
Cassel, Jean-Pierre 141

213

Chabrol, Claude 117, 125, 141, **175-176,** 187, **188-189, 195**
Chaplin, Charlie 13, **42-46,** 49, 50, **58,** 141, 151, 165, **192**
Chaplin, Hannah 42, 43
Charles I 136
Chaucer, Geoffrey 110
Chekhov, Anton 155, 202-3
Chytilova, Vera 34, **64, 70-71, 124-125, 193**
Cixous, Helene 63
Clair, Rene 7
Clark, Larry 149
Clementi, Pierre 133
Clinton, Bill 169
Clouzot, Henri-Georges **117**
Collins, Michael 182
Colonna 206
Conrad, Joseph 117
Corey, Isabelle 180
Corneille 148
Coward, Noel 128
Cowie, Peter 188-9
Cromwell, Oliver 121
Cronenberg, David 200
Curtis, Richard **154-155**
Crowley, Aleister 206
Cytherea 97
Dafoe, Willem 169
Dahlburg, Eva 117-118
Dahlstrom, Alexandra 149-50
Dali, Salvador 11, 12, 13, 14, 15, 17, 18
Dallesandrio, Joe 137
Damiel, Walter 110
Dangerfield, George 82
D'Annunzio, Gabriele 124
Danton, Georges 115, 190
Dashwood, Sir Francis 207
Dassin, Jules 39
Davidsen, Hjalmar 190
Davies, Carl 111
Davis, Bette 116, 204
Davy, Jean-Francois 169, **196**

Dean, James 205
Dearden, Basil 191
Debussy, Claude 55
De Carlo, Yvonne 205
Defoe, Daniel 167
DeLaurentis, Teresa 66-67
Delerue, Georges 205
Delius, Frederick 55
Delon, Alain 180
Demarbre, Lee 166
Demy, Jacques 47
De Palma, Brian 185
Depardieu, Gerard 190
Derrida, Jacques 63
Detmers, Maruschka 143-4
Diana. Princess 183
DiCaprio, Leonardo 152
Dickens, Charles 42
Dickinson, Emily 156
Dieterle, William 180
Dietrich, Marlene 105
Diogenes 146
Dior, Christian 147
Dix, Otto 184
Dizdar 158
Doblin, Alfred 184
Doillon, Lou 50
Donne, John 109, 206
Dorleac, Francoise 52
Dors, Diana
Dostoevsky, Fyodor 200, **202-203**
Dreyer 120, 121, 152, 190, **193**
Drouot, Claire 189
Drouot, Jean-Claude 189
Drouot, Olivier 189
Drouot, Sandrine 189
Dryden, John 116
Dudow, Slatan 80
Dufvenius, Julia 173
Dumont, Bruno 89

Eagleton, Terry 60
Ebert, Roger **23-27,** 133-4, 151, 167, 181, 183, 197
Edwards, Eric 101-104
Eisenhower, Dwight D. 82
Eisenstein, Sergei 7, 28, 119, 151, **192**
Eisner, Lotte 69
Ek, Anders 152
Elgar, Edward 55, 60
Eliot, T.S. 156, 169
Elizabeth, Queen 183
Ellis, Bret 152
Ellis, Sam 184, 197
Elsner-Sommer, Gretchen 69
Eluard, Paul 18
Engels, Friedrich 133
Ensslin, Gudrun 77, 139
Epstein, Marie **64, 69**
Euripides 39, 102
Fabre, Jean-Henri 11, 18
Farmer, Frances 148
Farrow, Mia 53, 140
Fassbinder, Rainer Werner 85, **130-131,** 137, 139, 157, 173, **176-177,** 184, 187
Fellini, Federico 187
Ferdinand, Archduke 142
Ferran, Pascale 55
Fieschi, Jean-Andre 171
Firth, Colin 154
Flaubert, Gustave 84. 111, 123, 160
Fleischer, Richard **136-137**
Flitterman-Lewis, Sandy 7, 63, 67, **69-70, 76,** 197
Ford, Henry 44
Forman, Milos 52
Forsa, Marie 97, 101, 103-4, 157, **177-178**
Foucault, Michel 65
Frame, Janet 165
France, Anatole 210
Franco, Francisco 12
Frankl, George 92, 94
Franz Joseph, Emperor 142

Freud, Sigmund 9, 13, 42, 57, 58, 82, 100, 111, 120, 121, 164
Frey, Sami 133, 135, 182
Furtwangler, Wilhelm 185
Gainsbourg, Charlotte 50, 168
Galgoczi, Erzsebet 73
Galloway, George 51
Gance, Abel 109, 115, 183, **192**
Gansel, Dennis **163-164**
Garbo, Greta **107-113**
Gaudier-Brzeska, Henri 56
Gegauf, Clemence 189
Gegauf, Daniele 188
Gegauf, Paul 188-9
Genet, Jean 28, 29, **59,** 84, 125, 171
George III 115
Gibson, Mel 203
Gilbert, John **107-113**
Gilles de Rais 125
Gillis, James 104
Giscard d'Estaing, Valery 48
Godard, Jean-Luc 7, 9, 22, 64, 123, 125, 126, 135, 150, 180, 187, **193**
Goebbels, Joseph 64, 113
Goethe, Johann Wolfgang von 10, 116
Goldman, Steven 75
Goodman, Paul 93
Gorbachev, Mikhail 149, 173
Goulding, Edmund 107
Goya, Francisco 164
Gozzi, Patricia 120
Graff, Cathja 97, 102-103
Graham, Billy 164
Gramsci, Antonio 44, 124
Grant, Hugh 154
Grant, Steve 78
Green, Eva 89
Gretowska, Manuela 207
Grey, Sasha **166-168**
Griffin, Susan 91, 94
Grosz, George 184
Hammond, Paul 11, 197

Haneke, Michael 145, 173, 179
Hardy, Thomas 165
Harrison, Cathryn 137
Harrison, Rex 137
Harrison, Tony **60,** 156
Harron, Mary **65, 79, 147-148, 152**
Hartmann, Geoffrey 9
Hasek, Jaroslav 125, 142
Haussmann, Baron 147
Hawks, Howard 123
Hay, Will 114, 184
Heath, Stephen 93-4
Heck-Rabi, Louise 71
Heflin, Van 117
Hempel, Anouska 130
Hepburn, Katharine 122
Herzog, Werner 177. 185
Hesera, Simon 53
Hindenburg, Paul von 81
Hirohito, Emperor 162
Hitchcock, Alfred **114-115,** 117
Hitler, Adolf 44, 65, 68, 80-1, 115, 125, 142, 162, 164, 190
Hokusai, Katsushika 199
Howard, Ed 133
Howarth, Troy 102
Hoyle, Brian **185-186,** 197
Hoyles, Alice 197
Hoyles, Dominique 197
Huillet, Daniele/Straub, Jean-Marie 179
Huppert, Isabelle **140-141, 175-176,** 177
Husak, President 70, 124
Huxley, Aldous 110
Hypatia 171
Irigaray, Luce 63
Jackson, Peter 177
Jack the Ripper 111, 184-5
Jacobsson, Lara 127
James II 143
Jancso, Miklos 71, **121-122,** 179, 180, 186, **192**
Jankowska, Jadviga 73

Jarman, Derek 55, **194, 195**
Jesus 18, 59, 91, 164, 199
Jires, Jaromil **131-132,** 137
Jogiches, Leo 78
Johnson, Samuel 165
Johnston, Claire 66
Johnston, Sheila 68, 72, 76
Jones, Ron 163
Jonson, Ben 200
Jordan, Jennifer 104-5
Jordanova, Dina **178,** 197
Josephson, Erland 181
Joyce, James 165, 173
Kael, Pauline **22-23,** 88
Kafka, Franz 44, 45, 46, 108, 125, 129, 132, 142, 165-6, **179,** 202-3
Kahane, Peter 144
Kaplan, Nelly **47-48, 182-183**
Kaprisky, Valerie 197, **200-201,** 203
Karina, Anna 123, 126, 179, 183
Karslake, Daniel **160**
Karyo, Tcheky 203
Kawalerowicz, Jerzy 56
Kazantzakis, Nikos 39, 40, 41
Keaton, Buster 45, 147
Keats, John 85, 129, **164-166,** 172
Kedrova, Lila 39, 40
Keiller, Patrick **147**
Keitel, Harvey 185
Kermode, Mark 154-5, 169
Kettle, Arnold 50
Keyes, Evelyn 117
Khan, A. J. 105
Kidron, Beeban **65, 78-79**
Kingsley, Charles 171
Kinski, Klaus **177,** 204, 206
Kirchell, Mark 144
Klinga, Elin 1151-2
Kluge, Alexander 125, **132-133,** 155, 179
Kluge, Alexandra 133, 179
Knightley, Keira 157

Koestler, Arthur 179, 180
Korzynski, Andrzej 208
Kosintsev, Grigori **195**
Kosminsky, Peter **160-161**
Kracauer, Siegfried 190
Kristeva, Julia 63
Kruger, Hardy 120
Krumbachova, Ester 132, 137
Kubrick, Stanley 9
Kurosawa, Akira **193, 195**
Lacan, Jacques 65
Laclos, Pierre Choderlos de 98, 160
Lafont, Bernadette 187
Laing, R.D. 137
Lambeti, Elli 39
Lang, Fritz 44, 52, 184
Lanzmann, Claude 59, **185**
Lass, Frances 74
Latour, Lucienne 197
Laure, Carole 133
Lautreamont, Comte de 36
Lawrence, D.H. 30, 47, 55, 105, 120, 126
Lean, David 181
Leigh, Mike **139, 143,** 156-7, **164,** 171, **181, 194**
Lenin, Vladimir 44, 49, 153, 162, 208
Lennon, John 186
Leroi, Francois 187
Levinas, Emmanuel 162-3
Levy, Bernard-Henri 162
Lewinski, Monica 169
Liebknecht, Karl 78, 80
Liljeberg, Rebecca 149-50
Liljedahl, Marie 97-100, 177
Lindberg, Christina 97, 100, 177
Lindblom, Gunnel 174
Lloyd, Harold 169
Loach, Ken **49-51,** 143, 156-7, **194**
Lonsdale, Michael 159
Losey, Joseph **116-117, 128-130, 140-141**
Louis XIV 115, 148

Lovelace, Linda 103
Lubitsch, Ernst 111
Lukacs, Gyorgy 179
Lumiere, Louis 57
Luxemburg, Rosa 65, 78, 80, 183
Lynch, David 200
MacCormack, Patricia 197
Mackenzie, Suzie 78
Maeterlinck, Maurice 126
Magritte, Rene 126
Makavejev, Dusan 7, **133-134, 178,** 184, 190, **192, 196**
Makhmalbaf, Hana 155
Makhmalbaf, Samira 155
Makk, Karoly **64, 72-74, 138,** 180, 186
Malle, Louis **137,** 187
Mankiewicz, Joseph **116**
Manson, Charles 52, 53
Mao Tse Tung 9, **66**
Marat, Jean-Paul 115
Marceau, Sophie 130, **148,** 197, 203
Marie Antoinette 115
Markham, Pippa 188
Marnay, Derrick de 114
Marvell, Andrew 85, 109
Marx, Karl 9, 57, 128, 153
Mascagni, Pietro 200
Maugham, Somerset 116
Mayakovsky, Vladimir 45, 146
Mayo, Simon 154
Mayovski, Claude 47
McCarthy, Joseph 141
McGovern, George 158
Meinhof, Ulrike 65
Melies, Georges 57
Melville, Jean-Pierre 180
Mendelssohn, Felix 13
Mendum, Mary 101, 104
Menzel, Jiri 124
Mercouri, Melina 39
Meshkini, Marziyeh **155**

Mesquida, Roxane 160
Meszaros, Marta **64, 71-74,** 138, **179-180**
Metzger, Radley 101, **196**
Meyer, Russ 85, 130, 137, **183-184**
Michelangelo 99
Miller, Claude **155**
Miller, Henry 92, 105
Millett, Kate 93, 165
Milton, John 158
Minelli, Vincente 200
Moliere 148, 203
Monod, Jacques 202
Monroe, Marilyn 116
Montaigne, Michel de 197
Montand, Yves 117
Moodysson, Lukas **149-150,** 168
Moreau, Jeanne 125, **140-141,** 186
Morgan, Robin 93
Mottram, Eric 12
Mozart 165
Muehl, Otto 28, 92, 133-4, 178
Mulvey, Laura 67
Murphy, Kathleen 36
Mussolini, Benito 12, 13, 14, 15
Nagy, Imre 179
Nasser, Gamel Abdel 180
Nebe, Chris 101
Neeson, Liam 154, 182
Neill, A.S. 58
Neill, Sam 198
Nemec, Jan 132
Nesbitt, James 182
Nezval, Vitezslav 132
Niblo, Fred 107
Nietzsche, Friedrich 18, 119
Nighy, Bill 154
Nilsson, Jessica **157-158, 196**
Nin, Anais 35, 92, 105, 110, 111
Nixon, Richard 9, 158
Nizan, Paul 163

Norstein, Yuri **60**
Nostradamus 203
Nykvist, Sven 25
O'Casey, Sean 143
Olin, Lena 173
Olivier, Laurence 206
Olofson, Christina 174
Orwell, George 49, 157
Oshima **28-31,** 37, **193, 196**
Ovidie 96, 158
Ozon, Francois 141, **151,** 155
Pabst, G.W. 109-110, 184-5
Papas, Irene 39, 40, 121, 122
Paradjanov, Sergei 162
Parc, Marquise Therese de 148
Pascal, Christine **176**
Pasolini, Pier Paulo 123-4
Patterson, John 88, 90
Paul II, Pope 208
Pawlikowski, Pawel **149, 194**
Peirce, Kimberly **151**
Pepys, Samuel 91
Petry, Iwona 197, **209**
Pialat, Maurice 49
Picasso, Pablo 95, 200
Pilbeam, Nora 114
Pinkerton, Nick 183
Pius XI, Pope 14
Plath, Sylvia 63
Polanski, Roman **52-54, 190**
Pompidou, Georges 47
Pontecorvo, Gillo **119-120, 193**
Pope, Alexander 116
Potter, Denis 156
Potter, Sally **155-157,** 168, 184
Powell, Michael **194**
Prevert, Jacques 131, 132
Proust, Marcel 35, 166
Prucnal, Anna 133
Puccini, Giacomo 87

Pudovkin, Vsevolod 9, 66
Quinn, Anthony 39
Rabelais, Francois 149, 206
Racine, Jean 111, 148
Radiguet, Raymond 143
Rank, J. Arthur 12
Rank, Otto 12
Ray, Man 14
Redgrave, Vanessa 122
Reems, Harry 103-104
Reich, Wilhelm **81-82**, 178, 190
Reinhardt, Max **195**
Remmele, Adam 81
Renoir, Jean 7, 52, **115-116**, 118
Resnais, Alain 119, 123, 126, 135, 180
Richardson, Amanda 65
Richardson, Natasha 155
Richardson, Tony 55, **125**, 156, **194**, **195**
Riefenstahl, Leni **63, 67-68**
Rimbaud, Arthur 36, 205
Riva, Emmanuelle 180
Rivera, Primo de 12
Rivette, Jacques 119
Robbe-Grillet, Alain **125-126**
Robbe-Grillet, Catherine 101, 125
Robespierre, Maximilien 115, 190
Roche, Henri-Pierre 187-8
Rocque, Francois de la 15
Rohmer, Eric 48
Rodin, Auguste 200
Roosevelt, Franklin D 141
Rosenbaum, Jonathan 132
Rossellini, Roberto 118, 123
Roud, Richard 171
Rougemont, Denis de 16, 17
Rousseau, Douanier 132
Rowlands, Gena 204
Rukar, Jeanne 14
Russell, Ken **55-56, 60, 194**
Sade, Marquis de 18, 36, 91, 94

Saeli, Marie 67
Sagan, Leontine **64, 68-70, 113-114,** 137-8
Sagnier, Ludivine 155
Saint-Just 115
Salome 111
Sanders, George 116
Sands, Bobby 182
Sarkozy, Nicolas 162
Sarno, Joe **95-106, 177-178, 196**
Sarno, Peggy 97-101
Sartre, Jean-Paul 156
Sautet, Claude **145-147**
Schloendorff, Volker 139
Schneider, Maria 89
Schneider, Romy 176-7, 197, 204-5
Schubert, Franz 15
Schygulla, Hanna **130-131,** 177
Sciamma, Celine 150, **161-162**
Scofield, Paul 147
Segal, Lynne 94
Sev igny, Chloe 151
Seyrig, Delphine 33, 34, **135-136**
Sgarsgard (Skarsgard), Stellan 185
Shakespeare, William 104, 109, 121, 128, 156, 200
Shaw, G.B. 143
Shelley, P.B. 122
Shepitko, Larissa **63, 68**
Shimkus, Joanna 128
Shklovsky, Viktor 63
Shostakovich, Dmitri 100
Sieglohr, Ulrike 75
Simenon, Georges 126
Sinyard, Neil 197
Sjoberg, Alf 74
Skvorecky, Joseph **70-71, 209-210**
Soderbergh, Steven **166-168**
Soederbergh-Widding, Astrid 74
Sokurov, Alexander **162-163**
Solanas, Valerie 65, 79, 91, 94, 147-8, 152, 191
Solas, Humberto **83-87**

Sontag, Susan 9, **21-22,** 27, 30, 63, 66, 93-4
Sophocles 156
Span, Anna 8, 88, 91
Stalin, Joseph 49, 60-1, 73, 124, 132, 153, 179, 190
Steadman, Alison 164
Steiner, George 92-4
Stendhal 122-3
Sterne, Laurence 173
Stewart, Alex andra 137
Strasberg, Susan 119
Straub, Jean-Marie 171, 179
Streitfeld, Susan 157, **186**
Strindberg, August 200
Stromerstedt, Monika 98
Sukowa, Barbara 78, 138
Svankmajer, Jan **60-61**
Swank, Hilary 151
Swift, Jonathan 139, 147, 149, 173
Swinton, Tilda 157, 169, **186**
Szabo, Istvan **141-142,** 180, **185-186**
Szapolowska, Grazina 73
Tarkovsky, Andrei 162
Tarr, Bela 126
Tatar, Maria 184
Tate, Sharon 52, 53
Tavernier, Bertrand 176
Taylor, Elizabeth **128-130,** 140
Taylor, Paul 77
Taymor, Julie **195**
Tchaikovsky, Peter Ilyich 55
Temple, Julien **194**
Teresa, Mother 50
Thalmann, Ernst 81
Thatcher, Margaret 147, 174
Theodorakis, Mikis 39
Thomas, Dylan 129
Thompson, Emma 154
Thompson, J. Lee 120
Thorez, Maurice 115
Thorsen, Jens Jorgen **196**

Thulin, Ingrid 21, 127
Tolstoy, Leo 107-108
Tornatore, Giuseppe 200
Toubiana, Serge 188
Tournier, Michel 125
Toussaint l'Ouverture 84
Trier, Lars von 29, 151, 157, **168-170,** 200
Trintignant, Jean-Louis 126
Trotsky, Leon 49, 63, 141
Trotta, Margaretha Von **65, 77-78, 138-139**
Truffaut, Francois 55, 64, 97-8, 110, 156, **187-188, 192,** 200
Trujillo, Marisol **60**
Trumbo, Dalton 117
Ullmann, Liv 20, 21, 24, 27, 130, 177, **180-181**
Unamuno, Miguel de 162
Ustinov, Peter 114
Van Gogh, Vincent 203
Varda, Agnes 33, 35, 47, 62, **64-65, 70-71, 75-77,** 79, **118,** 128, **175,** 179, **188-189,** 191, **193,** 197
Velasquez, Diego 86
Verhoeven, Michael 89
Vernon, John 134
Vertov, Dziga **193**
Vidal, Gore 158
Vigo, Jean 28, **58, 64,** 118, 150, **192**
Vinceandeau, Ginette 180
Visconti, Luchino 83-4, 89, 118, 124
Vittoria, Stephen **158**
Vogel, Amos 92, 94, 134, 197
Voltaire 140
Wagner, Richard 13, 14, 16, 17, 18, 110, 128, 185
Warhol, Andy 65, 79, 147-8
Wajda, Andrzej **189-190**
Warner, Marina 47
Watkins, Peter 7, 137, **153-154, 193, 194,** 197
Watson, Malcolm 197, **198-210**
Wedekind, Frank 184
Weir, Peter **137-138**
Welles, Jennifer 101, 104
Welles, Orson 179, **195**

Wenders, Wim 177
West, Mae 17
Wheatcroft, John 190
White, Patrick 137
Whitehouse, Mary 106
Widmer, Kingsley 126
Wiene, Robert **57-58, 190**
Wilde, Oscar 110
William of Orange 143
Williams, Linda 93-4, 96, 197
Williams, Melanie 197
Williams, Tennessee 128, 130
Winner, Michael 55
Winstanley, Gerard 136
Winstone, Ray 50
Winterbottom, Michael 89-90
Wiseman, Frederick 74-5
Wollen, Peter 63
Woodcock, Bruce 175, 197
Woolf, Virginia 156
Wyler, William 116
Yeats, W.B. 32, 143
Zamyatin, Yevgeny 44
Zbanic, Jasmila **158-159**
Zenovich, Marina 53
Zetterling, Mai **64, 74-75,** 79, 119, **126-127, 172,** 173-4, **190-191**
Zola, Emile 49, 50
Zulawski, Andrzej 169, **197-210**

Printed in Great Britain
by Amazon